Advan

"*Experience My Brand* is the perfect book for every C-level leader to devour and implement. Getting behind the hype and jargon, Joe digs into the math and return on investment metrics necessary to help organizations invest properly in customer experience management. This book is full and complete with examples, practical applications, and extensive financial analysis that make the decision making process easy for leaders interested in having their companies truly lead in customer experience and their market segments."

—*Tim Searcy*, CEO, Catalyst Solutions

Dear Julie,

May your life
be full of wonderful
and unique experiences

Best wishes,

Joe Tawfik
17/5/2017

EXPERIENCE MY BRAND

*How Successful Companies
Develop Loyal Customers
AND Increase Profits*

BRAND

JOE TAWFIK

RIVER GROVE
BOOKS

This publication is designed to provide accurate and authoritative information in regard to the subject matter covered. It is sold with the understanding that the publisher and author are not engaged in rendering legal, accounting, or other professional services. If legal advice or other expert assistance is required, the services of a competent professional should be sought.

Published by River Grove Books
Austin, TX
www.rivergrovebooks.com

Distributed by River Grove Books

Design and composition by Greenleaf Book Group
Cover design by Greenleaf Book Group
Cover images: ©iStockphoto.com/JJPan; ©iStockphoto.com/enisaksoy

Cataloging-in-Publication data is available.

Print ISBN: 978-1-63299-127-0

eBook ISBN: 978-1-63299-128-7

First Edition

This book is dedicated to my lovely wife Louise and our two wonderful daughters, Sophie and Isabelle. Together, you have given me the experience of a lifetime.

Contents

INTRODUCTION: *The Quest for Unique Customer Experience (CX)*

PART ONE: *Mastering CX Analysis, Measurement, and Design*

1	Strategic CX: Is Your Organization Ready?	9
2	The Financials of CX	27
3	Measuring Organizational Customer Centricity	57
4	Designing the Customer-Centric Organization	70
5	Mapping the Customer Journey	86
6	Aligning Initiatives to Achieve CX Objectives	124
7	Review: Ten Rules for CX Excellence	146

PART TWO: *Mastering Implementation of CX Initiatives*

8	CX Implementation Planning	156
9	Leadership for CX Excellence	174
10	Employee Engagement during CX Implementation	183
11	Scaling and Maintaining CX Excellence	196
12	Building the Right Organizational Structure and Governance Model	209
13	How to Innovate in Customer Experience	222
14	CX for the On-Demand Generation	235
15	Redefining CX for the Digital Age	249
16	Outsourcing and Other Implementation Options	263
17	Effective Governance of Outsourcing Relationships	278
18	Managing Outsourcing Relationships	286

PART 3: *The Future of Customer Experience Management (CEM)*

19	How Data Will Define the Future of CEM					298

20	How Technology Will Define the Future of CEM				310

21	The Impact of the Digital Workforce on CEM				328

22	Final Thoughts on Strategic CEM					343

APPENDIX									345

INDEX									349

CONSULTING AND RESOURCES						360

The Quest for Unique Customer Experience (CX)

This book simply presents the argument that if you are going to be successful in business today you have to embrace customer experience (CX) as your new mantra. Why? Because brands are no longer determined by advertising and clever marketing. They are *defined* by the collective experiences you provide your customers. Differentiating your brand in the marketplace requires you to provide a uniquely *branded experience* for your customers. The common attribute of all high-growth and profitable businesses with loyal customers is their masterful execution of branded experiences for their customers. Let me now explain why this topic is so important today.

In our digital era, the competition for market share and consumer loyalty has never been more fierce or complicated. Economists have described the digital wave of disruption as the Fourth Industrial Revolution,[1] because of the degree of change affecting so many aspects of industry, government, and consumers. Traditional industry built from brick-and-mortar business models has found that the commercial advantages it once held, thanks to captive markets and trade barriers, have all but disappeared. Organizations now compete in a global marketplace where physical barriers are no longer pertinent. Advancements in technology have enabled organizations to create new business models, products, and services that can distribute their wares anywhere—and do it all at lightning speed.

As these new competitors enter the marketplace, they erode market

....

1   The term was first used in April 2011 at the Hanover Fair, the world's biggest industrial trade show. By October 2012, the Working Group on Industry 4.0, chaired by Siegfried Dais (Robert Bosch GmbH) and Henning Kagermann (acatech), had developed a set of recommendations for companies implementing Industry 4.0.

share from traditional industries. Without legacy systems or business models, these new entrants are able to quickly win new customers by offering higher value offerings at lower costs. This is leaving brick-and-mortar businesses with a declining margin and lower profitability. Facing inevitable decline in profitability, these organizations are searching for ways to compete and regain market share.

What does this mean for your organization? How can you create a sustainable competitive advantage in today's business environment? The answer is straightforward, though not exactly simple: by forging a unique bond with your customers.

The key to this premise is that the *value* of customer experience resides in your customers developing a unique emotional relationship to your goods and services. A positive purchasing experience without a unique emotional relationship does not constitute a point of differentiation. A customer relationship based on transactional interactions without an emotional attachment is nothing more than customer service, and this is *easily replicable*.

On the other hand, a truly unique emotional bond with a customer can be difficult to replicate, because creating this distinctive relationship requires the core of your organization to change and move in a new direction. As difficult as the task may be, however, it is invaluable to your organization's bottom line.

What Is a Branded Experience?

Customer experience management is not about how you can delight a customer or how many smiley faces you can get on social media after a customer interaction. People often confuse customer experience with a modified version of customer service. This confusion can lead to the misunderstanding and incorrect positioning of customer experience within an organization.

Customer experience management is the process a company follows to forge an emotional and spiritual bond with its customers. Customer experience management aims to create a unique bias for an organization's products and services by meeting and exceeding customer expectations. Every interaction customers have with your organization, at every stage of their life cycle, shapes and determines the emotional relationship they have with the organization. Customers are loyal to your brand only when there is a very tight correlation between what your brand *promises* and what customers *experience*. Your company's ability to consistently deliver positive emotions builds a level of trust between brand and customer, and this trust fosters the long-term loyalty that supports the company's commercial success. The unique relationship established between the customer and the company from these experiences is what I term a branded experience. And to reap the rewards of the branded experience, your organization needs to develop and implement a CX program that will manufacture and maintain uniquely positive experiences for customers.

Customer experience, as a market differentiator, must be part of corporate strategy and embedded within a company's DNA. It does not belong to the contact center or marketing department. Once it resides in a "customer service department," it is ultimately isolated from the rest of the organization and will never be fully absorbed at root level. The inability to reach other areas of the organization will make CX nothing more than a "special project" designed to tick a box for the C-level team.

Customer experience management is part science and part art. As a leader within your company, to achieve CX excellence you must be part engineer and part circus entertainer. You need to master juggling a number of balls, and then add several types of fruit, and then swords. Circus jugglers are required to know the scientific attributes of each item they juggle in order to apply the right amount of force to keep them in perfect rotation. Likewise, we business leaders can juggle our customer experience items only when we take a scientific approach to understanding their unique attributes. Whether we are considering employees, business processes, technology, or leadership, each component has diverse characteristics that require specialized skill sets and focused attention to keep them working harmoniously toward delivering the desired customer experiences.

The story of CX is ultimately about how people can reorganize their work, behavior, and thought processes to achieve an extraordinary outcome for their customers and their organization. Throughout this book I will outline the unique attributes contributing toward the achievement of customer experience outcomes. We will explore the three key dimensions of CX excellence that require shaping if the organization is to achieve market differentiation:

- Employees
- Customers
- Leadership

Each of these dimensions influences your CX strategy, and none can be neglected or disregarded in the total equation. There are many moving parts in mastering CX management in order to achieve measurable and sustainable results. My goal is to guide you through these parts and along the journey toward achieving customer experience excellence, and to enable you to achieve a measurable return on your investments.

I have identified thirty key stages required to analyze your organization and its customers (the complete list is provided in the appendix), and provided a blueprint you can use to build a CX program to achieve a branded experience. Following the stages in this book will give you a solid business case for implementing and maintaining the program. Each stage has a desired output that signifies its successful completion. Together, the stages and outputs form a methodology for achieving strategic market differentiation in customer experience—in other words, to reach CX excellence.

The book is divided into three parts:

- Part One: Mastering CX Analysis, Measurement, and Design
  » This section will cover stages 1-20 of creating your branded customer experience.
- Part Two: Mastering Implementation of CX Initiatives
  » This section will cover stages 21-30 of building your CX program.

- Part Three: The Future of Customer Experience Management (CEM)
  - » This section will help you prepare for the future evolution of CX.

The aim of this book is to give you an understanding of what is involved in creating a uniquely branded customer experience as a strategic differentiator for your company. We will cover an initial analysis of your company's approach to customer experience, the design and implementation of an appropriate CX program, and issues surrounding post-implementation sustainability of the right branded experience for you. Whether you're an experienced practitioner of CX or a novice, you can apply the methodology, practices, and ideas in this book to any type of organization, from large publicly listed companies to small and medium businesses to government enterprises.

I have written this book based on both my direct experience with CX implementations and my research on the topic. If you follow the key stages and practices I outline, you can achieve extraordinary outcomes for your organization and customers. I hope you enjoy the journey, and I am confident that you will discover the success you seek.

Part 1

MASTERING CX ANALYSIS, MEASUREMENT, AND DESIGN

CHAPTER I

Strategic CX:
Is Your Organization Ready?

Many companies may think they are providing a strategic program of uniquely branded customer experiences, when in fact they are only delivering tactical, product-centric experiences. The fact is, a strategic customer experience can increase bottom-line profitability and provide other economic benefits to an organization that a tactical experience cannot. This chapter examines the two approaches to CX and reveals why the area of interest for business leaders is in the strategic value, and not the tactical value, of customer experience management.

Assessing CX Programs: Tactical vs. Strategic

The differences between tactical and strategic customer experience programs are linked to their primary objective. A tactical program will have a very specific objective limited to a particular area in the business that has an impact on customers. The strategic approach, on the other hand, requires a whole-company perspective. As we shall see, the results of each type of program contrast as much as their objectives do.

TACTICAL CUSTOMER EXPERIENCE

A tactical CX program tends to operate only within the defined problem area, without considering larger root problems. Rather than tackling underlying causes, a tactical program tends to focus on *symptoms* of the problem.

Take, for example, an initiative to increase customer satisfaction levels. A typical tactical customer experience program may focus on the training of contact center agents. This type of program does not consider the multitude of other factors that affect customer satisfaction in the contact center.

An organization that adopts a customer experience program for tactical purposes only will not be able to extract value in terms of the bottom line. Tactical CX management tends to end up as a feel-good exercise. Executives sponsoring a tactical CX program feel good about themselves because they are doing something that appears progressive and customer focused, and employees implementing it feel good because they are doing something positive that could help their career progression. However, the general outcome of tactical customer experience projects is short-lived and does not normally translate into an increase in overall profitability. Most tactical projects have a negative return on investment, because what is created is merely an ephemeral asset that soon dissipates, giving no sustainable or measurable value back to the organization. The return on the investment made is rarely realized.

Consider the remedial training programs that your company has delivered over the years and the long-term impact on results. Contact centers are a prime example. Results may temporarily improve, but rarely do they lead to any long-term commercial benefits for the company. Contact center agents typically leave the company after a short tenure or fall into old habits because the underlying root causes of the problem have not been fixed.

STRATEGIC CUSTOMER EXPERIENCE

A strategic approach to the same issue—customer satisfaction levels in the contact center—would address the issue from a different perspective, viewing it within a much larger framework by considering components such as the brand promise, customer research, business processes, organizational culture, and technology. If we apply a strategic approach to the contact center example, we would ask a number of questions to get to the underlying causes of customer dissatisfaction. We may uncover, for instance, that the underlying problem is not training but a poorly designed business process, and that only by fixing this process can we hope to remedy the customer problem once and for all.

Unlike tactical programs, strategic ones focus on the greater significance to the organization rather than on the short-term benefits to a particular department within the organization. Action would not be taken unless it would deliver long-term, sustainable value to the company. The myopic view of tactical programs prevents the broader perspective required to achieve sustainable benefits over a much longer period. While tactical CX programs focus only on symptoms, strategic ones fix the underlying *causes*.

This book is interested in the strategic potential of customer experience. The empirical evidence for companies delivering sustainable, differentiated customer experience and profitability is well documented and convincing. Research of over one hundred midsize and large companies shows that the companies that are able to translate customer experience into bottom-line profitability are the ones that deliver experiences of positive emotion at moments that matter to customers. They achieve this by closely matching, on a consistent basis, the value propositions most desired by their customers. This objective cannot be achieved by allocating the responsibility to a single or a few departments within a company. Instead, the strategic CX program requires a broad and structured approach.

The strategic value of customer experience as an economic booster is closely associated to a number of other dimensions in an organization, including three primary components:

1. Company processes
   a. Company strategy
   b. Back-office processes
   c. Front-office processes
   d. Technologies enabling the processes

2. Company environment
   a. Culture and people
   b. Operating structure
   c. Investment capability
   d. Employee engagement
   e. Senior executive leadership
   f. Product/service differentiators

3. Customers
   a. Customer profiles
   b. Customer values
   c. Customer feedback
   d. Customer expectations
   e. Customer engagement

All these moving parts exist in the organization and affect overall customer experience. The broad examination of all these components will help you identify the problem areas in your company and the most important values identified by your customers. The tactical approach—focusing on only a single or a couple of these components—simply will not achieve any long-term measurable benefits. It simply does not dig deep enough to spark the transformation required for a lasting, meaningful change in the customer experience. Business leaders need to be strategic in our approach, to ensure the initiatives selected are closely aligned with our brand's promise and address underlying problems preventing the company from creating a uniquely branded experience for customers.

Checklist: Evaluating Your CX Strategy

How do you know whether your company is providing not just tactical, product-centric experiences, but a leading, strategic CX program to your customers? By evaluating your organization's current processes and position on customer experience, using a brief, fourteen-question checklist. To help you determine in which direction to proceed, the checklist will identify possible challenges you may face as you prepare to initiate any new strategies.

These key questions are related to how your company is performing in the same market as your competitors relative to volume, value, and profitability of sales. Answering these questions will better prepare you to accomplish the rest of the tasks in this book.

I. ARE YOU WINNING NEW CUSTOMERS FASTER THAN YOUR COMPETITION?

Compare your figures on new customers with those of your competitors. In most industries, these numbers are relatively easy to source. If the information is not easily obtainable, however, I recommend undertaking market research to determine your competitors' activities and their success in winning new clients. The number of new customers acquired should include monthly, quarterly, and yearly figures.

2. WHAT IS THE VALUE OF YOUR NEW CUSTOMERS?

In some industries, a single sale could have a dramatic variance in value, perhaps even ranging in the millions of dollars. It's important to understand the value of the customers acquired, as this will enable you to undertake a more thorough comparison of your own company with others. The aim is to ensure you can compare your competitors' sales volume and value to your own.

3. ARE YOU WINNING AND RETAINING CUSTOMERS WITHOUT COMPROMISING YOUR MARGIN?

The gross margin achieved on the sales made will help you identify signs of market pressures driving your profitability downward. It may be difficult to obtain comparative figures on the profitability of your competitors. Publicly traded companies, however, issue financial reports (normally available in the investor relations section of the company website) that provide insights into gross margins achieved on sales.

The Importance of Comparative Analysis

Compare the trends of your closest three competitors with your own performance over the same time period a year ago. Also include in your analysis emerging competitors that are disrupting your competitive space with new business models and technology solutions. Nontraditional competitors should be squarely on your radar for this comparison, as the largest threat of market share erosion is likely to

---

Continued

come from a new competitor using digital disruption as a means to break into a lucrative marketplace traditionally held by brick-and-mortar businesses. Even though such competitors may not be one of your top three competitors, studying them can provide insights on their business model, customers, and market traction that will enable you to formulate a customer experience strategy to enable your own organization to remain competitive and profitable.

Your analysis should seek to identify the following key trends:

- Adoption rate of your products or services

- Profit margins

- Value per customer

- Total customers lost over a twelve-month period

If the outcome of your analysis reveals that your organization is experiencing lower margins, a lower adoption rate, or a reducing value of each sale, then you have identified the first good reason in your business case to read on and determine how customer experience can help remedy your situation. If your analysis leads you to conclude that sales are healthy and margins are at their peak, then you should be applauded for such an achievement.

4. HAS YOUR COMPANY FORMALLY EVALUATED ITS CUSTOMER CENTRICITY?

It's easy to claim your company is customer focused, but only by asking your team targeted questions can you determine whether team members truly know what it takes to be customer centric.

Numerous surveys can help you determine the level of customer-centric delivery within your organization and its various departments, and I recommend performing an analysis based on empirical evidence. One such study is the CCScore (customer centricity score), which measures the extent to which customer centricity could be experienced across all organizational units.

Swiss researchers released the CCScore (www.ccscore.com) in 2014 to provide organizations with greater insight on the areas they need to improve in order to become more customer centric. The researchers identified factors that form the basic building blocks for determining an organization's customer-centricity level. The factors are clustered into the categories of Leadership, Collaboration, and Implementation.

The CCScore is derived from a fifteen-question online self-assessment designed for all employees, plus additional questions that can be added to evaluate further attributes that are specific to the organization. The assessment takes less than six minutes to complete, after which you can further analyze the available data and make a benchmark comparison.

You don't have to use CCScore to achieve this step, but any organizational assessment you select must be based on scientific grounds.

5. DO SENIOR MANAGERS UNDERSTAND THE VALUE OF CUSTOMER CENTRICITY AND SEEK TO IMPROVE HOW THE COMPANY OPERATES?

Business leaders show varying levels of understanding of, and willingness to commit resources to, a customer experience initiative. Most C-level executives will acknowledge the need to be customer centric and the importance of customer experience to the organization. However, most executives lack an in-depth understanding of the real value of a properly functioning customer-centric organization. Even fewer executives truly understand what is required and how long it will take to achieve a level of customer centricity that translates into bottom-line profits.

The key to answering these two difficult questions is to determine the quality of sponsorship the C-level is willing to give, by examining four dimensions of executive involvement with a customer experience program:

a. Understanding
b. Commitment
c. Investment
d. Execution capability

There is a direct correlation between the full understanding of the value held by a truly customer-centric organization and the organization's ability to execute differentiated customer experiences. Executives normally fall into five categories based on the maturity level of their understanding and their capacity to support implementation of a strategic CX program. The key attributes defining each category are outlined in table 1.1:

TABLE 1.1: EXECUTIVE CX MATURITY CATEGORIES

Attribute	Category 1	Category 2	Category 3	Category 4	Category 5
Understanding	Product focused. No real grasp of the value of customer centricity.	Customer centricity is linked to transactions made by frontline staff.	Customer centricity is centralized and the domain of marketing or the contact center.	Customer centricity has been mandated by a board to be very important and is understood as a special project.	Customer centricity is in the company DNA, and influences the entire organization and what it does.
Commitment	Very little. Low priority given to changing existing practices.	Willing to focus on training of frontline staff as a means of improving the customer experience.	Willing to look at tactical projects that will improve a numerical score such as net promotor score (NPS) or voice of the customer (VOC).	Willing to invest in a customer experience project with the understanding that the company will be customer centric in 6-12 months.	Willing to engage in long-term project and properly address all facets of the organization to lead to a differentiated market position.
Investment	Minimal	Training of frontline staff	Will utilize specialist external consultants in a short-term project.	Will invest a larger amount over 6-12 months and employ a broader team.	Prepares for an investment over a 3-to-5-year period.
Execution	No additional resources allocated.	External training body or internal trainers dedicated to execution.	Small consulting team works with in-house staff.	Larger consulting resources work with dedicated or new resources.	Business transformation unit established and partnership formed with consulting firm to execute a change management program.

If the executive team falls into any of the first three categories, then education and time are required to reach a level of understanding where customer centricity is properly accepted as a strategic differentiator. Executives displaying the characteristics of category 4 or 5, on the other hand, are the ideal ones to methodically roll out a customer-centricity program that delivers unique, differentiated experiences to customers. Yet few executives are at a category 5 maturity level, ready to make the necessary long-term commitment in resources and funding in order to achieve a sustainable return on investment and transform their organization.

Choosing a single customer experience executive as an evangelist for the virtues of taking the deep plunge into mastering CX management—however committed he or she might be to customer centricity—is insufficient. The entire executive team must be on board, although ultimately the endeavor is still predicated on the understanding, commitment, investment, and execution capabilities of the organization's CEO. Without the determined support of the CEO for the long journey ahead, any attempt to become truly customer centric and to achieve elevated customer experiences will be wasted.

6. IS THERE A CUSTOMER-CENTRIC FRAMEWORK WITH CLEARLY ALIGNED MEASUREMENTS FOR ALL STAFF?

Your organization may claim to be customer centric, and may point to existing programs in place to monitor, measure, and address customer satisfaction levels. Perhaps your customer service activities are centralized according to the traditional model, and your measurement and monitoring are largely focused on frontline staff and the quality of their interactions with customers. This type of focus is not what I would consider to be true organizational customer centricity.

To achieve the strategic customer centricity that will allow your organization to compete in the age of digital disruption and global competitive forces, there must be decentralization of control over customer issues. A framework needs to be in place that stretches over the entire organization and dictates how and why people do things. Measurement of the impact on customers should include all personnel in an organization, including back-office staff. Without a framework and clearly aligned measurements for the entire organization, customer centricity will not achieve the intended economic benefits of any customer experience program.

The right framework and measurement system (covered in later chapters) will ensure an organization is able to adapt to the changing competitive environment and to address customer expectations more rapidly and effectively than an organization that retains a tactical perspective of customer centricity and confines customer issues to one or a few departments within the organization. The framework I will outline is designed to embed customer centricity into the DNA of the organization, making it the first and final thought in all executive decision making.

A review of how your organization treats customer issues will help you determine its views on customer centricity and will provide a reference point when designing your CX program.

7. CAN YOU DEMONSTRATE TANGIBLE BENEFITS FROM CURRENT CUSTOMER PROGRAMS?

A number of organizations have embraced packaged customer-centricity measurement solutions concepts such as net promotor score (NPS) or voice of the customer (VoC) as the basis for measuring customer experience. Later in this book, I will outline how these concepts can be incorporated into a customer-centricity framework. But despite claiming to be customer centric and focused on delivering an exceptional customer experience, the organizations using NPS do not necessarily realize any commercial benefits, even if their NPS score is high. Sure, they may be measuring personnel and their contribution toward customer satisfaction. But the focus for these organizations tends to be more on achieving a metric to earn a personal bonus than on delivering greater customer value.

The measurement of CX effectiveness should be directly linked to an organization's core customer objectives. For example, a start-up organization may be seeking to grow market share, whereas a mature company is more interested in retaining customers and increasing profitability from customer experience differentiation. If neither of these outcomes is achieved by existing CX programs, then there is room for improvement.

A review of your financial performance over twelve to twenty-four months should reveal whether your customer programs are achieving any commercial benefits. If profitability or market share has remained the same or declined, then you need to address the elephant in the room: Why continue investing in a program that is not yielding any commercial benefits?

8. HAVE YOU MAPPED CUSTOMER TOUCH POINTS AND
IDENTIFIED THE IMPACT ON CUSTOMERS' EXPERIENCES?

The customer journey normally begins outside the organization and then extends into the organization and beyond. Each touch point reveals an interaction with, and the subsequent impact on, the company's customers. Creating a map of how your customer experiences your products and services will enable you to tackle the issues that matter most to your customers. Identifying hot spots of heightened emotional pain and pleasure gives the organization the necessary insights to determine which areas are most appreciated by a particular customer segment and which could be revised or remedied.

Customer journey maps are essential to ensuring an organization has its finger on the pulse of its customers. Successful maps are dynamic, linked to analytics, and available in real time. Unfortunately, most organizations today conduct customer journey mapping that is created on applications not fit for the purpose, and is detached from customer analytics. This has rendered customer journey mapping a secondary tool that adds only a static view of the customer experience.

We will cover journey mapping in chapter 5, but the key at this stage is to understand if and how your organization currently performs customer journey mapping, whether such a program is older than twelve months old, and how your company integrates journey mapping with analytics and updates it to reflect different customer profiles. Most organizations exhibit weakness in this area. While customer journey maps are not the be-all and end-all of customer centricity, they are valuable tools when you are working toward elevating customer experience in your organization.

9. DO YOU HAVE A GOVERNANCE MODEL TO ENSURE
EXECUTION OF CUSTOMER-CENTRICITY OBJECTIVES?

Achieving true customer centricity requires a proper governance model and specialist resources to ensure the organization is continuously moving toward the desired customer-centricity objectives. A *governance model,*

20

which I discuss in greater detail in chapters 8 and 12, is a mechanism that allows a group of people with specialist skill sets to monitor, remedy, and advise the company on matters related to customer centricity and customer experience. The primary objective is to ensure, by applying a structured methodology, that approved initiatives are achieving their desired outcomes and addressing new issues.

Without the governance model in place, an organization is unlikely to adapt quickly enough to a changing marketplace. Consider a company like Uber, which has managed to manipulate both the demand and the supply side of hired ground transportation. Uber's customer-centric governance model has entirely changed the customer experience and expectations. Competing companies in ground transportation that retain their existing business model now find it more challenging to compete.

For organizations seeking to challenge new entrants like Uber, achieving a fast enough pace of change is possible only when a governance model is in place to monitor, guide, and influence the organization to achieve CX excellence. This governance model must include resources such as a chief of customer experience or a chief of customer, who will have enough influence over corporate strategy to enable the organization to change course with minimal resistance. For a company to maintain a competitive position in today's marketplace, change is a necessary constant. A department responsible for change management specifically is becoming an essential fixture in many organizations.

10. HAS YOUR COMPANY ASKED CUSTOMERS WHAT THEY THINK ABOUT YOUR PRODUCTS AND SERVICES?

Knowledge about your customers and how you are performing is an essential component of determining what your customers value most and like least about your products and services. Research should not be restricted to simple online surveys or phone calls. The aim of your customer research should be to arrive at a set of common themes that reveal what your key customer demographics value the most—what they define as a "great" customer experience from your organization.

One big mistake any customer-centric organization can make is to rely on secondary research, such as mystery shopping results or internal staff workshops, to determine what the customer experience is genuinely like. On the contrary, these methods lead to false conclusions and flawed strategic paths. Instead, I recommend face-to-face and group interviews that allow individuals to clarify and elaborate on various topics expressed by other customers. Direct research among your customers is a reliable means to gain the most insight into how they feel about your products and services, and how they are delivered. Without this direct feedback, your future program of customer-centricity initiatives would be built on a shaky foundation of uncertain assumptions.

II. DO YOU HAVE STRUCTURED PROGRAMS THAT TRAIN TEAM MEMBERS TO CREATE CUSTOMER EXPERIENCES?

Most organizations do regular training and coaching for their frontline staff, often out of necessity rather than for any developmental purposes. For example, a group of new recruits start and are trained to perform their new duties. Refresher training may be provided on an ad hoc basis, but the training tends to minimal, with no larger development objective in mind other than to perform a specific task well. While this training may be useful for production, it does little to improve customer experience. Sustainable customer experience stems from professional development training and coaching that is structured, multifaceted, and provided to all employees, including front- and back-office staff.

To master CX management, organizations need to reverse-engineer the desired customer experiences—by getting a good grasp of who your customers are, what they value most, and what emotional experiences they have at each key touch point with your company—to determine the type of staff training and development to provide. Only organizations that equip their staff with the necessary skill sets and competencies can properly address the changing needs of customers, deliver unique experiences directly linked to your brand, and position your brand in the marketplace as superior when compared with the competition.

12. HOW ENGAGED ARE THE EMPLOYEES IN YOUR COMPANY?

Employee engagement plays a vital role in the success of any customer-centric organization. The correlation is strong between employee engagement and practicing customer centricity, and studies undertaken by Harvard Business School (2005) and numerous other research firms have identified the link between highly engaged employees and the ability to achieve commercial success. Highly engaged employees work better together in teams, striving toward a common goal of delivering a uniquely branded experience. Highly engaged employees also are able to overcome obstacles and deal with change better than employees who don't care whether or not the organization succeeds in the marketplace.

It doesn't take much to realize that companies like Apple have been able to achieve astonishing commercial results because Steve Jobs and other CEOs had a highly engaged team of individuals who believed they could change the world. Apple probably would never have achieved the turnaround commercial results after Steve Jobs returned to leadership in 1997 had he not provided the clear vision and charismatic leadership that encouraged an extraordinary degree of engagement from his team.

Any effective customer-centricity plan must examine the company's employee engagement level and identify a plan to remedy any issues likely to inhibit the success of a transformative customer-centricity program. How engaged are staff with your company? Do you really know the "happiness factor" of your team members and the issues that have a negative impact on them? For example, if a staff engagement survey revealed a high level of dissatisfaction among staff because the health insurance plan had recently been downgraded, it would be futile to introduce a CX program that asks employees to go the extra mile for customers.

Employee engagement level is always a by-product of the organization's leadership style and workplace culture. Thus, leadership plays a fundamental role in customer centricity, as we will discuss further in chapter 9. Culture is also fundamental, and the ability to scrutinize and categorize the type of culture present in an organization is an important step toward understanding the extent of change required to achieve customer centricity. The majority of staff will need to become advocates for your brand by knowing precisely how to deliver uniquely branded customer experiences, and for this to occur, often a complete transformation in organizational behavior is required.

To achieve customer-centricity objectives, your organization may need to transition team members from traditionally accepted behaviors to new, customer-centric ones. This is no easy task. The process of change will encounter less resistance when the culture of the organization has fewer negative components working against those objectives. Organizations defined by staff working in silos, egocentric conduct, and using fear as a motivator are steeped in some of the cultural traits that are most difficult to overcome in order to achieve customer centricity.

13. ARE EMPLOYEES EMPOWERED TO DELIVER DESIRED CUSTOMER EXPERIENCES?

Employee empowerment is an essential component of any customer-centric plan for an organization. To ensure customers are not frustrated with their touch points and interactions, staff must be enabled to make decisions within defined guidelines. Imparting a decision-making process and a level of empowerment so staff members can take action and address a broad range of customer issues ensures the organization is able to meet one of the critical elements of any leading customer-centric organization: the ability to resolve issues quickly, efficiently, and fairly.

All too often, employees feel they are operating with their hands tied behind their back. Exploring the reasons behind this lack of empowerment reveals that it is rooted in legacy issues related to management, technology, and business processes. Some business models may feature a high degree of automation that does not require employee input. However, regardless of the level of automation or the need for higher management to be involved, every organization seeking a branded CX program needs to review how it resolves customer issues and look for ways to improve this.

14. DO TECHNOLOGY AND PROCESSES ENABLE TEAM MEMBERS TO DELIVER GREAT CUSTOMER EXPERIENCES?

Underlying every customer experience with your organization is a business process and a piece of technology supporting it. For example,

Wal-Mart has invested in technology and streamlining its business processes to deliver on its brand promise: "Save Money. Live Better." By lowering operating costs in its supply chain, the company ensures that its customers receive a consistent experience of cost savings. The evolution of customer expectations requires organizations across all industry sectors to review how they currently do business with their customers and the technology they use. Legacy processes and technologies could be key barriers to meeting the demands and expectations of a generation of customers accustomed to getting information and transacting business at any time of day via a multitude of channels.

Many CX practitioners highlight the importance of offering your customers an omnichannel strategy. This should certainly be a major consideration in your planning, but there is little point in deploying such an omnichannel strategy without first critically reviewing existing business processes and their impact on customers. I prefer a more holistic approach: Consider the business processes affecting customers either directly or indirectly. Can any processes be reengineered or eliminated? If you want to truly master customer experience excellence, you need to have a good grasp of all your business processes, and you must continually review and try to enhance them. You should be regularly asking, "Is this process really necessary?" and "How can we redesign this process to improve the customer's experience?"

Once you have performed a rigorous review of your business processes, with your customer research findings in hand, you will be able to identify what needs to change and also the specific technology you should deploy to support that change. Using techniques such as Six Sigma to develop a strong competency in process excellence will enable the organization to enhance existing processes. To achieve customer experience excellence, however, we need to go further—to the point where we completely rethink how to achieve a certain customer outcome, possibly by totally eliminating a preexisting process.

These fourteen self-evaluation questions are designed to identify the key issues at hand prior to the strategic implementation of a customer-centric CX program. By reviewing the questions and why they play an important role in preparing for your company's transformation, you can better understand whether your company is ready to embark on the journey of evaluation and change required for that transformation. Taking the time and effort to evaluate your organization's readiness for a strategic CX program will expose the areas that need the greatest attention and allow you to more easily prioritize and address them.

·············· **KEY LESSONS** ··············

- Two of the numerous approaches to customer experience in business are a strategic CX implementation versus a tactical CX focus. Evidence strongly suggests the strategic implementation of customer experience gives the greatest return on investment.
- Before implementing a strategic CX program, an organization needs to determine its readiness and ability to successfully attain a sustainable and differentiating market position in customer experience. During this self-evaluation, you will perform the following analysis:
  1. Review the pace of growth of your company compared with the competition's.
  2. Determine the value of winning new customers.
  3. Determine whether you are winning and retaining customers without compromising your margin.
  4. Determine the organization's level of customer centricity.
  5. Determine where the leadership team stands regarding a tactical approach to customer experience versus the strategic value of delivering a differentiated customer experience.
  6. Determine whether the company conforms to a customer experience strategy or framework that measures alignment to specific CX objectives.
  7. Determine the economic value generated from existing customer experience programs (if any exist). If there is no uplift in bottom-line results, there is room for review and improvement.

8. Evaluate customer journey maps, and determine how dynamic and functional they are in generating insights about your customers.

9. Determine whether a governance model is in place and which resources are appropriate in order to execute a strategic version of CX management.

10. Undertake customer research to determine your customers' sentiment about your company and products or services.

11. Determine whether a structured training and professional development program is in place to ensure that employees develop the right skills and are properly equipped to handle the customer demands.

12. Evaluate any fundamental employee engagement issues that need to be resolved.

13. Evaluate whether employees enjoy a high level of empowerment to resolve customer issues, and identify any legacy issues impeding fast, efficient resolutions for your customers.

14. Examine your business processes, and determine the level of effort required to review, reengineer, or eliminate them.

CHAPTER 2

The Financials of CX

Customer experience as a strategic initiative, or even as a tactical initiative, needs to have a distinct economic benefit on an organization, whether directly or indirectly. It is imperative that as a customer experience professional, you have a sound understanding of the key financial concepts that define and measure the success of CX management. If you fail to grasp these financial relationships, your efforts are in danger of being misguided.

This chapter covers the first four stages in your journey toward achieving CX excellence:

Stage	Desired Output
1. Identify whether your organization can benefit from improving its customer experience, and set your vision and mission for your program.	A comparative financial analysis of your nearest competitor, and a clear vision and mission for your program
2. Identify the financial areas you would like to generate a commercial benefit.	A financial analysis of customer metrics and the profit and loss statement
3. Identify by how much you would like to change the metrics.	Objectives and targets for each area selected for change
4. Provide a clear ROI for the investment in your customer experience initiative.	A summary of the net commercial benefits, required investments, and expected time frame for achieving the financial targets

Can Your Organization Benefit from a Strategic CX Program?

To identify whether your organization needs to make an investment in a CX program, and to employ the metrics that can best determine if your current efforts to elevate customer experience are yielding the preferred financial outcomes, you need to be equipped with some essential financial concepts. Some of the mathematics in this chapter may tempt you to skip this section altogether, but I encourage you to persist on this section of the journey, as it forms the very heart of the knowledge you need in order to build a sound business case for your CX program and to measure the outcomes of your initiatives.

As I mentioned in the introduction, mastering customer experience is part science and part art; making sense of the financials is no different. Although numbers may seem fairly well defined in their meaning, there is nearly always room for multiple interpretations and incorrect conclusions. Any discussion of customer centricity or customer experience should include a close examination of the financials before you decide what future steps to take. Regardless of the potential for misinterpreting the numbers, the core outcome of a CX initiative has to be the improvement of the financial position of the organization. Any other outcome is, in fact, secondary.

I am a firm believer in fact-based decision making. This is why my starting point in the evaluation process is the comparison of your financials to your competitors'. To determine your course of action, during this stage of the process you will need to collect facts by undertaking the following tasks:

- Identify your nearest competitors.
- Acquire the financials (yours and competitors') for profitability and customer acquisition numbers.
- Analyze and evaluate five CX metrics.

Facts may be misinterpreted if they are not in their proper context. In this chapter, I will outline the areas you must study to ensure that you carefully consider and interpret the facts. The objectives of this stage in the process are, first, to arrive at conclusions that properly reflect the current state of the business, and second, to create a vision and mission for your CX program that will properly reflect the strategic direction and objectives of your company.

COMPARE YOUR ORGANIZATION WITH ITS COMPETITORS

We're going to determine whether you can benefit from a CX program by comparing, using several factors, your business to its competitors. The aim is to get the closest like-for-like comparison by measuring your organization against its closest rivals in the same marketplace. For the comparison to be meaningful, your analysis must be based on organizations similar to your own.

Consider Market Maturity

Each organization belongs to an industry sector that is experiencing its own degree of maturity. A market's maturity can be broadly classified in one of four degrees: emerging, growing, maturing, and declining. Each level is characterized by a number of attributes such as the adoption rate by consumers, the size of the market, the number of competitors, and the typical profit margins achievable. Broadly, an industry is classified as mature if new customer acquisitions are slowing down and margins are shrinking. Conversely, an industry can be classified in the growing phase if it enjoys a high consumer adoption rate relative to the number of competitors in the marketplace.

In addition to considering the maturity of the industry, you must identify a competitor with similar characteristics in terms of size, positioning, and market offering. Comparing a start-up company to a 1,000-person organization that has been in business for twenty years would not be fruitful. A business operating in a new industry sector could be classified as emerging, and the addressable market size and opportunity for the organization are relative to the market share owned by the organization as compared with its competitors. So, if the addressable market has not yet gone to competitors, then it would be reasonable to assume the organization has significant potential to acquire a large number of customers.

Conversely, if an organization exists in a mature or declining industry sector where the addressable marketplace has already been saturated, then it faces a greater challenge in acquiring new customers. In either case, the only scientific method for properly evaluating the effectiveness of the organization is comparing it directly with its closest rival in the same marketplace.

The financial news often reports on Apple's growth compared with Samsung's and Microsoft's, or Verizon compared with T-Mobile. These companies are evaluated in tandem because they share many of the same characteristics and produce competing offerings for the same types of consumers. Since the number of available customers is largely dictated by the size of the marketplace and the level of industry maturity, the first metric to give us a glimpse into the health of an organization is the number of customers won in a defined period compared with the number a competitor won.

Analyze Whether Your Competitor Is Winning or Losing Customers

In the case where a start-up has entered or created a new business model, and thus there are no easy comparisons, the best metric to use regarding CX position is a review of the pace at which your competitor is winning new customers in the marketplace. This figure will provide you with an indication of whether the company has developed something that is resonating with customers and is gaining traction in the marketplace.

The ability to win new customers is only part of the equation, however. Your analysis also needs to include a comparison of how many customers were lost in the same period, applying the same methodology as for the number of customers won. The loss of customers is often more revealing about customer experience issues than the acquisition of new ones is.

Review Your Competitors' Profit and Loss Statements

Once you are able to analyze the numbers of customers won and lost, the next component to review is the organization's profit and loss statement (P&L). Your goal is to examine how the organization has performed over a longer term. A minimum twelve-month period is required to determine insightful trends. If the company is a start-up, then such a comparison may not be possible. In this case, the metrics related to customer acquisition become the most vital to determine future growth potential.

Assuming the organization has been trading for two years or more, however, you should compare key areas of the P&L. Answering some important questions will guide each area of investigation:

- **Revenue comparison**
  - » Is the rate of growth from the previous year reducing compared with previous years?

- » Does the twenty-four-month comparison show a decline in revenues?
- » Is the revenue growth skewed by an abnormally large singular sale?

- **Gross margin comparison**
  - » Is the operating margin increasing, decreasing, or the same as in previous years?
  - » How does the current gross margin compare with the competition's in the same time period?

- **Operating margin comparison**
  - » Is the gross margin increasing, decreasing, or the same as in previous years?
  - » If it has decreased, is this related to the cost of marketing, advertising, or promotions, or some other function?
  - » If it has increased, is this related to a reduction in headcount of supporting functions? If so, then how has this supporting function performed?
  - » Is the reduction in operating margin related to a new company strategy?

For each fact obtained about the metric under investigation, you should attempt to identify the most probable reason for this trend. Annual reports of publicly listed companies will document the main reasons. If you do not have access to annual reports, then consult with your CFO or CEO about the most probable reason for the financial metrics. It's more difficult to access information about competitors that are privately listed, but investigating secondary details, such as their numbers of clients and staff, can help you generate estimates for the figures you require. The Internet can be a powerful tool for accessing information from company media releases and websites. Or, for a fee, professional data providers such as Dun & Bradstreet can assist you with the necessary statistics to determine competitor analysis of private companies.

To clarify this exercise, consider an example of how to understand the different metrics. In table 2.1, I have taken two organizations in the same field and identified the variance in results for a number of measurements. The differences between the two companies reveal the most probable reason for the variance.

TABLE 2.I: COMPETITOR VARIANCE ANALYSIS

Measurement	Company A	Company B	Variance between Companies A & B	Most Probable Reason
New customers won over a 12-month period	354,250	210,156	41%	Company A is winning 41% more customers than Company B, which indicates it has a value proposition with greater appeal than its immediate rival's.
Customers lost over a 12-month period	79,054	175,067	-55%	Company B had 55% more customers leave than Company A. This mass defection indicates a better offer is available elsewhere.
Revenue change over a 12-month period	12%	5%	58%	With fewer defections, Company A had a 58% better revenue result.
Gross margin change over a 12-month period	-24%	-2%	92%	Company A saw a 24% reduction in gross margin, a change that is 92% lower than its nearest competitor's. Company A appears to be winning clients by reducing prices.
Operating margin change over a 12-month period	-28%	-4%	86%	The operating margin has dropped by 28% for Company A, indicating that its marketing costs have increased. Compared with Company B, it appears to be focused on winning market share over profitability.

From the analysis, you can draw some broad conclusions about the competitive environment and the marketplace for both companies. For example, Company A and Company B appear to be operating in a crowded marketplace. Winning new customers has come at a high price for Company A. The organization has had to lower prices, sacrifice gross margin, and at the same time reduce operating margin to fund the advertising and promotions it leveraged to win new customers.

Although Company B has won fewer new customers and lost more existing customers, it still has maintained most of its operating margin.

Company B has not engaged in a price war with Company A. Instead, it appears Company B has made a conscious decision not to try and salvage price-sensitive customers. Instead, Company B has determined the value of the customer segment it has lost to Company A, and has opted to protect its margins instead of investing in initiatives to win back customers.

Case Study: Digital Disruption—
Going After Market Share Instead of Profits

A long-held belief in business is that in new markets, the key is to win market share by sacrificing short-term profitability. Amazon is a prime example of a company in a new industry sector that has publicly gone after market share over profit. CEO Jeff Bezos believes the global e-commerce market is enormous and a business's main focus should be to win and retain customers. Amazon has been winning market share largely by attracting customers with its strong value propositions. Lower prices and convenience are the main appeal. Delivering on these simple customer promises is no easy task.

Amazon is continually reinvesting its thin profits back into the organization to maintain its lower prices and convenient delivery practices. It holds fast to a long-term plan, anticipating a future where the marketplace has matured and Amazon becomes the leading player in market share. If Amazon's infrastructure is built up to service this marketplace, then it would be reasonable to argue that the company would stop investing the same amount into supporting its customer promises. At this point, patient investors would expect to receive a windfall in profits. Amazon is still a work in progress, and it will take some time to truly verify if the company's strategy delivers future profits by sacrificing in the short term.

Company A's strategy would not work well in a mature market that is saturated by many players with strong customer value propositions. The battle for market share leads to lower margins for all contenders, and the reward of downstream profits is remote because the value proposition is largely based on price reductions.

Opportunities exist in mature markets for a new player to enter with a completely new value proposition from that of all the incumbent players. An obvious example is digital disruption, which is now occurring at a rapid pace in almost every industry sector. It is important for CX professionals to calculate the value of customers in their industry sector using metrics and methodologies applied by start-up companies in the digital disruption space. By applying the same numerical treatment to your customers, you will be able to determine the investment needed to improve your customers' experience—and achieve the return on investment from your efforts.

FIVE METRICS FOR IDENTIFYING CUSTOMER EXPERIENCE ISSUES

Once these financial figures are gathered and these questions answered, the next step is to establish whether your organization has a potential customer experience issue that is, or could be, affecting the bottom line. To explore this further, you need to review five key metrics to ascertain potential areas for improvement in the organization. You should use them to determine your company's maximum investment in any CX program and to calculate financial targets for that program.

1. Current cost to acquire a new customer (CAC)
   CAC is defined as follows:

   $$CAC = sum\ of\ all\ sales\ \&\ marketing\ expenses\ /\ number\ of\ new\ customers\ added$$

   Simply applied, a company that is spending $1 million annually in marketing expenses and is able to acquire 500 new customers would have a CAC of $2,000.

2. Customer lifetime (CL)
   CL is how long you can keep a customer before he or she leaves your organization. To understand a customer's value to the organization, you need to know the length of time the individual interacts with you as a customer. CL can be gleaned from your annual or monthly churn rate.
   Some organizations, particularly those that see themselves as a single sale business, may find this seemingly simple task quite difficult. However, every organization does have a CL, even if it has not

thought about its customers in that way. For example, a government entity providing power to customers may be a monopoly, but it also has customers constantly connecting and disconnecting power, and thus a CL is associated with its customers. A cohort of its customers over a period of time would reveal an average churn rate.

Customer lifetime can be calculated using the following formula:

$$CL = \frac{1}{customer\ churn\ rate}$$

Using the formula, and hypothetically applying an annual churn rate of 10 percent to the power company's customer base, the CL would be ten years. So on average, the power company would be billing the same customer for ten years.

3. Customer lifetime value (CLV)

CLV is how much a customer will spend with the company during his or her CL. Four key inputs are required in order to arrive at this metric, generated using historical figures or future dates based on predictions. Often organizations should calculate both historical and predictive CLV because the current pace of change in the marketplace means historical CLV is unlikely to provide a reliable metric when formulating business decisions for the future. There are numerous ways to calculate CLV; two common methods are outlined here.

a. Historical CLV

Using historical data to determine the CLV has limitations: It reveals only what the customer was worth to your organization in the past, not what the customer will be worth in the future. However, you must calculate historical CLV to ensure that any predictive calculations using forecasts are as accurate as possible.

When you know what the customer is spending over a period of time, you can calculate historical CLV as follows:

historical CLV = (sum of all transactions made) x gross profit margin

So if a customer spends $21,000 in sales over a seven-year period at a gross margin of 30 percent, then the historical CLV for the customer is $6,300.

b. Predictive CLV

In this calculation you are seeking to predict the future value of each customer to the organization. Predictive CLV is complex and requires a number of factors to calculate it, including

- the lifetime of a customer in months (MCL),
- the average gross margin on the products or services the customer buys (AGM),
- the number of repeat purchases on a monthly basis (MRP), and
- the average expenditure per transaction (AET).

When you know these figures, you can calculate predictive CLV using this formula:

$$predictive\ CLV = ((MRP \times AET) \times AGM\%) \times MCL$$

For example, assume the following about customers of a telecom company on a contracted plan:

MCL = 120 (ten years)

AGM = 30% (assumed)

MRP = 1 (the customer is billed only once a month)

AET = $300 (assumed monthly plan cost)

In this case, application of the formula would be as follows:

CLV = ((1 x 300) x 30%) x 120

The predictive CLV for the telecom company is therefore $10,800 per customer.

This simple application of the formula depicts the basic aspects you must consider when calculating CLV. Yet every organization has unique attributes to consider. The aim is to customize the formula to best suit the typical conditions of your organization. Once you have a grasp of how to apply the formula best suited to your organization, you then need to contemplate how many customer profiles you should apply to your analysis.

Every organization intending to undertake a predictive CLV should also reflect on other typical business factors and premises, such as the following:

- Revenue may be expected to expand on an annual basis. To factor this into your calculation, a simple method for determining the value is to multiply the percentage increase of annual growth to your predictive CLV figure. For example, say your estimated annual revenue growth is approximately 20 percent. Multiplying the $10,800 CLV by 20 percent gives us $2,160, so the new CLV would be $12,960. This is a simple estimate and is not intended as a precise prediction, because it makes assumptions such as customer growth being consistent over the lifetime of the customer.
- Revenues may be expected to shrink over the long term. To factor this into your calculation, use a similar application as with expansion revenue, instead subtracting the expected decline from the predictive CLV figure. For example, the $10,800 CLV decreased by 20 percent gives us $2,160, so the new predictive CLV would be $8,640.
- Because of inflation, future capital does not hold the same value as today's capital. To determine the net present value of predictive CLV, you need to apply a discount rate to the amount the customer is likely to contribute in the future. For example, if inflation is running at an annual rate of 3 percent over a 10-year period, the future CLV of $10,800 would have a present value of $8,036. A number of Excel formulas and online calculators can calculate the net present value for you.

4. Customer contribution to returns on investment (ROI) as calculated later in this chapter.

   Not every customer type has the same customer lifetime value, so to design an effective program that generates economic benefits for your organization, you need to dive deeper into your customer segments and identify their contribution to your bottom line. For example, you may discover a segment of customers who have a rather low CLV because they are highly price-sensitive and show little loyalty. The decision to invest in this particular customer segment should be easier because the ROI to build emotional allegiance to the brand will not pay off. This customer segment is best acquired and retained by simply providing the lowest price in the marketplace. Thus, having the lowest price is considered the best possible customer experience for this segment, and by providing lower prices or perceived value, you will be achieving your customer-centricity objectives for these customers.

5. Customer retention cost (CRC)

   During the customer lifetime, there may be additional costs related to customer retention that are not captured as separate items in the company's profit and loss statement. These costs affect the company's profitability and overall bottom line, and should be taken into consideration using the following formula:

$$CRC = \frac{total\ retention\ expenditure}{total\ customers\ retained}$$

   If the total customers retained in twelve months equal 200,000 and the total retention costs are \$5 million annually, then the cost to retain a single customer is \$25 per year. If this were a fixed cost, then using our telecom CLV example, the cost of retention over the ten-year lifetime would be \$250. Subtracting this amount from the CLV calculation would offer a better sense of the value of the customer.

   These five key metrics are designed to ascertain potential areas for improvement in your customers' experiences—where you should focus in order to maximize your company's investment in CX. After completing your financial analysis, you should be in a position to articulate what high-level strategic objectives you would like to achieve from your customer experience program.

DEFINE YOUR VISION AND MISSION FOR YOUR CX PROGRAM

As I've mentioned, CX excellence is all about delivering the values considered most important by *your* customer. These values may be either actual or perceived. CX excellence is also about being able to endow your customers with well-targeted experiences that are closely aligned to your organization's strategy and mission.

Start with a vision for your CX program. The vision should provide your overarching objective by stating the optimal, desired future state. For example, the vision for the CX program for Company A might be as follows:

> *Our vision is to become recognized by customers and competitors as the leading CX company in the US mobile marketplace.*

For this vision to be effective and accepted within the organization, it needs to align with the overarching corporate vision. For instance, if the large-scale vision for the company is specifically about excelling in product offerings to the marketplace, then you should adjust the CX vision so it reflects how the CX program will contribute to achieving this larger objective.

Next develop the mission for your CX program. The mission should state *what* your program will do to achieve the future vision, *who* it's for, and *how* it will achieve its goals. The mission for Company A might be as follows:

> Our mission is to generate new, sustainable economic benefits for the company by providing the most valued experiences for our customers. These experiences will differentiate us in the marketplace, enabling us to deliver a uniquely branded experience for US mobile customers.

Whatever the vision and mission statement you decide on, make sure they have strategic dimensions that properly reflect the broader focus of your organization. Once you write your mission statement, you will have a much clearer notion of what you are trying to achieve with your CX program. It will help you brainstorm initiatives and prioritize them in later stages of the process.

Which Financial Areas Do You Need to Change?

The ultimate aim, of course, is to supply the organization with sustainable economic benefits on a consistent basis. So your goal is to position customer experience within the organization as a strategic imperative that, if executed properly, will add real economic value to shareholders in terms of bottom-line profits and increasing the enterprise value.

The economic benefits you seek from an effective customer experience program require that you make changes to key customer metrics. A CX program that fails to make these changes will fail to have a positive effect on profitability or the organization's value. When there is no direct correlation between the company's customer-centricity efforts and measurable commercial value, a CX program is in danger of becoming a tactical initiative like "delighting the customer" or "encouraging customer feedback."

A strategic CX initiative should seek to demonstrate the following economic outcomes:

- Reduce the cost of customer acquisition.
- Increase the number of customer acquisitions.
- Reduce the customer churn rate.
- Increase the frequency and spend of each transaction.
- Increase the customer lifetime.
- Reduce the cost of support and retention.

All these outcomes are measurable and have an impact on both profitability and enterprise value. To achieve these outcomes, you will need to include a number of different initiatives in your case for a transformational CX program.

For example, building stronger emotional ties with customers helps develop loyalty and leads to an increase in advocacy. The advocacy sought is an increase in word-of-mouth referrals about the company and its products and services. The increase in word-of-mouth recommendations leads to

- reduced cost of customer acquisition (because existing customers are doing the work for your marketing department), and
- increased customer acquisitions (because your marketing department is still winning new customers using traditional methods, and additional customers are coming from the word-of-mouth referrals).

By analyzing customer metrics in your financial statements and those of your closest competitors, you will be able to identify weak areas. Once these have been identified, you can isolate the areas that need changing to improve your commercial results. You can then proceed to the next stage and begin quantifying the degree of change for each area.

How Much Would You Like to Change Company Metrics?

This stage of the process is often the most intensive; it will largely dictate what you focus on as you move forward with your CX program. Always err on the side of conservative targets. As a guideline, your business case should not exceed a 20 percent increase in customer numbers, nor should it be based on a more than 20 percent net increase in profits. The return on investment needs to be clear and realistic. A business case that promises to deliver improvements across all financial metrics will be less believable than one based on more attainable, cautious objectives.

This process will require multiple revisions until you feel the desired economic outcomes are sensible and achievable. During this stage, you are simply identifying the financial impact you wish to achieve with the CX program. You are not yet in a position to answer the question of *how* you will achieve this.

The metrics you select for change should depend on your particular organization and should reflect both the organization's goals and the external dynamics of the marketplace. These changes will be based on a number of variables, such as:

- Existing revenues
- Market size and opportunity
- Market saturation
- CL and CLV

For example, let's evaluate the metrics of a start-up company with little or no revenues, whose offering appeals to a largely untapped marketplace. The start-up would focus its efforts and investments on increasing customer acquisition by refining its existing offerings and winning market share. Without an existing budget to adjust, the start-up would be forced to allocate investment funds to increase its rate of customer acquisition. Investing in increasing the number of customers will improve the valuation of the enterprise, thus allowing it to raise more capital in the future. With the increase in capital, the start-up would be able to allocate more funds for its customer retention costs and then could build on its customer acquisition costs within an established support network.

Determining the quantity of change needs to be tailored to your current circumstances and your company's capacity and appetite for transformation. In any situation, the key to determining the quantity of change is to ensure you have the underlying financial facts outlined in this chapter to support your rationale for the quantity of uplift you hope to achieve.

What Is the ROI for Your CX Initiative?

The most important variable in this stage is the expected duration for achieving the desired financial outcomes. In the example used earlier, the US telecom company adopts a twelve-month period to achieve its financial objectives. The time you allocate to achieve these objectives will depend on a wide range of variables:

- The financial budget allocated for the program
- The degree of change required for your financial metrics
- The amount and depth of the work required in your organization

- The pace of change the organization can achieve during your program
- The degree of support received from the leadership team

All these factors relate to the period required for economic benefits to be achieved, and will depend largely on the company's appetite for and capability to change. As a guide, no term should be lower than eight months, and the average duration before achieving the financial objectives is eighteen months. If the targets are more aggressive, then the terms could be as high as thirty-six months or more.

Now let's move on to a discussion of how to come up with an appropriate ROI.

CALCULATING CX VALUE FOR ESTABLISHED COMPANIES

Every organization, based on the type of industry sector and the maturity level of the marketplace, has different potential to attract and retain customers. I will use a conservative hypothetical example to illustrate the economic benefits of a strategic customer experience program. Any commercial organization (other than a start-up) is valued in the marketplace based on either its free cash flow, multiples of its earnings, or multiples of its revenues. For this exercise we will use one of the most common valuation methods: multiple of earnings. More specifically, the valuation is a multiple of earnings before interest tax depreciation and amortization (EBITDA). If we assume our telecom company is making $40 million in EBITDA, and the marketplace estimates it is worth ten times that amount, then the valuation of the telecom company is $400 million.

Despite ample studies on the commercial benefits obtained from companies able to deliver differentiated experiences for their customers, we will adopt a conservative approach in our example. So, assuming we can make only a positive 2 percent increase in the EBITDA of the telecom company, the value to the organization would be as follows:

- New EBITDA: $40.8 million
- New enterprise value: $408 million

So, in this example of the telecom company, the 2 percent increase in EBITDA has had a positive commercial benefit equivalent:

- $800,000 increase in profitability
- $8 million increase in enterprise value

The total commercial benefit to the organization is $8.8 million. This amount will determine what investment should be made when implementing customer experience initiatives. This telecom company example highlights the importance of knowing the EBITDA multiples used to value your organization in the marketplace.

Assuming Company A is a publicly traded telecommunications company, we can access its annual report to shareholders and learn the following:

TABLE 2.2

	Actual Figure	Variance on Previous 12 Months
EBITDA	$ 1,199,999,999.97	-28%
Enterprise Value Based on 12 Times Earnings	$ 14,399,999,999.64	-17%

If you are unable to determine the enterprise value because the organization is not publicly traded, then you can use the following table as a high-level guide:

TABLE 2.3

Company Type	Method of Valuation	Multiple
Privately traded, revenues of $1M–$5M	Free cash flow	3
Privately traded, revenues of $7M–$15M	Free cash flow	5
Privately traded, revenues over $20M	Free cash flow	7
Technology-based start-up, in a high-growth sector	Future 12-month revenues	5
Non-technology start-up	Future 12-month revenues	0.5

CALCULATING CX VALUE FOR START-UP COMPANIES

Customer experience excellence tends to be an obsession with start-up organizations because they are normally challenging in a market dominated by brick-and-mortar organizations, and providing a new business model or service offering. They are able to win over customers to their new way of doing business only by having something substantially better than what the incumbent players have.

Start-up companies, especially technology ones, rarely use EBITDA as a measure for valuation. Start-ups will tend to use a combination of their intellectual property, future recurring revenues, market opportunity, and number of customers. The multiples used for many tech companies tend to dwarf those of brick-and-mortar companies if they have the potential to scale up quickly without incurring proportional costs, so the ability to acquire customers rapidly or to increase recurring revenue can have a profound effect on technology start-up valuations.

The amount of investment a start-up organization should make in a strategic customer experience program will depend on a number of variables:

- The net CLV of customers
- The cost of customer retention
- The number of employees in the organization
- The depth and saturation of the marketplace
- The organization's current rating on customer centricity (the lower the rating, the greater the change, which will consequently impact the cost)
- The level of understanding and commitment by the CEO and C-level regarding implementation of a strategic CX initiative
- The organization's ability to implement change management
- The number of new resources required, whether hired directly or via external consultants

For start-ups, how much will be invested in your CX program ultimately depends on the investment capital available and the orientation of the business. For example, if the start-up is largely consumer oriented, then it should allocate a larger portion of its budget to a customer experience program that will help differentiate a new entrant into the marketplace. A technology-centric start-up may need to allocate most of its budget initially for research and development, but it will need to shift focus toward customer experience later if it wants to acquire and retain customers for its technology. Either way, customer experience has to be a primary concern for any start-up wanting to win market share. The ROI for a start-up is clear when you apply the methodology to determine your CX program budget, because there is a direct link between the objectives of the program and the increase in profitability and enterprise value.

STRUCTURING YOUR BUDGET

The budgeting process for your strategic CX program will require you to gather more detail about the resources and costs of completing the analysis and design of your initiatives before you reach the implementation stage.

There are three phases for any customer experience project, and a different amount will be allocated for each. As you are making the budget, use the following benchmarks to ensure you are not under- or over-allocating parts of the budget:

- Analysis: 10 percent
- Design: 20 percent

The analysis and design phases are typically conducted by the same staff to ensure the final design of the program will accurately address the issues identified during the analysis phase. There is also some overlap in the timing and tasks of the analysis and design phases, especially in those processes required to create your customer journey maps. As you move back and forth between analysis and design, it is helpful and efficient to have one group of resources for both phases.

The successful creation of your customer experience program will depend largely on the expertise you have on hand. To complete the analysis and design phases effectively, you should budget for the following key resources or services:

- Senior customer experience strategy consultants
  (from one to ten, depending on the size of the organization)
- Customer research organization
- Organizational customer-centricity evaluation
- Workshop facilitator
- Project manager

These resources should be provided by one organization, or perhaps two at the most, to avoid conflicting directions during both analysis and design phases.

There are a number of different approaches to creating and implementing a CX program. As owner of the program, you should lead the direction and ensure your methodology follows the steps outlined in this book, so that you achieve your financial and strategic objectives. Overall, the resources during the analysis and design phases should not amount to more than 30 percent of the total budget.

- Implementation: 70 percent

Many people make the error of under-budgeting for the implementation phase of their initiative, and end up with a greatly designed program that never achieves any objectives because implementation never really gets off the ground. Allocating the largest portion of the budget (70 percent) to implementation ensures your program can execute your initiatives.

Presenting Your CX Case Effectively

I have outlined the first four stages required to build a business case for a strategic implementation of customer experience: identifying whether, how, and by how much your organization can benefit from such a program, and providing clear ROI goals for the program. Now you must present, in a coherent and logical manner, what you have discovered about your company's need for strategic CX. By considering all these components, you can communicate a well-considered financial plan to your CEO and board of directors that supports your initiative and provides a return on investment specifically defined for your organization.

No board of directors or CEO should make a commercial decision of this nature without sound evidence. Rather than generalizations, you need evidence based on hard facts about how the CX initiative will lead to economic value. A good business case will incorporate an understanding of the decision makers' perspectives and will hit on the right mix of facts and foresight to convince the CEO to proceed. Finding this balance is the artistic aspect of making a business case for CX.

Let us return to the case of the mobile telecom company used earlier, and identify whether it can benefit from improving its customers' experiences. I will review the four stages (as described at the start of this chapter and in the appendix) you need to arrive at measurable, specific financial objectives that you can use to make a case for customer experience at your company.

STAGE I: DETERMINE WHETHER THE ORGANIZATION COULD BENEFIT FROM IMPROVING ITS CUSTOMER EXPERIENCE

Pegging your company against your closest rival will give you the necessary insights to determine your main problem areas and what changes you should make. In each measurement area, you should examine the variance between two companies (one of which is your own) and then deduce the most probable reason for the variance.

Now let's return to the previous analysis we did earlier in this chapter. From the competitor variance analysis (table 2.1) of the two telecom companies, we can draw the following conclusions:

- Company A is winning new customers by lowering prices, but it is also sacrificing margins. It is focused on winning market share over profitability. Company A seems to be product centric and spending marketing dollars on the wrong customer segments. Company A would benefit from becoming customer centric, focusing on what its customers value most and on how to retain them for longer without dropping margins.

- Company B has not engaged in the price war initiated by Company A. It has lost a larger number of customers but has marginally sacrificed profitability. Company B could improve the customer experience to retain more customers and also extend their lifetime value.

Furthermore, we can draw the general conclusion that both companies could benefit from elevating their customers' experiences. These organizations are both operating in a saturated, mature marketplace, so product differentiation is difficult. Still, they could differentiate themselves by delivering unique propositions that are highly valued by profitable customer segments.

STAGE 2: IDENTIFY THE FINANCIAL AREAS YOU WOULD LIKE TO CHANGE TO GENERATE COMMERCIAL BENEFIT

For this stage, you will need to collect the financial measurements relevant for the proposed CX initiatives. Since your goal in a strategic adoption of a customer experience program is to increase commercial value to the organization, your aim should be to identify the components most likely to improve commercial results.

In the case of Company A, it is winning a large number of customers by sacrificing margins and profitability—by increasing marketing costs and also reducing operating margin by 28 percent from the previous year. From this synopsis, we can hypothesize Company A's problem areas as follows:

1. High cost to acquire a customer
2. Poor targeting of customer segments
3. Poor profitability on products or customers
4. Lower-margin trend that is not sustainable over the long term
5. Mature or saturated marketplace with aggressive competition

To gain a better understanding of the problem areas, we need access to the customer metrics relevant to Company A. Using the formulas provided in this section, we can determine that Company A has the following values and variances over a twelve-month period:

TABLE 2.4

	Actual Figure	Variance on Previous 12 Months
Cost to Acquire a Customer (CAC)	$ 650.00	18%
Customer Lifetime (CL)	5.6 years	-12%
Historical CLV	$ 7,920.00	-5%
Predictive CLV	$ 7,130.00	n/a
Customer Retention Cost (CRC)	$91	2%

The cost to acquire customers has increased by 18 percent in the past year, confirming that the marketing department has increased spending to acquire new customers. Meanwhile, the CL and the historical CLV have both reduced over the twelve-month period, putting further pressure on the company's ability to extract profits from existing customers.

On first review, the positive CAC variance may seem to contrast with the number of customers lost over the twelve-month period. Company B had 55 percent more customer defections than Company A. Why? If Company A is experiencing fewer defections in the past twelve months, when it lowered prices but also experienced lower CL and CLV, the likely answer is that Company A is winning price-sensitive customers with little loyalty to the brand. These volatile customers are moving every time there is a lower price offer. This reduces the overall CL for Company A, which is why it is facing trouble with operating margins and profitability.

We can also see that there is only a 2 percent increase in retention costs. Company A is focusing on winning new, low-profit customers, and is not focusing its efforts on retention or increasing profitability.

We can conclude that the current strategy for Company A is not sustainable. By continuing on this course, the company will further reduce its margins and will continue to attract unprofitable customers at a high cost.

To remedy the situation, Company A needs to focus on the areas that will have the greatest positive commercial impact:

- Reduce the cost of acquiring new customers.
- Increase the number of profitable customers.
- Reduce the number of profitable customers lost every year.
- Increase the customer lifetime and the predictive value over the period.
- Increase gross profitability and operating margin.
- Increase the cost of retention to secure profitable customers.

These areas need to change for Company A to rectify its current issues and generate sustainable commercial results.

STAGE 3: IDENTIFY HOW MUCH YOU WOULD LIKE TO CHANGE THE METRICS

As I stated earlier, the amount of change applied in each area will vary depending on the company. A basic rule is to apply percentages that have been previously achieved by your company or your nearest rival, keeping in mind that conservative figures are more likely to be believable by senior executives.

Going back to our example of Company A, I have demonstrated how you can generate substantial economic results with zero financial investment, simply by adjusting budgets and changing focus areas. In the case of Company A, our telecom organization, I have applied minor changes to customer acquisition, customer retention, and customer lifetime, all with no new investment from the company. Instead, we decided to find the money for our program by marginally reducing the existing budget allocated for customer acquisition. The spare capital is used to totally fund the proposed customer experience program.

In this example, Company A seeks a minor uplift in gross profit margin, even though customers are currently spending the same amount on an annual basis. The EBITDA margin has not changed either. The metrics we wish to change with the CX initiative are outlined in table 2.5:

TABLE 2.5: METRICS AND FINANCIAL TARGETS

CUSTOMER WINS AND LOSSES

Metric	Company A: Current State	Objective	Financial Target
Total customers	6,702,197		
New customers won over a 12-month period	354,250	Increase new customers by 10% on previous year results.	Achieve 35,425 new customers.
Customers lost over a 12-month period	79,054	Reduce lost customers by 5%.	Achieve 3,952 more customers retained.

CUSTOMER VALUE

Metric	Company A: Current State	Objective	Financial Target
Customer lifetime in years (CL)	5.6	Increase lifetime of customer.	Increase lifetime to 6 years.
Annual spend per customer	$3,978.79	No change.	No change.
Gross profit per customer per year	$1,273.21	Increase GP amount based on 39,377 acquired and retained customers.	Based on new revenues, achieve an additional $25.46 in GP per customer.
Historical CLV	$7,920.00		
Predictive CLV	$7,130.00	Increase predictive CLV.	Increase CLV to $7,639 (achieved by increasing lifetime from 5.6 to 6 years—no difference to customer annual spend).
Cost to acquire a customer (CAC)	$650.00	Reduce CAC by 1.4% to fund the CX initiative. The goal is a 0% increase in the cost base.	Achieve new cost to acquire: $640.09 per customer.
Customer retention cost (CRC)	$91	Increase retention cost by 10% to fund the cost of the CX initiative.	Achieve new retention cost: $100.10 per customer.

COMPANY PROFITABILITY

Metric	Company A: Current State	Objective	Financial Target
Revenues	$26,666,666,666	Based on 39,377 new or retained customers, and on average yearly spend of $3,978, the revenues would increase by $156,675,781.	Revenues to increase by $156,675,781.
Gross profit margin	30%	Improve GP margin by 6.5% over the previous 12 months.	New GP target is 32%.
Gross profit amount	$7,999,999,999.80	GP amount to increase based on total of new customers acquired or retained.	Increase GP by $50,136,250 from new customer revenues plus 2% increase on total EBITDA margin, taking total increase in GP to $583,469,583.
EBITDA	$1,199,999,999.97	Increase EBITDA.	Increase EBITDA by $87,520,437 (proportional increase to change in GP).
EBITDA margin	15%	No change.	No change.
EBITDA multiple used for valuation	12x	No change.	No change.
Enterprise value based on 12 times earnings	$14,399,999,999.64	Increase in enterprise value.	Achieve new enterprise value: increase by $1,050,245,249 (based on increase in EBITDA).

STAGE 4: SUMMARIZE AND PROVIDE A CLEAR ROI FOR THE INVESTMENT IN THE CX PROGRAM

Our CX program for Company A is going to focus on acquiring and retaining more profitable customers and on reducing the costs associated with acquiring price-sensitive customers who easily churn. The initiatives for the program will be self-funded by adjusting the existing cost budget.

If the program achieves its objectives, it will be able to increase the bottom-line EBITDA by $87,520,437. The cost of the program is to be funded from a minor reduction of 1.4 percent ($9.10) from the cost of acquiring a new customer. Reallocating the funds to the retention bucket means we now have $60,989,993 ($9.10 x 6,702,197 customers) to use for our CX program. The cost of the program is recouped in 8.4 months through the increase in monthly EBITDA ($87,520,437/12 = X monthly EBITDA); then divide the cost of the program by the monthly gain to get your ROI in months ($60,989,993/X monthly EBITDA).

The increased profitability also increases the enterprise value by over $1 billion. We are not including the increase in enterprise value into the ROI, as we want to measure only the capital return against actual cost incurred in the same time period. The net economic value from the program in the first year is $26,530,444. The summary of the financials for the program and ROI should be depicted as follows:

Cost of Program	$ 60,989,993
Increase in EBITDA	$ 87,520,437
Increase in Enterprise Value	$ 1,050,245,249
Net Economic Value in Year 1	$ 26,530,444
Period to Achieve Outcomes	12 months
ROI	8.4 months

Once you have completed these stages for your CX business case, you are ready to move on to designing your customer experience initiatives to meet the financial targets you have set. After sketching the outline for your program, you will need to return to the financial metrics you have set in order to review and potentially revise them. The revision may require you to change your objectives and targets to more accurately reflect the program you have designed. As with the implementation of most large projects, starting off with high-level financial targets and objectives is the key to determining the scope and depth of your program.

KEY LESSONS

- Strategic customer experience should always have a direct economic benefit to the organization.
- Any strategic customer experience discussion should begin by examining the key financials of the company.
- A comparison of the organization to its closest rival helps determine whether the organization can benefit by improving the customer experience.
- An analysis of a company's profit and loss statement and underlying metrics such as the number of customers and gross profit margin will help identify the areas to target for improvement.
- Incumbent players in mature markets need to apply the same methodologies used by start-ups when determining the value of a differentiated customer experience.
- Key calculations must be made to determine the investment amount and the areas targeted for change:
  » Cost to acquire a customer (CAC)
  » Customer lifetime (CL)
  » Customer lifetime value (CLV): both historical and predictive
  » Expansion or declining future revenues
  » Net present value of predictive CLV
  » Customer retention costs (CRC)
- The economic value of a customer experience program has to benefit areas of the business directly related to its profit and loss statement and/or the enterprise value.
- Strategic CX should aim for the following changes:
  » Reduce the cost of customer acquisition.
  » Increase the number of customer acquisitions.
  » Reduce customer churn rate.
  » Increase the frequency and spend of each transaction.
  » Increase the customer lifetime.
  » Reduce the cost of support and retention.

- Developing the best business case for customer experience will depend in part on a number of nonfinancial forces, such as external market conditions and internal organizational dynamics.
- There are four stages to determining your customer experience financial objectives:
  - » Stage 1: Identify whether your organization can benefit from improving its CX, and then develop a vision and mission for your CX program.
  - » Stage 2: Identify the financial areas you would like to change to generate commercial benefit.
  - » Stage 3: Identify how much you would like to change the metrics.
  - » Stage 4: Summarize and provide a clear ROI for the investment in the CX program.

CHAPTER 3

Measuring Organizational Customer Centricity

Now that you have completed the financial analysis and identified the areas you would like to change with your customer experience initiative, the next step in the process is to determine the scope of the initiative. Then you can outline how you will achieve the changes required to reach your financial objectives.

This chapter covers stages 5 and 6 of the customer experience management process:

Stage	Desired Output
5. Evaluate the organization to determine how customer centric the employees are.	An empirically based analysis identifying problem areas in the organization
6. Identify the impact of the lowest-scored components on customers and the company.	An analysis outlining the impacts and their underlying causes

Adding Substance to Your Business Case

In the previous chapter, we identified the customer metrics we wanted to change to increase telecom Company A's bottom-line profitability and enterprise value:

- Increase the number of new customers by 10 percent over the previous year's results. This equates to 35,425 new customers.
- Reduce the number of lost customers by 5 percent over the previous year's results. This equates to 3,952 additional retained customers.

- Increase the customer life cycle from 5.6 years to 6 years.

These three changes to Company A's customer metrics need to achieve the following financial targets:

- Increase revenues by $156,675,781.
- Increase gross profit margin to 32 percent.
- Increase total gross profit by $583,469,583.

We decided to base our proposed customer experience initiative on zero new investment, funding it instead by adjusting future budgets. We determined that by reducing the cost of acquisition by just 1.4 percent (equating to $9.10 per customer) and allocating these funds to the retention bucket, we could fund a new CX initiative with an annual budget of $60,989,995.32.

So, what's next?

A $60 million reallocation of budget is not going to just happen because you have completed the financial analysis exercise and you think improving the customer experience is a great idea. You will need to add more substance to your business case so it's well thought out, based on financial data, and convincing to the C-level audience. To do this, you will need to compile some additional evidence. The main types of evidence for your business case should include the following:

- Employee customer-centricity score (discussed in chapter 1)
- Financial analysis (discussed in chapter 2)
- Customer research and key findings (discussed in chapter 2)

From this evidence you will be able to draw conclusions that will build a strong case for your program. Your conclusions need to have a direct link to the facts you gather; otherwise the business case will miss its objective. Consider the example from chapter 1: It would be erroneous to conclude that a lack of training among employees of the contact center was the cause of a decrease in customer satisfaction. Without a direct causal link that is well supported by customer-based facts, the conclusion will be flawed and could lead you to focus on the wrong areas of your business. Investing your energies and the company's funds in fixing the contact center is unlikely to achieve your financial objectives. Unless you have performed a proper root cause analysis, any remedy you apply will not be long term and will not lead to any measurable, sustainable improvements in customer experience.

The objective is to design a case for your customer-centricity program that is well targeted, achieves sustainable changes, and meets the financial targets within your set time frames. It's important to identify the specific areas in the organization that you will need to address to accomplish your objectives. To achieve this outcome, you will need to undertake a fact-based evaluation of the organization to determine the level of centricity among the company's employees.

How Do You Evaluate Customer Centricity?

Customer centricity as a strategic imperative must be embedded in an organization's DNA, and the individual parts that make up a company's DNA are its employees. So, to design a highly effective customer-centricity initiative, we must first examine the employees of an organization and become acquainted with their perspective: What do they think about customer centricity? How do they strive to achieve it?

There are several ways to evaluate employees' customer-centricity levels, but my recommendation is to use a scoring system based on empirical research and conducted by a credited research group, such as the CCScore discussed in the previous chapter. This score, and insights gathered from the survey, will enable you to make decisions based on sound evidence. The primary goal of your employee evaluation is to identify the scope of work required to achieve your CX objectives.

The employee evaluation should identify insights about the organization along various organizational and demographic variables:

- Individual departments
- Roles and responsibilities
- Age
- Gender
- Job tenure

After the analysis is complete, you should have a more comprehensive understanding of the areas and departments you need to address to achieve your customer experience objectives.

An evaluation using the CCScore methodology, for example, will provide you with a breakdown of the components that drive customer centricity in your organization. The areas identified in the standard CCScore system that are useful in any evaluation of customer centricity are as follows.

LEADERSHIP

- **Prioritization.** Customer orientation is perceived as top priority in the company.
- **Openness.** The company culture encourages employees to be innovative and independent.
- **Enabling.** Management has given the employees the necessary tools to be customer focused.
- **Commitment.** Management champions a customer-focused approach with their actions.
- **Incentives.** Management prioritizes customer-satisfaction goals as well as financial or technical goals (sales goals, sales targets, time-to-market, releases, etc.).

COLLABORATION

- **Tolerance.** Employees can express their opinions freely and are encouraged to try out new things.
- **Learning culture.** The firm is continuously developing its products, and continuously integrating customer and employee feedback.
- **Persistence.** Once decisions are given the green light, they are put into action.
- **Cross-functionality.** Teams work impartially across organizational boundaries; there is no silo mentality.
- **Alignment.** All business units are constantly in contact with customer touch points.

IMPLEMENTATION

- **System support.** All systems, processes, and channels are designed to successfully support customer satisfaction.
- **Customer insight.** The employees really understand the needs of the customers; information on customer insights is available.
- **Experience design.** The desired customer experience is clearly defined from start to finish. The experience is in place, and everyone is familiar with it. Everyone knows their role in the customer experience chain.
- **Customer integration.** Customer input is integrated in the development of new products and service solutions.
- **Personal responsiveness.** Employees can respond to customer feedback in real time with individual solutions.

Your organization's size will determine how far you will drill down to identify where these issues are coming from. For example, you might be able to identify a correlation between employees' tenure and why employees scored low for the Enabling component of the CCScore questionnaire. Employees who have been in the organization for only a short time may feel less enabled by the leadership team to achieve customer-centricity objectives than do their colleagues who have long been a part of the organization. An insight like this allows you to better target the group of employees who feel less enabled in your organization and help them achieve customer-centric objectives.

An independent research firm like CCScore will provide your organization's customer-centricity results and their impact from a best-practice perspective. The firm will identify how close or far your organization is from total customer centricity. The evaluation exposes the problem areas in your organization that shift focus away from best serving your customers.

What the evaluations won't tell you, however, is the underlying reasons for the problem areas. To find these out, you will need to undertake a root cause analysis of the results.

Performing a Root Cause Analysis

Once you get the results of your employee evaluation regarding customer centricity, you will need to perform a root cause analysis to identify the specific areas and actions you should undertake to achieve your financial objectives. Without a proper root cause analysis, your efforts will likely focus on fixing only the symptoms of the problem rather than its underlying cause. Focusing on the symptoms may provide you with a short-term improvement, but the problem is guaranteed to return if the fundamental problem remains.

A Root Cause Analogy, Part I: Going Beyond Symptoms

The usefulness of a root cause analysis is best illustrated using the analogy of a medical condition. A patient who is sweating is displaying a sign of an underlying problem. The sweating is a direct result of a high fever. If we focus our energy on reducing the fever by placing the patient in a cold bath, it will provide the patient with immediate relief. But have we fixed the underlying cause of the fever? No.

A good doctor would conduct further tests to identify the cause of both the fever and the visible symptom (the sweating). A blood sample test could identify a bacterial infection in the patient's bloodstream as the cause of the fever. If this is the correct diagnosis, it would lead the doctor to the right prescription that would eliminate the problem for the patient.

In this example, we can clearly identify the sweating as the symptom of the problem, the fever as the problem itself, and the bacterial infection as the underlying cause of the problem. We could even go a little deeper to find and remedy the *root cause* and ensure the problem never occurs again. To achieve this, we need to ask why and how the bacterial infection was picked up by the patient.

Root cause analysis aims to identify the origin of a problem and understand why the problem occurred. Root causes in organizations usually fall under three key categories:

- **Physical causes.** Tangible, material items that have failed in some way.
- **Human causes.** People did something wrong, or did not do something that was needed. Human causes also typically create physical causes.

- **Organizational causes.** A system, process, or policy that people use to make decisions or do their work is faulty.

To perform a root cause analysis you need to take the following critical steps:

1. Identify the problem.
2. Collect facts about the problem and its impact on the customer and organization.
3. Analyze the problem and possible causal factors.
4. Identify the root causes of the problem.
5. Propose and implement a remedial plan.

There are a number of techniques for executing a proper root cause analysis. Popular approaches include using cause-and-effect diagrams or the "Five Whys" to derive your underlying causes. To use the latter method, we ask, "Why?" at least five times; each time we answer our "Why?" question, we question that answer again, until we uncover our root cause.

A Root Cause Analogy, Part 2: Applying the Five Whys

Returning to our analogy of a medical condition and diagnosis, applying the Five Whys technique leads to the underlying cause of the patient's visible symptom of sweating:

1. Why is the patient sweating? He has a fever.

2. Why does he have a fever? He has a bacterial infection.

3. Why does he have a bacterial infection? He received a cut while working in the garden.

4. Why did the cut lead to the bacterial infection? He did not immediately clean the dirt from the cut.

5. Why did the cut have dirt in it? He was not wearing gloves.

It's important to know that the solution to the sweating is twofold: We need to eradicate the bacterial infection causing the fever that creates the sweating, and we need to ensure that the patient is not cut while gardening again. To solve the first problem, we can prescribe antibiotics. If we are going to do our job properly and make sure the patient does not have a recurring problem, however, we will need to solve the second problem, too, by working out the best way to ensure the patient wears gloves the next time he is working in the garden soil.

Continued

We may decide that it's not enough to simply request that the patient wears gloves next time. Instead, we may take a more decisive course of action by showing him extreme examples of what could happen to him if he contracted another such infection. If we do this, we are essentially choosing to remedy the patient's carelessness by educating him, in the hopes that a more explicit medical perspective will make certain the patient is highly unlikely to repeat the same carelessness. This two-prong approach—addressing both the immediate and the ultimate underlying causes of the problem—is the only way of ensuring its long-term eradication.

In the case of our customer-centric evaluation of the organization, you will need to unearth the problem and the likely causal factors before we do the root cause analysis. An effective way of approaching this is to apply a matrix and a scoring scale to determine the impact of each problem area. Table 3.1 uses the categories from CCScore to determine the causal factors hampering customer centricity in a manufacturing and retail company. You can replace these with any alternate ones used to measure customer centricity and still apply the same methodology to complete the matrix and uncover possible causal factors.

How would you apply this analysis at this stage of the process? Let's imagine a company that has been in business for fifty years and has recently been experiencing declines in revenues and lower sales per customer. To demonstrate the application of my CX program in other industries, instead of a telecom company, let's take the example of a company focused on manufacturing and sales of physical products (Company C). The company produces household appliances such as stoves, washing machines, and fridges. After much debate the leaders have decided to undertake a customer-centricity evaluation of their company. They have used a CCScore measurement system and have received scores for each department and also for the whole company. Now they need to identify the components with the greatest impact on the company and the customer, and the likely root causes associated with these issues.

At this stage, we are still not identifying any actions that we will take to achieve our financial goals. Instead, the approach adopted in the organizational evaluation of Company C in table 3.1 is merely to allocate a simple weighting category depending on the range of scores received from the survey. The areas identified in the standard CCScore system that are useful in any evaluation of customer centricity are Leadership, Collaboration, and Implementation. In the CCScore system, for example, where scores can range from -100 to +100, we can allocate the following categories:

- **Low:** Scores from -100 to +30
- **Medium:** Scores from +31 to 60
- **High:** Scores from +61 to 100

The logical path to better customer experiences is to remedy any issues prohibiting employees from achieving this goal. The analysis of the organization will help determine where "surgery" is required. From a practical perspective, any category rating of Low will trigger the Five Whys technique to determine root causes. Although the Medium and High categories could also be analyzed in this manner, we shall focus on the components that scored lowest in our customer-centricity evaluation.

TABLE 3.1: ROOT CAUSE ANALYSIS

LEADERSHIP

Component	Score	Impact on Customer and Company	Possible Causal Factors	Underlying Root Causes
Enabling	Medium			
Openness	Low	The company is likely to become less competitive, as it isn't open to new ideas such as digital transformation. Customers will also be affected because they will not receive the benefits of any new ideas.	The company believes its products and business model are the best in the marketplace.	There is no diversity at the board level. The company is very patriarchal and is led as such.

Continued

Component	Score	Impact on Customer and Company	Possible Causal Factors	Underlying Root Causes
Prioritization	Low	Leadership has not properly communicated the importance of customer centricity. Customer loyalty is lower than the competition's.	The company leans toward being product centric.	The company's historical competitiveness has been in its product design. The company is fearful of moving away from what has traditionally worked.
Commitment	Medium			
Incentives	Low	The lack of prioritization of customer satisfaction goals has reduced the company's ability to satisfy customers as the competition does. Customers feel the company is focused only on its own benefit.	Incentives are all based on department deliverables and not on customer satisfaction.	Historically the company has achieved commercial success by encouraging internal competition among departments.

COLLABORATION

Component	Score	Impact on Customer and Company	Possible Causal Factors	Underlying Root Causes
Persistence	High			
Learning Culture	Medium			
Tolerance	Medium			
Cross-functionality	Low	Departments still operate in silos, which impedes communication. Customers feel the impact because issues take longer to resolve and doing business takes a lot more effort.	The company operates as a hierarchy, with clear divisions between departments.	Getting products out in the marketplace as quickly as possible was a differentiator, so dividing labor by departments worked well in the past.
Alignment	Medium			

IMPLEMENTATION

Component	Score	Impact on Customer and Company	Possible Causal Factors	Underlying Root Causes
Experience Design	Low	There is no clear design for what the ideal customer experience should be like. Employees do not know their role in delivering customer experience. Customers encounter a mixed experience when dealing with the organization.	No one in the organization is responsible for the end-to-end customer experience design.	The company has differentiated itself on products designed by its engineers, so little focus has been given to building customer experience design.
Customer Insight	Low	Employees are not receiving important information about customers and their experiences. For customers, the same pain points keep recurring.	No one in the company is translating the data into meaningful customer insights.	The leadership team sees little value in this data, because this is an engineering-led company.
System Support	High			
Customer Integration	Low	The company seeks minimal input from customers when releasing new products. Product releases are met with a mixed response from customers. Customers receive inconsistently designed goods from the company, which damages its image as a quality-focused company. Customers complain when products don't achieve expectations.	Designs of products are driven by an engineering team. The CEO gives the team full autonomy to design products with little customer input.	There has been little competition for the company's products in the past, so customer input was not considered vital.
Personal Responsiveness	Medium			

The findings described in table 3.1 illuminate the problem areas in the organization that have the greatest impact on customers. By using this format to identify the causal factors and the underlying roots of the problems, we can efficiently pinpoint the correlation between the two. This enables us to characterize the changes required to make the company more customer centric. This type of analysis also prevents us from ascribing problems to specific individuals in the company or reaching hasty conclusions not based on factual evidence.

Performing an evaluation of your organization's customer centricity is critical if you are implementing a strategic rollout of CX initiatives, because your ultimate aim is to implement a change in the organization that will achieve financial goals and be sustainable in the long term. The evaluation may seem like an unnecessary task, but when you are asking for millions of dollars and promising your program can deliver real, bottom-line financial benefits, you need to supply the necessary empirical evidence to show that your program will not waste company funds.

This chapter has outlined how to efficiently and effectively identify root problems in your company that prevent customer-centric best practices. This is a critical step in building the case for your strategic customer experience program. Without it, you will be presenting a flawed business case for a tactical program that will not produce the desired long-term results. Problems will reoccur if underlying organizational issues are not fixed. By finding and fixing the stumbling blocks that prevent your employees from practicing customer-centric behaviors, you will be safe-guarding your customers' branded experiences and thus long-term, sustainable commercial results for your organization.

Identifying the root causes, however, is just the first part of the equation. The primary objective of this stage of the process is to provide you with evidence about what needs to change in the organization to ensure long-term transformation. This exercise will ensure that the organizational initiatives in your business case are appropriately targeted and will avoid inappropriate expenditure of your budget on initiatives with a poor correlation to your program objectives.

The next chapter provides you with the second part of this analysis: an exercise that requires you to identify the financial impact these issues will have on your CX program if it is left unattended.

--------------------------- **KEY LESSONS** ---------------------------

- The DNA of the organization is made up of its people, and to embed customer centricity in the organization, you must identify the fundamental areas that need to change.
- To make permanent changes that can achieve sustainable financial results, you must single out the underlying root causes of problem areas in the organization.
- A scientific evaluation of the organization's customer centricity is required in order to establish empirical evidence for a convincing argument in favor of customer-centric initiatives.
- Each evaluation should be customized to include organizational and demographic variables so you can achieve comprehensive insights.
- Undertaking a root cause analysis is critical for identifying the origins of any problems and for circumventing a focus on only the symptoms of the problem.
- There are five key steps to performing a root cause analysis, and several techniques (such as the Five Whys) for reaching the underlying problem.
- By applying a root cause analysis to the customer-centricity evaluation results, you can identify specific areas to target and include in your final business case for your CX initiative.

CHAPTER 4

Designing the Customer-Centric

Organization

After you evaluate how customer centric the organization is and identify the root causes preventing full centricity, you need to design a series of initiatives that will impact the weak areas you found. Every organization will need to customize its CX initiatives based on the findings from its customer-centricity evaluation. Still, certain objectives, such as employee and organizational engagement, should apply to most organizations. The objectives you select for your organization will allow you to measure your progress and know whether you are achieving your targets.

This chapter outlines stages 7 and 8 of the CX management process:

Stage	Desired Output
7. Identify the areas within the organization that will have the greatest impact on your financial goals.	A list of organizational areas targeted for change as part of your customer experience program
8. Identify what actions you will take to achieve the changes in the organization you desire.	A list of actions you will take to remedy specific areas in the organization that affect customer experiences

The Value of Employee Engagement

Employees are the lifeblood of any organization, and changing processes without first examining employee engagement is a fundamentally flawed approach. No organization can deliver consistent, uniquely branded experiences to customers without a strong, united understanding and belief in what the company has to do and why. Employees who are not highly engaged cannot concentrate on a common cause. Failing to address employee engagement levels is the equivalent of ignoring the root cause of a key customer experience issue.

A highly engaged employee cares about the organization, its customers, and how his or her work affects both—and may even become a true ambassador for your brand. A disengaged employee, on the other hand, is self-interested and has little emotional ties to the company, its customers, or its objectives. An organization with highly engaged employees will be able to unite around common goals. An organization with employees operating on different agendas or displaying minimal care toward organizational objectives is unable to elevate customer experience.

Many organizations that desire to be more customer centric invest a significant amount of money in designing and implementing customer experience programs, yet still fail to achieve any positive outcome. Their investment fails primarily because they focus their attention on customer issues and ignore the employee side of the equation. Only by effectively addressing both sides of the CX equation can your organization transform itself and realize substantial economic value.

Two notable research findings, from Harvard Business School (2005) and Gallup research (2013), document the economic benefits intrinsic to an organization that effectively addresses both sides of the equation. These studies provide evidence of the correlation between engaged employees and customers and economic benefit. The Harvard Business School found that in more than two thousand companies, those with highly engaged employees and customers were 40 percent more financially successful than the baseline representing the average results of the companies.[2] The Gallup organization, after reviewing more than twenty-five million employee responses from 140 different countries, concluded that getting employee and customer engagement right leads to 240 percent more lucrative business-related outcomes.[3] Organizations that only maximize either customer engagement or employee engagement can experience growth in the short run, but they will be unable to sustain it over the long-term horizon.

....

2　John H. Fleming, Curt Coffman, James Harter, "Manage Your Human Sigma," *Harvard Business Review* (July 2005): 8.

3　Gallup, *State of the American Workplace Report 2013: Employee Engagement Insights* (page 55), accessed November 28, 2016, http://www.gallup.com/strategicconsulting/163007/state-american-workplace.aspx.

CAUSES OF EMPLOYEE ENGAGEMENT PROBLEMS

According to Gallup's global research into the state of employee engagement levels, a company may be unable to inspire the desired engagement levels among its employees for a number of reasons:

1. **The organization selects the wrong people.** Companies that don't know what type of people are suited for their particular environment end up hiring and retaining the wrong people.

2. **Managers do not empower employees to make a difference.** Employees who feel they lack control and are unable to make a difference are unlikely to embrace the company philosophy and go the extra mile.

3. **Strategy and leadership are not properly communicated.** When leaders fail to articulate how the company vision is linked to the employees' efforts, employees feel underappreciated and lack motivation to take proactive action to achieve results.

4. **The organization focuses on employee weaknesses instead of strengths.** Companies can't achieve their growth potential when they have performance management programs focused on penalizing employees who are weak rather than encouraging and rewarding them for strengths.

5. **The organization doesn't align employee accountability and performance to the company mission.** Companies that fail to align individual and team performance to the company goals, and to embed employee engagement in the overall performance criteria, will achieve substandard results because employees lack clear focus.

6. **The company doesn't consistently communicate with or encourage employees.** Companies that do not regularly express their appreciation of their employees' value, tout the importance of engagement, and lay out a path for regular improvement have failed to create a learning environment that fosters growth and increased engagement.

7. **Employee development is not readily available.** For companies that neglect to invest in their people, provide adequate learning opportunities, and invest in well-defined skills development programs for their people, there is little hope for greater employee engagement.

HOW TO ENGAGE YOUR EMPLOYEES

The link from highly engaged employees to brand ambassadors is not a given. To ensure engaged employees go on to deliver an exceptional customer experience, your company needs to employ a number of initiatives:

1. Acknowledge that all employees play an important role in effecting the desired customer experience.
2. Ensure that your brand identity is clear and consistent.
3. Communicate your brand values and promise regularly to all employees in simple ways.
4. Use simple tools to communicate your brand values and their relevance in various departments.
5. Regularly evaluate and assess your employees' understanding of your brand values and the promise to your customers.
6. Ensure that every employee, regardless of department, understands his or her impact on your customers.
7. Recognize employees who properly display your brand values in a public forum.
8. Ask employees regularly for their opinions on how to improve the customer experience.

Employees are the key to achieving sustainable market differentiation. To capitalize on this opportunity, your CX business case needs to outline how the organization can establish an environment that fosters and rewards employees for delivering your desired customer experiences, and how it can develop employee brand ambassadors capable of championing and elevating your branded version of CX.

The Power of Organizational Engagement

Improving your company's employee engagement is a precursor to mastering organizational engagement, which in turn is a precursor to achieving commercial benefits from consistently great customer experiences. To fully engage the entire organization, however, we must first attempt to understand what an organization *is*.

Business theorists examining modern organizations often mistakenly apply nineteenth-century theories about the importance of the division of labor. Departmentalizing the organization into separate, hierarchic groups leads to a false understanding of the organization as a lifeless machine that can be controlled through the manipulation of levers and buttons. We live in an era that is centered on how well we can package our goods and services and consistently deliver great experiences for our customers. We live in the age of connecting things to each other: people, organizations, nature, machines. To be properly connected to our customers, we need to view the organization as a single organic, living-and-breathing entity.

The classic definition of *organization*—a single entity that has a collective goal and is linked to an external environment—is well suited for how we need to understand a company. The word is derived from the Greek word *organon*, itself derived from the better-known word *ergon*, which means "organ." As with any organ in the human body, the organization is composed of cells (employees) that define its characteristics and its relationship to the external world. And like an organ, your company can properly operate only when all its cells are appropriately nourished, perform well collectively, and harness the power of positive energy.

INDIVIDUAL ENGAGEMENT

An individual is fully engaged when he or she performs a task with complete physical stamina, mental focus, emotional connection, and spiritual alignment. When all these components fall into place, the individual performs optimally and produces superior results. High-performing athletes have mastered the art of complete engagement: the ability to eliminate distractions and follow a structured, comprehensive training regimen that prepares them mentally, physically, and emotionally for competition.

In *The Power of Full Engagement*,[4] Loehr and Schwartz explain that full engagement is inextricably linked to the management of energy levels across four dimensions: physical, mental, emotional, and spiritual. They highlight that individual engagement requires a careful balance between

....

4   James E. Loehr and Tony Schwartz, *The Power of Full Engagement* (New York: Simon and Schuster, 2005).

training and recovery to build the capacity to achieve a higher goal. Any individual with aspirations larger than their current achievement must train in various dimensions to expand their ability in proportion to the task. This training should use a structured routine and include periods of recovery to ensure the individual does not burn out. The number of hours in the day is finite, so this objective is less about time management and more about managing energy to most effectively achieve a higher goal.

I've borrowed the concepts presented in *The Power of Full Engagement* for our discussion on organizational customer centricity because I believe leadership of high-performance companies is equivalent to training a high-performance athlete.

ORGANIZATIONAL ENERGY

Once you accept the organization as a single, animated unit akin to the human body, you can begin to drive yours in right direction. If the individual employees are the cells, then collectively these building blocks compose and operate as different types of tissue (departments). Not all the cells (people) are the same, as they belong to different tissue (departments) and perform different functions. However, they need to cooperate and serve a common goal. If one tissue area in an organ becomes diseased, then the whole organ will eventually stop functioning.

The following questions can help you examine and maintain the health of your organization:

- How must you regularly maintain it to keep it going?
- How much rest does it requires every day for proper recovery?
- How can you train it to perform above its current capacity?
- What types of disease can stop it from functioning properly, and how should you treat the disease should it occur?

The same thinking applies to the energy level of your organization, which reflects the collective output of its people and technology. Is your organization strong and healthy, ready to run a marathon? Or does it get winded and slow after a short sprint, or suffer an injury when its various parts fail to cooperate? Your organization's energy level determines the following:

- Its optimal daily performance
- Its ability to achieve certain goals with existing resources without burning out
- Its ability to outperform the competition
- Its ability to remain focused on achieving its goals even when confronted with obstacles, problems, and competing agendas

CX excellence requires consistent high performance from an organization and its people. This can only be achieved when the organization's energy levels are managed well, just as a high-performance athlete manages the body's energy.

THE POWER OF POSITIVE ENERGY

A high-performing athlete requires multiple sources of positive energy to operate at the levels required to win. Positive energy for the athlete flows from the perception of opportunity, adventure, and challenge. Negative energy is perceived in terms of threats, danger, and fear over one's survival.

Only when an athlete is able to harness positive energy can he or she perform at the top levels. The athlete has to master harnessing the power of positive energy across all dimensions of energy by maintaining the following:

- A carefully balanced diet, to ensure proper nourishment and hydration
- A routine training program that builds endurance and increases skills
- Predefined recovery periods that allow the athlete to rest
- Dedicated time to connect with loved ones, to ensure healthy emotions and attitude
- Mental exercises, to increase focus on the task
- A clear spiritual connection to the athlete's underlying goal or purpose

Positive energy is multidimensional. You cannot harness the power of positive energy by simply focusing on a single dimension. For example, it would be unreasonable to expect employees to be fully engaged at work if your organization requires them to work ten or twelve hours every day.

The time spent at work is time taken away from family or physical recovery. The overconsumption of energy at work will eventually lead to burnout and poor performance.

Leaders of customer-centric companies are masters of positive energy across all dimensions. They harness the four dimensions of engagement—physical, mental, emotional, and spiritual—and treat their organization like a high-performing athlete. They know when to exert and require high levels of energy to build capacity in their people that will transform work habits and behaviors. And they make sure their people have appropriate time for family, recovery, and recharging so they can perform at the next sprint or marathon.

Designing and Implementing an Employee Engagement Program

What drives high-performing athletes to wake up at 4 a.m. and spend 90 percent of their time training for the mere *hope* of winning a competition? Is it the dream of winning, of standing on the podium and being recognized as the best? Is it the possibility of celebrating success with family or loved ones? Or is there also another key driver for the athlete, a higher-purpose goal? For champion athletes, their belief system centers on the desire to reach the goal they have set for themselves. It is their flame, the spark or glow that lives deep within, driving them on to blazing success. And customer-centric organizations strive to kindle that same flame within their people.

IGNITE THE FLAME

An organization will never be able to achieve full engagement without creating a belief system that cultivates a strong spiritual connection with its people. The values of the organization need to be properly connected to its employees and excite them. The belief system provides the foundation for *why* that organization's employees behave in a certain manner. And that foundation supports two pillars: the company's vision and mission. Your organization's vision and mission need to inspire people into action—to be the fire from which your employees can light their flame. If either component is missing or not shared by all employees, the flame of engagement will be ineffectual.

FUEL THE FLAME

Once you have lit the flame of engagement within your employees, you need to know how to fuel it so it can grow. Your mission and values need to spread so they touch individuals and profoundly change them. Fueling the flame is difficult, and will be covered in greater depth in part two. For now, fueling the flame requires a leader to achieve the following:

- Develop an implementation plan that includes training for all dimensions of the organization.
- Ensure mentoring and coaching is implemented across the organization.
- Practice positive energy rituals to regularly spread positive energy.
- Plan to eliminate barriers to engagement, such as negative habits that distract people from their objectives and waste or contaminate positive stored energy.

The flame needs fuel to survive. As a leader, you need to understand what the fuel looks like and then effectively spread it throughout the entire organization. Every employee needs to know what the higher purpose is.

The story of the cleaner at NASA sums up the importance of higher purpose. Prior to the launch of Apollo 11, some generals visited NASA and saw a cleaner in the hallway. They asked the cleaner if he knew what his job was. Did the cleaner reply, "To sweep the floors," or "To empty the garbage"? No. The cleaner replied, "To help put a man on the moon."

Only when all employees enjoy clarity and conviction around the higher purpose of their work will the organization generate the necessary momentum required to achieve its customer experience objectives.

MAINTAIN THE FLAME

Once you have ignited and fueled the flame of engagement, you need to maintain it or else it will run out of fuel, become extinguished by internal organizational negativity, or be overshadowed by a more dominant competitor.

Maintaining the flame requires leaders of customer-centric organizations to ensure the established higher purpose is top of mind for all employees. You must develop an ongoing plan of periodic exertion and recovery that reminds employees of the importance of carrying out their tasks. You must help employees see the fruits of their efforts, which will encourage them to maintain the energy levels required to achieve high performance.

As with the high-performance athlete, to ensure that employees are fully engaged, your organization should provide the following:

- Education about physical and mental health, so employees understand the importance of eating, exercising, and sleeping properly
- Opportunities for physical exercise throughout the day
- Fresh food and beverages at the place of work, including healthy items on any menu
- Programs that focus on helping and caring for others, to develop employees' emotional capability
- Collaboration with colleagues to increase employees' capacity for decision making, increase focus and creativity, and encourage them to define clear priorities for tasks
- Events for corporate recovery, including socializing
- A work environment that encourages creativity and innovation
- A culture that is focused around customer experiences

Each employee plays an important role in ensuring the organization achieves its higher goals. An effective leader has his or her pulse on the energy levels of the staff. A great leader acknowledges that people will not always be positive and that personal issues will interfere with the company's objectives. They recognize this as an expected barrier, and introduce programs to help employees deal with emotional distress and get them back to positive, high-energy levels.

CHANGING ATTITUDES TAKES TIME

The success of any program designed to attain an organization's specific customer-centricity objectives hinges on how closely that program can leverage well-entrenched employee values and beliefs. In fact, an organization that lacks any consistent values or beliefs is easier to refocus toward customer centricity than one with a strong legacy culture rooted in a long, cherished history.

The strategic organizational changes you seek are unlikely to occur over the same period you have set for your financial objectives. The time it takes to achieve these deep, multilayered cultural changes depends on the size of your organization and its customer-centricity score. Typically, the larger the organization and the more deep-seated the legacy issues, the longer it will take to achieve desired outcomes. It may take twelve months, or it may take three to five years. Numerous variables will determine the time frame in which your organization can achieve sustainable market differentiation through your strategic CX program. You may be able to reduce this time frame by providing a structured process for your employees to follow and specific knowledge about how to apply what works.

Allocating Actions for Organizational Change

You now understand the importance of directing an organization toward customer centricity, channeling the energies of employees toward a common goal, and removing any obstacles to adopting a customer-centric attitude. Now you need to propose changes you can make to your organization to increase employee-engagement levels and eliminate those challenges to your employees' customer centricity.

To figure out what changes you need to make, return to the root cause problems you identified in the lowest-scoring areas of your organizational evaluation (see table 3.1) and consider their impact on your financial objectives. Make sure you document this process—again, I recommend using the CCScore system of Leadership, Collaboration, Implementation, or an equivalent system—as your notes will help you determine what actions to take.

Reviewing your organizational evaluation, decide which weak areas to address. Again, we can prioritize those areas with the greatest impact by using our simple three-tier measure (Low, Medium, High). After we've applied the measure, we can begin allocating actions to each area.

Review the example in table 4.1, again using the household goods manufacturer and retailer (Company C): a simple matrix table (borrowing the underlying root causes from table 3.1) identifies each area's financial impact and the proposed actions to strengthen these weaknesses.

TABLE 4.1: ORGANIZATIONAL ANALYSIS

LEADERSHIP

Component	Score	Underlying Root Causes	Impact on CX Financial Objectives	Priority	Actions
Enabling	Medium				
Openness	Low	There is no diversity at the board level. The company is very patriarchal and is led as such.	Getting the business case for the CX program through the board. Without proper implementation, financial sustainability will not be achieved.	High	Convince the CEO of the plan, and ensure he/she sponsors the program at board level.
Prioritization	Low	The company's historical competitiveness has been in its product design. The company is fearful of moving away from what has traditionally worked.	Without effective prioritization around customer-centricity objectives, the program will not meet its objectives within the set time frames.	Medium	Once ideal customer experiences at each touch point have been designed, deploy a structured communication plan to all staff and departments.
Commitment	Medium				
Incentives	Low	Historically the company has achieved commercial success by encouraging internal competition among departments.	Misaligned incentives will shape the behavior of staff and undermine the shift toward the desired customer-centricity objectives.	High	After designing KPIs, require the CEO, CFO, and HR director to sign off on new KPIs and incentives plan.

COLLABORATION

Component	Score	Underlying Root Causes	Impact on CX Financial Objectives	Priority	Actions
Persistence	High				
Learning Culture	Medium				

Continued

Component	Score	Underlying Root Causes	Impact on CX Financial Objectives	Priority	Actions
Tolerance	Medium				
Cross-functionality	Low	Getting products out in the marketplace as quickly as possible was a differentiator, so dividing labor by departments worked well in the past.	Without the cooperation of a number of department heads working toward achieving the customer-centricity objectives, the financial objectives will not be met.	High	In the short term, establish a CX task force to work on collectively achieving financial objectives. In the medium term, reevaluate the organizational structure to enable cross-functional teams.
Alignment	Medium				

IMPLEMENTATION

Component	Score	Underlying Root Causes	Impact on CX Financial Objectives	Priority	Actions
Experience Design	Low	The company has differentiated itself on products designed by its engineers, so little focus has been given to building customer experience design.	Without CX design, the organization will be unable to deliver on its brand promise or to provide customers with the products and services they value most.	High	After designing a CX program, ensure a structured training and mentoring program exists to communicate the desired employee behaviors and outputs required to achieve the program's objectives.
Customer Insight	Low	The leadership team sees little value in this data, because this is an engineering-led company.	Without meaningful customer insights, the CX program will not enable the organization to track and monitor progress.	Medium	Design an easy-to-understand dashboard for new customer metrics, organizational KPIs, and tracking against targets.
System Support	High				
Customer Integration	Low	There has been little competition for the company's products in the past, so customer input was not considered vital.	Customer acquisition, retention, and CLV targets will not be achieved unless the organization is able to modify its products and services to more accurately deliver customer values.	High	Gather customer research to identify (1) key pain points along key customer touch points, and (2) feedback on products and services. Design a new process to ensure customer input is gathered prior to manufacture or release of any products or services.
Responsiveness	Medium				

I have used the following methodology to allocate action items that will address the underlying root causes identified in the previous chapter's exercise (table 3.1, Root Cause Analysis—Leadership, Collaboration, Implementation), which determined areas in the business hampering the practice of customer centricity:

- Take the root cause analysis from the previous exercise (table 3.1), making sure to focus on the lowest-scoring customer-centric areas first.
- Identify the likely impact each area, if they are left unchanged, will have on your CX program objectives.
- Allocate a simple Low, Medium, or High value to represent the degree of impact on your objectives.
- Allocate proposed actions (perhaps in a brainstorming session) that need to be taken to remedy (or lower the risk inherent in) the issue that is likely to prevent your program from reaching its objectives.

At this stage, the list of actions you are proposing does not need to be comprehensive. Your goal is to build a reasonable outline of the changes you suggest for your organization. Once you are able to get sign-off to begin implementing your plans, the details will follow. The degree of detail applied at this juncture largely depends on the leadership team requirements. Some organizations may require more information, while the format outlined in table 4.1 will be sufficient for others.

If there are scores below the median score in more than half of the areas measured, you may need to apply your analysis at the departmental level. Later in the process, once you have built your program, you can review your design and identify stakeholders and resources. In chapter 6: Aligning Initiatives to Achieve CX Objectives, I outline the process of reviewing your program to ensure you are selecting the initiatives most likely to achieve your desired objectives.

Don't rush into trying to identify the resources yet. The picture is still half complete.

You have been able to complete the organizational side of the case for your CX program by completing the following steps:

- Undertaking an evaluation of how customer centric the organization is
- Identifying low-scoring areas and their impact on both the customer and the organization
- Undertaking a root cause analysis to identify problems' origins
- Examining the root causes, and identifying their impact on financial objectives
- Identifying high-level actions needed to ensure customer-centric organizational focus and engagement

Your focus on the employee and organizational sides of customer experience, before you embark on the customer side of the equation, stems from the important role employees play in achieving sustainable and differentiated experiences. A purely tactical program would focus solely on the customer side of the equation, without addressing root cause problems in the organization that create customer pain points. The strategic program you have begun to design, on the contrary, aims to cut off the fuel supply to the organizational engine that generates those customer pain points.

Having accomplished the first part of your design, you are now in a position to focus your attention to the customer side of the equation in the next chapter.

KEY LESSONS

- Employee output has to be aligned with what your customers value most rather than what the organization thinks.
- Organizational focus is required in order to gain momentum around common customer experience goals.
- Employees must have a united understanding of objectives and believe in the underlying values and beliefs of the customer experience program.

- Research studies provide evidence for a correlation between the economic value of organizations and highly engaged employees and customers.
- Highly engaged employees can more easily become brand ambassadors.
- The organization is like a high-performing athlete: It requires management of energy levels across four key dimensions: physical, mental, emotional, and spiritual.
- Leaders of great customer experience companies are masters of positive energy.
- Full organizational engagement will not occur without a belief system that has a strong spiritual connection with its people.
- Full organizational engagement needs to address employees' overall health, including the work environment, collaboration, and culture.
- Eradicating barriers that impact your customer-centric goals helps ensure full organizational engagement.
- To set priorities and actions, identification of the likely impact of the organizational root cause problems on set financial objectives is required.
- The actions chosen to remedy the problem areas should achieve greater focus and organizational engagement.

CHAPTER 5

Mapping the Customer Journey

After developing an understanding of the organizational and employee sides of customer experience, it's time to shift our focus toward customers. In order to understand, evaluate, and enhance the experience for your customers and prospects, you need to acquire a more comprehensive understanding of your customers' experience when they interact with your organization and its products and services. The insights gained from this process will help you determine areas needed for change, and monitor and measure how any changes impact the customer over time.

One of the ways to gain these insights is to design a *customer journey map*, which will identify the actions needed to address specific customer issues and to convert them into new, positive experiences. This chapter covers stages 9 through 16 of the CX management process:

Stage	Desired Output
9. Map your customer journey.	A comprehensive customer journey map that incorporates all customer touch points
10. Evaluate your customers to determine what they value most and what they like least.	An empirical analysis based on customer research that identifies customer values and problem areas
11. Evaluate what your competitor's customers like least about their products or services.	Identification of marketplace gaps that are opportunities to win new customers
12. Summarize your customer research, and identify the areas you wish to improve with a weighted system.	A weighted list of customer issues that form part of the case for your CX initiative
13. Use the customer research to allocate a ratings score to each touch point in your journey map, identifying which have the most negative impact.	Identification of the organizational pain points that should be remedied to elevate customers' experiences
14. Use the competitor research to identify opportunities to win new customers.	A list of new initiatives that are likely to lead to new customers

Stage	Desired Output
15. Use the breakdown of the reasons customers left in the previous year to identify the top 2–5 reasons.	A list of the top pain paints to rectify in order to improve retention
16. Use a breakdown of the top customer values and initiatives to win new customers, and identify the 2–5 points that are most likely to generate new customer wins to include in the business case for your CX program.	A list of the top new customer value initiatives that will lead to achieving your customer acquisition figures

What Is a Customer Journey Map?

Understanding the overall experience of your customers and prospective customers when they encounter your brand is an essential element of your quest to achieve your primary objective: creating a truly unique emotional bond between those customers and your organization. If you are to succeed in enhancing that experience throughout the entire customer life cycle, you need to evaluate where you stand and where you're headed, by creating a customer journey map.

A customer's journey is the sum of the key phases he or she goes through when deciding to purchase a particular type of product or service from your organization. A customer journey map documents the key actions taken by the customer and the emotional impact imposed by the company during the interaction. This tool will provide you with insights that will allow you to track and adjust the customer experience over time.

From an organization's perspective, the journey map illustrates what triggers will lead to new customers and the likely reasons you retain or lose existing customers. The process of documenting the customer journey map is akin to a detective making an investigation into a reported incident: You aim to identify the cause-and-effect relationship between what act occurred, the actions of the individual who committed the act, and the motives behind the individual's actions. Detectives investigate a case by tracking every interaction that could explain the events leading to the act. They pay careful attention to the timing of each interaction and to the emotions that could plausibly explain the suspect's actions.

Fortunately, your job is not as difficult as a detective's. You are able to return to every customer scene and observe actual interactions your customers have with the organization. Your ability to build a convincing case is made significantly easier by the body of evidence you can accumulate to achieve a comprehensive, empirically sound understanding of your customers and the various cognitive and emotional dynamics motivating their actions.

Before you start the process of documenting and evaluating the customer journey, you should carefully consider certain attributes of your customers and your organization:

- **The unique stages in your customer life cycle.** Each customer life cycle will vary depending on the type of organization. For example, the life cycle of a patient in a hospital would be very different from that of an online gaming company client. Your customer journey map must reflect the customers particular to your organization.

- **Variations between customer segments.** You may need multiple journey maps to reflect the different segments within your organization's customer base. Even though there will be common aspects for all of your customers' journeys, there are likely to be significant differences in how each group of customers interacts with the organization too. For example, older customers may choose to call a toll-free number when researching your product, while a younger segment will exclusively use the Internet. Some will use a combination of devices and channels to achieve the same outcome; they may start using a mobile device to search, then move to a desktop to view short-listed products, and then finally move to a retail store to examine products more closely. Your customer journey map should address all the customer segments relevant to your organization.

- **Variations in time frame.** Each customer interaction will vary in terms of length of time; impact on the customer; and the processes, people, and technology used by the organization to achieve an outcome. Some interactions may be transactional in nature and last only a couple of minutes; others could last an hour or more. The impact will also vary based on how your customer values the expected outcome of the interaction.

- **Your customer's thinking, emotions, and behavior.** Using internal organizational resources to determine customer behavior and feelings without incorporating or addressing actual customer feedback is simply a waste of time; it would provide a skewed view of your customers' actual experience. Instead, you will require qualitative and quantitative customer research data to pinpoint the feelings, thoughts, and actions specific to your customer.

All these characteristics should be carefully considered and captured in the evaluation process as you begin the customer journey mapping exercise, to ensure the validity of the results.

Creating Your Customer Journey Map

Now that you've considered your particular customer segments from a detective's point of view, using the guidelines listed in the previous section, you're ready to start mapping your customer journey. You can be sure to achieve the desired outcome from your journey mapping exercise—creating a better experience for customers—by following some clearly defined steps. As you will see, this ten-step process will permit you to extract the greatest value and design a better narrative for your customers.

STEP I: TELL YOUR CUSTOMER'S STORY

There are several types of maps you can create to analyze certain customer metrics. We are going to create an experience map. As we go through the various stages of creating this map, I will highlight other maps you may wish to consider if you require a better understanding of the principal issues negatively impacting your customers' experiences.

An effective experience map should provide a narrative of the customer and describe the story behind what or who has an impact on the customer, how that impact is generated, and why. In this story, the customer is the hero, and you need to see your hero triumph. Without that happy ending, your organization can't get its "happily ever after." Your hero will decide to leave you and join an organization able to deliver a narrative with better emotional outcomes, and your own organization will not achieve its financial targets.

Organizations need to become master storytellers, able to engage their customers in a way that makes them the center of the narrative and the ultimate benefactor. The hero, in classic narratives, is required to take a journey, overcome obstacles, and ultimately triumph. Eventually the hero achieves some form of self-discovery that places him or her in a better state than when the story first began. Breaking this down in terms of the customer journey mapping exercise, it is clear that you must answer the following questions about your hero and their story:

1. Who is your hero, and what are their key characteristics?
2. What is the current narrative of your hero?
3. What obstacles are preventing your hero from achieving their goals?
4. What is your hero's ideal happy ending?
5. What is the better state desired by your hero?

Analyzing the classic narrative reveals that an organization can ultimately deliver a satisfying emotional outcome by rewriting the customer narrative to remove obstacles so your customers easily progress through the story and achieve a new happy ending.

STEP 2: DEFINE THE GOALS OF YOUR MAP

Every map needs to have clear objectives and a good understanding of the audience for which it's intended. The goals of the customer journey map should align with your high-level vision for differentiating your organization's customer experiences. You should be clear about the audience and purpose of the map, internalizing goals such as the following:

- Better understand customers' needs, emotions, and behavior throughout their life cycle.
- Educate your organization about the different stages of the customer's journey and how the customer is affected by the organization, so you can align the organization with customers' issues.
- Identify the moments that matter most to your customers, and

design a new experience for them based on their values and your brand promises.

- Record and measure the impact on your customers and your organization from any proposed changes to your customer's narrative.
- Help your employees develop customer-centric thinking based on your organization's ideal customer experience.

By documenting the desired objectives of this mapping exercise, you will be able to more easily complete future steps in the process.

STEP 3: RESEARCH YOUR CUSTOMERS

In any well-written story, the author normally begins by researching key characters, places, and things, and any historical facts relevant to the narrative. You should do the same for your customer narrative. Collect research about relevant current customer experiences, including a combination of both quantitative and qualitative data from customer surveys, direct face-to-face interviews, blind observation of customers interacting, and so forth.

Isolate any phrases customers use if they seem to represent a general attitude held by the majority. For example, pay close attention to such statements as "I hate having to take a ticket and wait a long time for my number to be called," because this identifies a problem area that is likely to affect many customers. These kinds of insights will be valuable when you map the customer journey around negative touch points and want to reflect customers' feelings.

Your research should examine not only what frustrates and obstructs your customers during their experience, but also what they value most during their journey with your organization. In order to create an accurate and compelling experience for your customers throughout their journey, you must know what makes them happy at various touch points. Remember, customers pay prices based on perceived value, so if they don't value your proposed changes, your CX program will not generate any economic benefit.

Aim to answer the following key questions about your various customers:

- What do they think at key stages of the customer life cycle?
- What do they feel at touch points with your organization?
- What actions do they take at various points along their customer journey?
- What do they like least about your products and services?
- What do they like most about your products and services?

Each organization will elicit variations on these questions, but the essence of the research is the same. Any customer research should seek insights about your customers' strongest emotional responses to your products and services. Identifying the strongest emotional responses will help you narrow down the areas that need change to achieve the highest return on investment. Knowing what emotional response customers want throughout the customer journey will enable you to create a branded experience in the marketplace.

STEP 4: IDENTIFY YOUR CUSTOMER SEGMENTS

Once you have gathered your research, you can begin to distinguish different types or segments of customers and organize your customers according to their segment. Gaining that insight into your customers' frustrations, obstacles, and values will help you create an ideal customer experience narrative for each particular segment.

Armed with a deeper understanding of your key customer segments, you can now try to identify the customer segments most likely to have an impact on your financial objectives. For example, if your preliminary review reveals a segment of customers who are highly profitable but don't represent a large percentage of your clientele, then you may want to propose creating a new, compelling narrative that would attract more customers from this segment. Conversely, your evaluation may have uncovered a segment of customers you are losing; now you can begin to research the obstacles leading to this trend, so you can take action to eliminate these obstacles and achieve your retention targets.

Customer research plays an integral role in ensuring the case for your customer experience initiative remains well targeted to various customer segments and thus more likely to achieve your financial objectives.

STEP 5: SELECT CUSTOMER SEGMENTS TO MAP

By this step in the process, you should already have a good idea as to which customer segments you wish to create journey maps for. The customer research likely helped narrow your choice. You should prioritize the segments for your journey maps around three considerations:

- Your financial objectives
- Your preexisting knowledge about your customers
- Your research findings

Keep in mind which segments are likely to enable you to create a uniquely branded customer experience and ultimately achieve your financial objectives. Remember to include your largest customer segment in your journey mapping, in addition to any new segments you may have uncovered in your research. If you don't include your largest segment, you face the danger of designing a new experience that will alienate the majority of your customers. And if you fail to consider your newest customers, you risk missing out on a potential opportunity to capture new areas of the market.

STEP 6: DEFINE THE PHASES OF YOUR CUSTOMER JOURNEY

Each organization's customers will experience different phases throughout their life cycle. For instance, a government agency and a car dealership provide very different goods and services, and thus a very different series of touch points, for their customers. What all customer journeys have in common, regardless of the type of organization, is that the journey is a narrative with a beginning, a middle, and an end. In business, everything prior to the purchase of an item can be considered the "beginning." Everything that happens after purchase is considered the "middle." And the "end" of the narrative is when the customer either decides it's time to repurchase or no longer has any use for the item.

The phases you define need to cover the two primary dimensions of customer economics: acquisition and retention. Examples of functions for acquisition include awareness and purchase; functions for retention also include service and support. For a typical commercial organization, the customer journey would move through the following ten phases:

1. Past experiences
2. Customer need
3. Awareness
4. Research
5. Selection
6. Purchase
7. Receipt
8. Use
9. Maintenance and support
10. Recommendation

At times these phases may appear distinct, but when you examine the customer's journey more closely, you may find an important phase in the experience that will color your perception of how you need to change a particular organizational process.

Most customers probably would declare the awareness phase as the starting point in their journey with your organization. However, a deeper understanding reveals that the path starts at a much earlier phase: past experiences. This phase is crucial, particularly for some types of organizations, because it sheds light on the customer's need for the item, which triggered the search to fulfill that need. Understanding a customer's past experiences can help you design a better experience during the awareness and research stages of the customer life cycle, by incorporating positive emotional triggers from past experiences.

When you have outlined the various phases of your customer journey, flag those you want to analyze more deeply—particularly those phases that correlate to your financial objectives and your customer research findings. For example, if you have set a retention target and have identified that a disproportionately large percentage of customers are leaving the relationship shortly after the use phase, you need to determine the reasons why they are leaving at that particular time. Researching customers who no longer interact with your organization can provide valuable insights about how to alter your existing customer experience journey so it is closer to your ideal. Similarly, a closer look at prospects and at competitors' customers will help you alter the dynamics in a particular phase of your own customer journey so you can positively influence your customers' experiences.

STEP 7: DEFINE THE DIMENSIONS OF YOUR MAP

Outline the dimensions of the customer's journey you wish to document and analyze at each phase of that journey. Because you are creating an experience map, your organization should seek to customize the dimensions for the experience map to suit not only your industry sector, but your desired financial outcomes. Some dimensions—customer need, customer touch points, business processes, enabling technologies—should be investigated in all experience maps. I suggest placing these dimensions under the broad categories of cause and effect, as this will help you understand the primary relationships that define customer experience. So you want to outline the elements of cause and effect that define the customer's experience, and then you must analyze the aspects that need to change. By identifying cause and effect factors up front, you will get to the root causes of problems faster.

For example, in the table below we can easily identify that a business process (cause) has the primary impact on the customer (effect). This helps us focus on the specific nature of the business process responsible for impacting our customers and the underlying root causes of why this process was designed in such a manner.

Cause	Effect
Customer need	Customer takes action
Customer touch point	Experience layer
Business process	Touch-point impact
Enabling technologies	Business process design

One of the problems in many customer journey maps is the inability to figure out how to rectify a root organizational problem that creates a poor customer experience. Maps, too, often do not incorporate business processes and enabling technologies. Your analysis will be incomplete if you don't explore these critical dimensions. Though you don't want to jump to conclusions, it's worth mentioning here that the majority of customer issues are rooted in poorly designed business processes or inferior technology.

STEP 8: DEEPEN YOUR MAP THROUGH A SERIES OF WORKSHOPS

By now you will be in position to start adding the detail required to bring your customer narrative to life. I recommend using a workshop methodology to capture the insights about your customer that provide the depth necessary for your analysis to meet your strategic objectives.

As you prepare to conduct the workshops, there are a number of issues to consider. Some of these are simply based on logistics, such as *Where should the workshops be? How long should they last?* Other issues require you to consider strategy and how best to achieve your objectives for the map.

Workshop Logistics

Logistical considerations for your workshops include the following:

- **Room size.** The room should be large enough to accommodate the number of attendees, so people don't feel cramped and uncomfortable.
- **Workshop length.** I recommend workshops no longer than three hours in duration on a single day. In three hours, you can harness the best from people in a concentrated time frame and still let attendees return to their daily work commitments for half of the day.
- **Size and format of map.** Consider the size and format of the map you'll be making. Allow yourself plenty of room to add multiple Post-it notes, markers, and pictures along the way. Generally, 10 to 13 feet (3 to 4 meters) of wall space is sufficient to place your map. I also recommend starting off using handwriting (analog) before moving your map to digital format, so users can easily add and subtract elements as the map is being created. Working together to create an interactive and visual experience will engage the participants and make them feel included.

- **Facilitator and scribe.** The facilitator of the workshop should not be the scribe, as this can slow down the brainstorming process. Whoever is the scribe should capture participants' insights while the facilitator drives the group's thought process. Throughout the workshops, the facilitator should always focus the discussion around the characteristics of the topic and should prevent participants from digressing or reaching a false conclusion. To achieve this, the facilitator should always remind participants of the following elements:
  - » *The customer persona.* As I pointed out earlier, different customer segments may have different experiences along their journey, so don't try to use a single persona to define all your customers.
  - » *The brand promise and attributes.* Participants should keep in mind how the brand attributes are reflected throughout the customer journey, so the experiences or touch points remain consistent with the brand—and so you end up creating a uniquely branded experience overall.
  - » *Target KPIs and relevant financial objectives.* Participants should be reminded of the relevant commercial objectives you wish to achieve.
  - » *Trends from customer research, the marketplace, and internal metrics.* The intelligence you have gathered is going to be important in highlighting an area of importance and fostering further discussion.

The focus of the workshops is to have targeted discussions during which you can extract from participants the required insights that will enable you to complete a draft of the customer journey map for a customer segment and ensure it aligns with your brand promises. The workshop leaders, the map's presentation, and the time and place of the workshop are all logistical considerations to be worked out for optimal results.

Strategic Aspects of the Workshops

In addition to considering the logistical aspects of the workshops, you should think about the strategic ones:

- **Pre-workshop organizational communication.** When you advertise the workshops to the rest of your organization, the tone and type of communication sets the scene. Try to get the CEO to sponsor the workshops and highlight your project's importance and objectives with the rest of the organization. It is natural to expect a level of disinterest in your project from stakeholders who are needed at the workshops, but C-level endorsement and communication will help eradicate any resistance you may encounter.

- **Pre-workshop reading material.** You should also carefully consider the material you prepare for your attendees. It should contain sufficient workshop information, but not too much information that preparation becomes daunting—or that the workshop itself seems repetitive. You should provide a summary for each of the following types of information:

  » The map's goals
  » The type of map being created, and the various phases it will cover
  » The customer segments the workshop will map
  » Your customer research findings

  The last thing you want is for participants to arrive at the workshops without any knowledge of what is expected from them. In this case, shooting from the hip does not count as contributing but instead leads to poor input during the workshop and less of a chance of achieving a valuable final map. Pre-workshop materials enable participants to prepare to contribute to the workshops.

- **Workshop attendees.** Who should attend these workshops? Your initial meeting should include senior leadership of the organization, ensuring there is buy-in for future workshops and the time commitment they require. Other attendees should be selected based on their ability to influence future changes in particular areas. By the time you reach the workshop stage in the process of creating your customer journey map, you should have an idea of

the pain points for your customers. Senior representatives should
be present at that phrase of the journey, because later you will most
likely be asking them to change a component over which they have
control. Involving them in the process lets you gain their buy-in
and plant the necessary seeds for change early, thus minimalizing
resistance further downstream.

- **Third-party involvement.** Also consider inviting any third-party
  organizations or consultants you have engaged with on this project. Their attendance may be valuable if they are able to focus the
  brainstorming, by highlighting important topics and research findings from your organization and other industry sectors. The external expert will also help validate the conclusions reached around
  various life cycle stages, and visualize how the newly designed
  journey is most likely to achieve the financial objectives. An objective point of view also can raise the level of confidence among
  attendees and can reduce debate or confusion around whether
  some conclusions are appropriate. An external expert's validation
  may even influence your CX initiative's implementation.
- **Style and design elements of the map.** Before creating the map,
  you need to strategically think about its graphic layout. Confirm
  the outline and the format prior to the workshops. You can identify some components of the experience map beforehand, such as
  the emotions of the customer. Other components may not be as
  forthcoming, so go back to the goals of the map as you contemplate an effective style. A well-styled map will offer clarity and
  streamlined communication around specific dimensions, making it
  accessible to a wider audience. Your map's design should incorporate the following elements:
  - » *Pictures.* Pictures can easily display important markers in a map:
    a stage in the life cycle, a strong emotion, or a significant inter-
    action. Using appropriate visual imagery will make a map more
    approachable and communicate its message more effectively.

» *Keywords*. It's easy to write a one-pager about each phase of the customer journey, but selecting a few keywords that capture the essence of what you wish to communicate is much more effective. Keywords can concisely summarize and pinpoint a message, allowing participants to isolate the main issues at each customer interaction and develop an appropriate response for each phase of the journey.

» *Customers' words*. Wording from a customer's perspective is more powerful than something made up by workshop participants. Customers' words should be used at key touch points to summarize what is going on from the customer's point of view.

» *Logical order*. Laying out the various components of the experience map in a logical order will afford the reader a better understanding of the relationship among all the map's components. Any reader of the map should arrive at the conclusions intended by the workshop participants, without having been present at the workshop. The logical flow of components will also expedite the types of correlations that can be drawn and enable the team to undertake a root cause analysis more easily.

• **Structure of the map.** You need the map to assist you during organizational change and to help shift the organization toward becoming more customer centric. To do this, I recommend you create two maps that appear side by side (see table 5.1). The first map will outline the current customer journey as currently experienced by a chosen customer persona. The second map will guide you in redesigning the journey of the same customer persona, with the goal of achieving an experience more in line with what the customer values most and what expresses the brand in a more defined manner.

TABLE 5.1: CURRENT EXPERIENCE MAP VS. NEW EXPERIENCE MAP—TEMPLATE

Current Experience Map	New Experience Map
Customer need that is driving the action:	What values highly regarded by the customer have not been met?
Emotional and cognitive expectations valued most by a customer:	Why does this moment matter to the customer?
Customer interaction at a touch point:	What are the opportunities to improve this interaction?
Emotional and cognitive responses of customer: • Emotions • Cognition	What is the ideal experience we would like to give our customer?
Attitudes driving customer behavior:	How is the new experience going to meet an emotional need?
Typical behavior of customer after interaction:	How is the new experience likely to change the customer's behavior?
Organizational impact from the interaction:	What are the likely financial benefits?

- **Map time frame.** Allocate a typical time frame for the customer to complete each phase of the life cycle. For example, does the typical customer research for ten minutes or ten days before taking appropriate action? Understanding the duration of each phase allows the workshop participants to better understand the importance of various phases for the customer in relation to your products and services.

During the workshops, it's not important to get all the required detail in exactly the right format. At a later workshop, new insights may surface that may add greater understanding on a topic. This is normal when addressing a topic for which there are many relationships and possible conclusions. Returning to your map on a regular basis to check the documented outcomes will ensure you can fine-tune any aspect until you are satisfied.

Case Study: Customer Mapping and Eliminating Bill Shock

Before mobile carriers started practicing customer centricity and using best practices in customer experience, they thought little about their practice of issuing a single, monthly bill to a customer. Mobile carriers had no idea this was a problem until they captured the real-life experiences of their customers. Customers using mobile data roaming were hit with exorbitant changes that didn't equate to the amount charged on the monthly bill. Customers were often caught unawares and were unpleasantly surprised when they received the bill with these charges added on. This became known as bill shock.

By undertaking a root cause analysis and discovering the root causes of many customer complaints, the mobile operators developed new business processes and introduced new technology to ensure customers were made aware of costs prior to receiving the bill. Carriers even went as far as calling any customer with an unusually high spend, to try and resolve the issue before it become a negative customer experience. Mobile carriers realized it was more profitable to absorb some of the costs incurred by the customer than to lose the customer due to bill shock.

STEP 9: EVALUATE YOUR CUSTOMER'S CURRENT JOURNEY

Now that you have documented the different phases of the customer journey, the next step is to evaluate these experiences in an attempt to weigh up the impact on the customer and organization. This evaluation will provide opportunities to create a new narrative for the customer. Ultimately, with customer experience, we are trying to manipulate the situation to elicit a more favorable behavioral response. Simply put, we want to change our customers' behavior.

The journey map for your customer persona should include all the relevant information required to assess the impact of certain moments or phases of the journey. Using the map, you should be able to evaluate which changes to these moments are most likely to yield your desired financial outcomes. Any change in the customer journey should be based on empirical evidence generated from your customer research and from internal customer metrics. Armed with this specific data, as you address the various phases and interactions in the customer journey, you can more accurately create hypotheses about the outcomes you expect if certain elements were changed.

The evaluation process should begin by first examining which moments along the journey elicit the strongest emotions from customers. Evaluate both ends of the emotional spectrum, because strong emotional responses are the main drivers behind how people behave. The language in survey results or interview questions will help you determine whether the moment mattered to the customer or not. Consider the following examples of descriptive words you may find in your research that indicate a strong emotional response:

Positive Emotional Response	Negative Emotional Response
Happy	Angry
Delighted	Hate
Love	Frustrated
Thankful	Embarrassed
Ecstatic	Shocked
Secure	Annoyed
Comforted	Any swear word used to describe a feeling

Your focus should always be to isolate the moments of strong emotion and explore the dynamics of the situation. Some companies remove from their reports any survey answers with offensive language, but this is a grave mistake. A negative experience presents you with an opportunity rather than a problem. Anytime customers use swear words to describe how they feel is a great opportunity to identify a moment of high impact. I recommend always prioritizing the negative experiences over the positive ones, as negative emotional forces generally have a far greater impact on a customer's behavior.

STAGE: PRODUCT RESEARCH

Customer Profile:

Millennial generation, highly reliant on mobile devices, uses the Internet to research and buy goods. Expresses opinions of products on review websites.

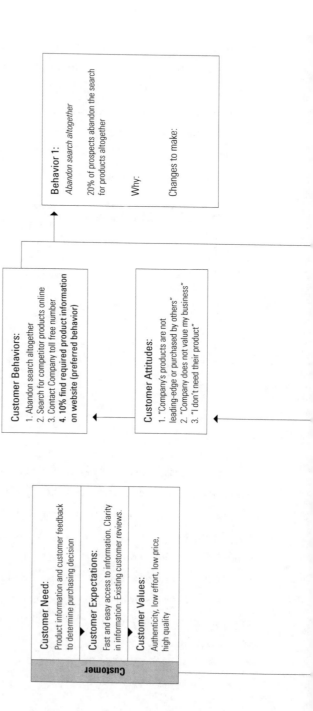

Customer Behaviors:
1. Abandon search altogether
2. Search for competitor products online
3. Contact Company toll free number
4. **10% find required product information on website (preferred behavior)**

Customer Attitudes:
1. "Company's products are not leading-edge or purchased by others"
2. "Company does not value my business"
3. "I don't need their product"

Behavior 1:
Abandon search altogether

20% of prospects abandon the search for products altogether

Why:

Changes to make:

Customer

Customer Need:
Product information and customer feedback to determine purchasing decision

Customer Expectations:
Fast and easy access to information. Clarity in information. Existing customer reviews.

Customer Values:
Authenticity, low effort, low price, high quality

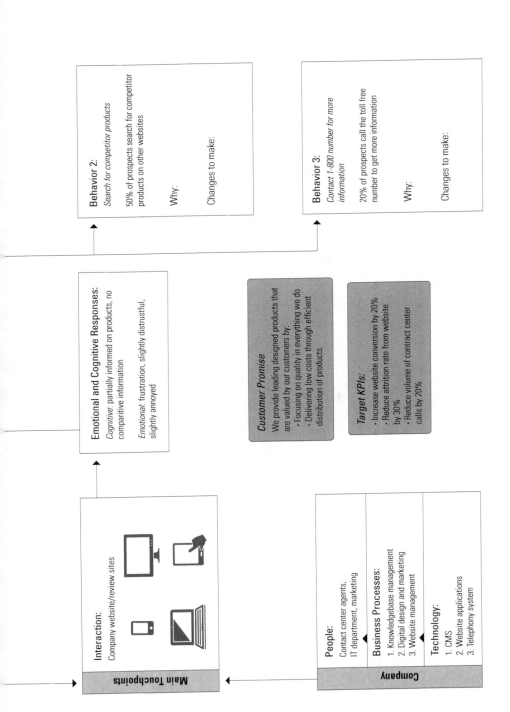

Behavior 2:

Search for competitor products

50% of prospects search for competitor products on other websites

Why:

Changes to make:

Behavior 3:

Contact 1-800 number for more information

20% of prospects call the toll free number to get more information

Why:

Changes to make:

Emotional and Cognitive Responses:

Cognitive: partially informed on products, no comparitive information

Emotional: frustration, slightly distrustful, slightly annoyed

Customer Promise

We provide leading designed products that are valued by our customers by:
- Focusing on quality in everything we do
- Delivering low costs through efficient distribution of products

Target KPIs:
- Increase website conversion by 20%
- Reduce attrition rate from website by 30%
- Reduce volume of contract center calls by 20%

Interaction:

Company website/review sites

Main Touchpoints

Company

People:

Contact center agents, IT department, marketing

Business Processes:
1. Knowledgebase management
2. Digital design and marketing
3. Website management

Technology:
1. CMS
2. Website applications
3. Telephony system

Case Study: Airline Customer Journey Map

Recently, an airline decided to reduce costs by no longer providing any trays or side dishes for their meals. After undertaking customer research, the airline found that a customer segment was expressing disappointment and anger when their meal arrived and did not meet expectations. This particular customer segment of an airline has certain cognitive and emotional expectations around receiving a meal on a long-haul flight. The deviation between customer expectations and what is actually delivered by the airline produced the strong negative response from customers.

The airline's research highlighted that mealtime was one of the few pleasures that this segment of customers could enjoy on an otherwise long, boring, and uncomfortable flight. Customers perceived a high degree of value from the meal and, feeling cheated by the airline, later looked for another airline that delivered better value, in their perspective. The cost savings by the airline may have amounted to a few dollars per meal, but the impact on the airline was the loss of a profitable customer segment.

Instead of subtracting from the meal, the airline could have differentiated itself by adding elements to the meal that would have made it a talking point among customers after the flight. By understanding what customers value most, the airline has the opportunity to use the mealtime as a key touch point that can lead to loyalty and advocacy. Increased loyalty would far outweigh the up-front cost savings of the reduced meal service. It's ultimately a simple equation that is not properly understood unless you undertake the journey mapping exercise.

One of the main customer experience practices I have tried to dispel is the concept of trying to "delight" more customers without first identifying and eliminating negative moments currently experienced by customers. Rather, your approach must be to prioritize the most negative experiences first, with the aim of turning them around by either fixing the underlying problem or completely redesigning a new experience.

A medical response in the brain further validates the wisdom of prioritizing the moments that create the strongest negative emotions. When a person experiences an emotionally charged event, the brain releases dopamine into his or her system. This chemical reaction makes the event easier to remember with accuracy than an event that occurs without attendant strong emotions. This is why I recommend always starting off with identifying all the highly impactful negative moments before trying to delight your customer. The concept of delighting customers is often incorrectly associated with *satisfying* customers. Focusing on satisfying customers does nothing to create an emotionally charged event capable of becoming memorable for the customer. Too often, any positive experience is easily negated by a negative experience.

The underlying cause of emotionally charged events, both positive and negative, is surprise: when an individual experiences surprise from an interaction that does not conform to preconceived expectations. The element of surprise is what creates the emotional charge. To achieve a "delightful" moment for a customer, there has to be an element of surprise in surpassing the expectations of the customer. Often the delivery of such a positively charged event is much more difficult to achieve than people may realize. It requires employees of the organization to be customer centric and highly empowered to resolve customer issues. This is certainly achievable, but it should become part of your longer-term objectives rather than your immediate ones. I would always recommend dealing with highly charged negative moments first, and looking for innovative solutions that could transform them into highly charged positive moments.

STEP 10: CREATE A JOURNEY MAP FOR YOUR CUSTOMER'S NEW EXPERIENCE

The design of your future customer journey map—the new experience map (table 5.1)—should be based around a series of questions that need to be answered in order to reach a new experience that will achieve your financial objectives. The questions are designed to help the organization prioritize the changes required to achieve the desired commercial outcome. They aim to ensure minimal resources are wasted in changing elements of the experience that are not tied to the desired financial outcome, which could mean a wasted investment that costs the organization rather than benefits it. The new experience map should incorporate the elements outlined in the template.

From the data collected around the dimensions you captured earlier (in step 7 of your customer journey map process), you should be able to prioritize the particular moment or touch point by knowing the financial impact on the organization. If the impact is directly related to one of your financial objectives, then the experience or touch point has to be higher on the priority list so that you can focus on changing it.

Contemplating the design of your future customer experience will enable participants to better appreciate the end game of the workshops and the final desired outcomes. Completing the new designed experience will be the task in the next step of the process. For now, you can begin adding substance to the new experience map, which should be sitting opposite or adjacent to your current journey map. You should be drawing on the data captured in the current experience map—the negative moment in the customer's journey—and answering the new experience map's questions. Table 5.2 illustrates this process using a hypothetical negative interaction with a financial institution:

TABLE 5.2: CURRENT EXPERIENCE MAP VS. NEW EXPERIENCE MAP—EXAMPLE

NEGATIVE MOMENT 5:

Customers of a financial institution expressed anger when they are called by a collections team if they are a couple of days late paying their credit card bill.

Current Experience Map	New Experience Map
Customer need that is driving the action: • Need to buy goods and services now in a convenient and effortless manner	Values highly regarded by the customer but not being met: • Effortless • Control
Emotional and cognitive expectations valued most by a customer: • Freedom, convenience, flexibility, control, clarity	Why this moment matters to the customer: • Customer feels the call is confrontational. They have to explain themselves to the collections officer. Call is also unannounced; it catches them off guard.
Customer interaction at a touch point: • Customer has to stop what they are doing, take call, and explain the reasons they are late on monthly bill. Collections officer is unfriendly and only interested in a commitment to make a payment. Late fees are also applied.	What are the opportunities to improve this interaction? • Create an interaction that is effortless, non-confrontational and places the customer in control, but at the same time reduces the late payment and fees.
Emotional and cognitive responses of customer: • Emotions: Anger, embarrassment, surprise • Cognitive: The card is costing me more money than other ones	What is the ideal experience we would like to give our customer? • (brainstorming stage)

Current Experience Map	New Experience Map
Attitudes driving customer behavior: • "They treat me poorly and don't value me as a customer"	*How is the new experience going to meet an emotional need?* • The experience will give the customer control, respect their time, and align with their emotional need to be free
Typical behavior of customer after interaction: • Replace the card with an alternate financial institution's credit card	*How is the new experience likely to change the customer's behavior?* • The customer will become more loyal to the brand as they feel more valued • They will continue using the card and with fewer late payments
Organizational impact from the interaction: • Customer monthly spend is reduced by 50% • 10% of customers called by collections team stop using the card altogether	*What are the likely financial benefits?* • Increase in revenues • Increase in customer retention

At this point in the process, you do not need to apply specific financial targets that we expect to achieve from our modifications. All you need to do is identify what would change the customers' behavior and how this new behavior is likely to benefit the organization financially.

Using the example in table 5.2, we can quickly isolate the negative interaction that should be changed to elicit a positive emotional response: The call made by the collections officer is having a detrimental impact on customers, and the consequential financial impact to the organization is far greater than the benefits gained from calling the customer.

To rectify this problematic interaction, we begin completing our new journey map. In the new journey we don't know *how* we will achieve our new experience, but we can outline *what* we want to achieve. Our analysis has identified that the customer values mostly the freedom, convenience, and control the card provides. We also identified that the customer values a low-effort relationship when transacting with the bank. The collections call achieves the opposite, taking away what is most valued by the customer: freedom. The new experience, if it is to elicit a positive emotion, needs to deliver on the primary benefits the customer values most.

Once you rewrite the narrative of the customer journey to more accurately and consistently reflect your organization's brand promise, you can begin to create differentiated and uniquely branded experiences for your customers. Redesigning any negative moments for the customer so these interactions fulfill emotional needs instead of frustrating them is the overarching objective that makes your organization more customer centric.

Using Your Map to Create a New Customer Journey

Designing a new experience is perhaps one of the most important parts in any customer experience initiative. This next step in the process draws on the creativity of the team as it explores the multiple options available to rewrite the narrative for your hero. All the steps you have taken lead you to this stage: ensuring the stakeholders are armed with the necessary information to help shape the customer's new experience so it achieves the desired financial outcomes for the organization. Customer experience practitioners need to become experts with a finger on the customers' pulse, knowing exactly how they are likely to respond. To be successful at creating your new customer experience, however, you should possess not just your customer research and your internal metrics, but also knowledge of mega trends in the marketplace, changing consumer expectations, how your competitor manages similar customer moments, and whether you have any rising competition.

THE BRAINSTORMING PROCESS

This brainstorming part of the process is all about creativity, innovation, and a wide range of skill sets. You don't want to invite a large team to this workshop; instead, find members in your organization known for their creativity and deep knowledge of customers and your competitors. These are the people who will help you redesign the customer experience.

Your methodology should follow a logical progress from high concepts to clear action items for implementation. You should outline a clear objective about the problem you are trying to fix, to ensure all participants are able to brainstorm about the same topic with a unified purpose. During the brainstorming process, you should be collecting ideas from all stakeholders, ensuring no concepts are dismissed. Encourage creativity. Thinking outside normal comfort parameters will help you innovate.

At the same time, try to structure the workshop. Establishing structure is fundamental to ensure participants are focused. It's also important to frame the brainstorming within a narrative context, identifying how and why the customer is affected at various points during the overall journey. The opportunity exists to rewrite the narrative in a way that enables your hero to overcome the current obstacles and propels that hero effortlessly along a path toward a happy ending—not just for your customer, but for the organization.

Try not to overanalyze the thoughts captured from the team. If you attempt to put too much detail in your new proposed idea and then find out you can't meet the detailed demands, you are in danger of maintaining the status quo and not proceeding any further. The aim at this stage is simply to establish which ideas are worthy of testing.

After collecting the ideas from all team members, you will need to prioritize the ones you want to explore further, by asking the team how they would respond to the proposed change. The changes generating the strongest response are the ones that should be given priority. Also include a high-level estimated cost to implement the idea—if not now, during the brainstorming period, then at a later stage if the idea is short-listed.

For our credit card customer's problem, we would create a grid to evaluate the effectiveness of each short-listed solution (see table 5.3). Then you can further narrow the options most likely to achieve your financial outcomes.

TABLE 5.3: NEW CUSTOMER MOMENT EVALUATION

Customer Moment Dynamics	New Customer Moment Dynamics
Customer moment: Collections agent calls customer because of late payment and requests commitment to pay.	*New moment:* No call is made to the customer. A mobile phone application is created that alerts the customer of due dates and amounts owed, and provides resources such as budget settings to control expenditure on the card.
Problem: Customers stop using the card, and some leave the bank altogether.	*Solution outcome:* Customers keep using the card, stay longer with the bank, and reduce late payments.
Why does this occur? Customers get angry when they receive the call and embarrassed when they have to explain why they are late making payments.	*What is the likely new customer behavior?* Customers feel they are in control of their finances through the new app and decide to make the card their primary one. They show it off to their friends and tell others how easy it is to control their spending.

Continued

Customer Moment Dynamics	New Customer Moment Dynamics
What customer values are we violating? Desire for freedom, control, and low effort.	*What customer values will be achieved?* Control, freedom, and effortlessness.
Who or what is creating this problem? Collections team. Billing technology.	*How does this solution compare with the competition, mega trends, and brand values?* Mobile applications are popular with the customer segment. The application would be a first among current competitors. The solution is consistent with bank's brand values.
What is the cost to the organization? The reduced spending and lost customers are estimated to cost the bank $5,000,000 every year.	*Who and what are needed to achieve this?* IT director, head of digital, marketing director, CEO, billing team.
	What is the estimated cost to implement this? The estimated cost to implement is $500,000.

In the example, the brainstormed idea is not based on fixing the existing problem by changing aspects of the process. This certainly could have been a possibility, and the team may have brainstormed the idea of simply changing collections agents' attitude or tone when making the call, or foregoing the need to get a commitment to pay from the customer. Instead, the entire process of making calls for late payers has been eradicated. The chosen solution used another, and often more rewarding, approach to changing moments of negative interaction in the customer's journey: Completely rewrite the experience by changing the entire process altogether.

In the brainstorming workshop, the team may have argued that making the outbound call is an outdated course of action, is obtrusive to the customer, and violates both what the customer expects and what the brand stands for. By rewriting that part of the story for the customer, the organization now has not only the potential to solve a current obstacle in the customer's journey, but the opportunity to create a differentiated and branded customer experience.

When evaluating your brainstormed ideas, be sure to reference the financial KPIs and targets. This will help the team better appraise the version of the story most likely to achieve the set commercial objectives. In our example, we may argue that if the solution's cost is estimated at

$500,000, and if only 50 percent of our customers change their behavior by keeping the card, then the investment would yield a $2 million benefit to the bank (50 percent of the $5 million minus the cost of the application at $500,000). From a high-level perspective, the idea has a strong business case because it is well supported with research on the use of mobile applications by the particular customer segment in question. The innovation around expenditure control also contributes to the customers' need to have greater control in their relationship with the bank.

Short-listed ideas may themselves require further brainstorming and scoping to determine their feasibility. Viability needs to be determined before the idea progresses to the testing stage. For example, the idea of building a mobile application may not be deemed viable if we discover that in order to achieve the desired outcome, the entire billing system would also need to be upgraded at a cost of more than $5 million.

If you uncover a major hurdle, you may wish to look at how the idea can still achieve its objectives but with a slightly different design. Continuing the example, we may still find we can build an application, but we don't have to integrate it into the billing system. Perhaps we can still achieve the majority of the outcomes by integrating with the CRM system at a lower cost. If the case is strong, then look for options to achieve the desired narrative for your customer.

TEST THE NEW EXPERIENCE

Before heading down an expensive path to change the customer journey, you should test your idea. Just as a newly developed drug must be tested on patients to determine whether it will achieve its desired outcomes and if there are any side effects, the redesigned customer moment needs to be tested on the target customer segment. The test should aim to replicate the new moment as closely as possible to learn whether the expected results are likely to be achieved if the solution were rolled out in full production.

During the testing stage, you are trying to measure emotions and changed behavior of customers, not seeking absolute guarantees that the change will meet the desired objectives. You are largely seeking validation that a high percentage of the test group, representing your customer segment, would behave according to your expectations. You can use observations and customer surveys from a statistically acceptable cohort to reach the evidence required to validate or disprove the idea.

When a new technology is being conceived as part of the solution, the approach would be to create a low-cost prototype. The prototype should show how the technology would look and operate, to give your test group a good sense of its potential value. A low-cost prototype of our mobile app, for example, will help validate the application and its various features before our organization commits to costly development. The prototype ensures your application is being built with customer validation, by showing you whether customers want or use the expensive features you conceived.

Testing results will lean toward either validating or disproving your new idea, and unless the idea has convincingly tested well among your customer segment, you should not pursue it further. A marginal improvement in the customer experience is unlikely to yield the desired results you are after. As stated earlier, only strong feelings about an experience can persuade people to change their behavior.

Case Study: Banks Shifting Customer Behavior

The adoption of online banking came about largely because banks used this concept of negative experiences to their advantage. Banks wanted to shift customers from using costly physical branches with tellers to using online banking and the contact center. They decided that to wean customers away from branches, they had to deliver a highly impactful and negative experience.

Banks began to ensure limited staff members were allocated to branches so that lines started to get longer. Wait times for teller service left customers frustrated and angry with the experience. The underlying premise to this strategy was that although lines at the branches were bad, customers would not go through the trouble of actually switching banks because the lines were not bad *enough* to cause them to abandon the bank for a competitor. The tactic worked, and the majority of bank customers today do at least some of their banking online.

Using this concept of negative experiences to their advantage may have worked for banks in the past, when competition was more limited. But this strategy is unlikely to work today, as competition has increased and switching banks has been made a lot easier with technology.

The final step in the testing process, before going into full production and rollout, is validating the financial metrics most likely to be affected by the change. If you have been following the process outlined so far in this book, there should be a direct correlation between the customer moment you are redesigning and one or more of the financial targets you set at the beginning of the process.

The results from your test should enable you to calculate the most likely financial outcome of the proposed change. Different organizations will go to varying degrees of depth to achieve these calculations. Using statistical modeling, for example, you can apply a regression analysis to your test results to predict the most probable financial impact. Since this book is not about statistical analysis, I will not attempt to outline this in-depth technical approach, but I recommend that you engage with an expert who is trained in statistical modeling if you decide to do so.

The level of analysis used during your test phase will largely depend on the resources you have available. A larger organization is likely to have more resources at its disposal than a smaller one, and because its investment is also likely to be larger, it is more likely to take an in-depth approach to analyzing financial impact. Numerous variables can shape the success of your customer journey change. Going back to our example of a financial institution handling late credit card payments, the mobile application may have tested positively with the test audience, but if it's not properly promoted or distributed to the target customer segment, it will not achieve its desired financial objectives.

If you want to apply a high-level analysis to determine the viability of your new, changed moment, then creating different scenarios is the best approach to determine what percentage of changed customer behavior is required to get the necessary return on your investment. Applying these different scenarios will also help you discover the minimum levels of changed behavior required to break even (see table 5.4). In addition to giving a broad overview of the metrics defining the success of your change, taking the median result from this analysis will enable you to define the most likely contribution the change will make toward achieving your financial objectives. At a later stage, you will need to determine whether the total investment committed for the change is likely to give the organization new financial value.

Using our example about the mobile app replacing a collections call, we could apply the following analysis:

TABLE 5.4: NEW CUSTOMER MOMENT FINANCIAL ANALYSIS

Variable	Existing Moment Profitability	Net Gain	Customer Losses (Retention)	Customer Acquisition
Current loss to organization from existing customer negative moment	-$ 5,000,000.00		- 15,000.00	- 9,000.00
Cost of changed new moment	-$ 500,000.00			
Gain/loss if 0% change	-$ 5,500,000.00	- 10%	- 15,000.00	- 9,000.00
Gain/loss if 10% change	-$ 5,000,000.00	0%	- 13,500.00	- 8,100.00
Gain/loss if 20% change	-$ 4,500,000.00	10%	- 12,000.00	- 7,200.00
Gain/loss if 30% change	-$ 4,000,000.00	20%	- 10,500.00	- 6,300.00
Gain/loss if 40% change	-$ 3,500,000.00	30%	- 9,000.00	- 5,400.00
Gain/loss if 50% change	-$ 3,000,000.00	40%	- 7,500.00	- 4,500.00
Gain/loss if 60% change	-$ 2,500,000.00	50%	- 6,000.00	- 3,600.00
Gain/loss if 70% change	-$ 2,000,000.00	60%	- 4,500.00	- 2,700.00
Gain/loss if 80% change	-$ 1,500,000.00	70%	- 3,000.00	- 1,800.00
Gain/loss if 90% change	-$ 1,000,000.00	80%	- 1,500.00	- 900.00
Gain/loss if 100% change	-$ 500,000.00	90%		
New Moment Financial Summary				
Median financial gain/loss	-$ 3,000,000.00	40%	- 7,500.00	- 4,500.00
Financial gain	$ 2,000,000.00		7,500.00	4,500.00
Program financial targets	$ 10,000,000.00		17,000.00	15,000.00
% of total target from the initiative	**20%**		**44%**	**30%**

This simple analysis enables you to quickly pinpoint the breakeven point (10 percent change of behavior)—the impact on your retention and acquisition figures. It's not a comprehensive analysis; however, it is very useful to know what percentage of customers changing their behavior would affect your financial outcomes and help you achieve your targets.

Our example is essentially a sensitivity analysis that seeks to understand the likely impact in different scenarios. Using the median as the expected case, we can determine that the change could contribute to 20 percent of our profitability target, 44 percent toward our retention target, and 30 percent toward our customer acquisition target. At first glance including an acquisition target may appear to be an error, because the collections agents are largely having an impact on existing customers. The evidence presented later in this book, however, should convince you of the impact on customer acquisition due to negative word of mouth by customers affected by poor experiences. The analysis assumes the bank is losing out on securing nine thousand new customers every year because of negative publicity caused by the collections call.

With customer experience, it's important to always consider the domino effect. The impact does not just end with one domino falling. Rather, the impact is generally felt across multiple areas, such as the following:

- Revenues
- Cost of sale
- Gross margin
- Net margin
- Brand equity
- Customer retention
- Customer acquisition

It is essential that you perform analysis prior to pulling the trigger on implementation of any new CX initiative. Before deciding on which new experiences to implement, you will need to undertake this analysis for each of your proposed changes. By doing this exercise, you will be able to determine whether you are likely to achieve your targets for the allocated budget or whether you need to do some revisions. You may need to revise your budget and targets, or perhaps you can tweak the moments you wanted to change for the customer. Taking a pragmatic approach toward what stays or what goes is pivotal as you try to achieve a sustainable commercial benefit by selectively elevating experiences for your customers.

Rolling Out the New Experience

Once you have decided which moments you would like to change and defined how you wish to change them, it's time to prepare for the implementation of the new experience. This topic is covered in more detail in part two of this book, so here I will only summarize the areas that influence—and are influenced by—the successful rollout of your newly changed customer moments.

EXAMINE THE RISKS OF ROLLOUT

The rollout of your CX initiative should consider the applicable risks associated with the rollout and the actions needed to mitigate these risks. The initiative may affect a large group of customers, or all customers, so you should implement an awareness campaign to educate them about the change. There are a number of issues you must consider to ensure the rollout of the initiatives achieves its objectives:

- Stakeholders
- Customers impacted
- Employees impacted
- Technology used
- Business process changes
- Training required
- External parties needed for rollout
- Marketing of initiative
- Risk mitigation
- KPIs and measurements

During the implementation of any new customer experience initiative, company leadership needs to measure the impact on customers to assess whether the initiative is meeting its objectives or should be changed to align with customer expectations. Where the impact is significant or a large customer base is involved, the approach to mitigate risk will normally involve a staged or staggered rollout so any problems do not affect all your customers. In technology rollouts a beta version typically is released prior to a full production release. The beta testing identifies and rectifies any bugs, mitigating risk and increasing the chances of achieving the desired experience outcomes.

DIGITIZE YOUR MAPS FOR COLLABORATION AND MEASUREMENT

Once you have implemented the changes to create a new customer narrative for your targeted customer segments, you need to monitor and measure the customers' experience effectively throughout the life cycle so you can identify opportunities for further enhancement.

You should have two customer journey maps completed for every particular customer segment you have identified as being important to achieving your financial and strategic objectives: one map that represents the current customer journey, and another that represents the ideal customer journey (see template in table 5.1). Because you make these maps through collaborative efforts in your workshops, they are probably paper based (as recommended earlier in this chapter). It's now time to convert these maps to digital format.

There are a number of software programs you can use—for example, IBM's Journey Designer, Mapovate, UX360, Visual Paradigm, and Suite CX. Ideally the software should capture customer sentiment along the customer journey in real time. It also should give your customers the opportunity to directly input how they feel about a particular interaction and any changes they would like to see. Ideally your software will help you work in a collaborative way with your customers and employees to ensure the new customer journey is achieving its objectives for both of you.

Leading organizations understand the importance of treating the customer as another type of "employee" and regularly consult with their customers before bringing out new products and services or changing aspects of their customer journey. Having a system that enables you to incorporate customers' feedback into the design process in real time will enable your organization to be more responsive and take meaningful, targeted action.

Measure the Effectiveness of Your Customer Journey Maps

The final step in your customer journey mapping exercise is to create and then monitor some key performance indicators (KPIs) and targets so you can measure how the organization is performing. KPIs keep people focused on what is important and hold them accountable for their contributions. To ensure the organization achieves its objectives, be sure to provide your team members with clear and updated information on how they are progressing.

Make Sure KPIs Align with CX Objectives and Are Achievable

The KPIs you set should be achievable, realistic, and aligned to the organization's strategic goals. KPIs never work when there are too many of them or the targets are unrealistic. Discuss with stakeholders—as many of them as possible—to ensure quicker adoption of the KPIs and respective targets. The inclusion of multiple stakeholders in the KPI- and target-setting stage will facilitate the rollout of the proposed customer moment changes and also help shape the organization's customer-centric behavior.

I would warn against setting a single measure such as the net promoter score (NPS) as the sole measure to determine how well an organization is performing. Too often this approach leads employees to focus on the score to the exclusion of all else. Having only one measure in place doesn't necessarily make them more engaged or in tune with customer issues.

Instead, I prefer to see metrics that are specially focused on what the customer values most. Many organizations change their KPIs around customer values after undertaking a comprehensive customer journey mapping exercise with the goal of elevating the customer experience and making the organization more customer centric.

Case Study: Call Centers and KPIs

For many years, call centers modeled their behavior entirely around operational efficiency and how quick they could complete a call. It wasn't until customer experience became a topic of interest, and customer surveys identified what customers value most, that customers were revealed to be dissatisfied with many call centers delivering highly efficient call handling.

Customers felt rushed, as though agents were not properly addressing their requests. Often they would have to call back several times to get the issue properly resolved. Research done by many organizations confirmed that customers really wanted to get their query properly addressed the first time. They actually didn't mind waiting a few more seconds, as long as they got an attentive and highly competent agent on the other end to resolve their query.

This insight led many call centers to change their primary, efficiency KPIs into outcome-based KPIs. Today, first-call resolution has become the dominant KPI in many customer-centric call centers, because it focuses the agents of the center on what customers value the most: taking the time to get the job done right, the first time.

In the example of the credit card collections call, we deemed that the values most appreciated by the customer segments were low effort, convenience, freedom, and control. If we take these values and apply them to the new experiences with the software application, we can create KPIs and targets for the key stakeholders as follows:

TABLE 5.5: KEY STAKEHOLDER KPIS AND TARGETS

Customer Value	KPI	Target	Department Responsible
Low effort	Software accessibility	Any version of the software must never require the customer to access any feature by clicking more than two times.	IT
Convenience	Software interoperability and uptime	Any version of the software should be available on all popular platforms and should contain the same features and customer information. Server uptime should be greater than 99.999% to ensure customers can conveniently access their accounts at any time.	IT/Network
Control	Account controls	Any version of the software should provide customers with full control over their account, including limiting expenditure.	IT

These are three KPIs that ensure the redesigned customer moment specifically achieves its objectives and delivers the value we had planned for the customer. Creating KPIs and targets around specific moments that matter, as opposed to having a generic measure such as NPS, keeps the organization focused on delivering real value back to the customer.

The customer journey mapping exercise becomes a powerful tool when you can redesign organizational KPIs around very specific, high-impact areas in the customer journey. Customizing the KPIs for each department, whether or not it is customer facing, will make this metric relevant and will empower department heads to focus on the necessary activities that lead to the desired experience.

KEY LESSONS

- The *customer journey* refers to phases each customer goes through when deciding to purchase a particular type of product or service.
- The journey map, from an organization's perspective, addresses what triggers lead to the acquisition of new customers and the retention of existing customers.
- You can design an effective customer journey map using the following process:
    1. Tell you customer's story.
    2. Define the goals of your map.
    3. Undertake customer research.
    4. Identify your customer segments.
    5. Select the customer segments for mapping.
    6. Define the phases of the customer journey.
    7. Define the dimensions of your map.
    8. Create the map through a series of workshops.
    9. Evaluate the current customer journey.
    10. Design a new customer experience.

- Test the new experience before your rollout.
- Digitize the customer journey map so it can be collaborative and you can measure the effectiveness of your changes.
- Set and measure your new experience against organizational KPIs and targets.

CHAPTER 6

Aligning Initiatives to
Achieve CX Objectives

The business case for your CX program should be taking good form and providing a more comprehensive picture of areas you need to address and how you will go about achieving your desired outcomes. To complete your case, you will need to identify opportunities on both the customer and the organizational sides that will finalize your design. These opportunities do not present themselves easily, but if you have completed the stages outlined in previous chapters, you should be in a position to identify gaps in your plan.

It's now time to step back and take a look at the full picture of your design, and to evaluate what aspects of it are risky and need adjustment or new initiatives. Stages 17 through 20 are about aligning your plans and objectives in order to finalize your CX program prior to implementation.

Stage	Desired Output
17. Review your top customer acquisition and retention initiatives, and identify how you can achieve any defined cost or improved margin targets.	A list of initiatives to achieve your cost reduction and/or improved financial targets
18. Summarize all initiatives to achieve your financial targets, and allocate time frames and resources to complete them.	High-level time frames and a list of how resources for each initiative's completion are allocated

Stage	Desired Output
19. Using the organizational evaluation for customer centricity, identify the top 2–5 areas you need to change to achieve sustainability for your CX initiative.	A list of the key organizational changes needed to achieve sustainability for your CX program
20. Design a customer-centricity program specifically addressing the areas in the organization most likely to impact sustainability of any financial benefits generated from your CX initiative.	A program designed to permanently change the key areas identified in the organization as impacting improved CX sustainability

Performing a Gap and Opportunity Analysis

Before you can finalize your CX business case, you need to complete a number of analyses to ensure you have properly considered any issues identified in earlier stages and aligned the initiatives to your CX objectives. The first such task is a gap and opportunity analysis, which will examine the initiatives for both the organization and the customer. Using a similar methodology, you will take the matrix table you developed in chapters 3 and 4, and build on it by adding new criteria for analysis and evaluation.

REVIEWING YOUR ORGANIZATIONAL INITIATIVES

Review the organizational part of your plan first. For this current analysis, you will flesh out the details related to additional resources, costs, and expected benefits of the actions you wish to take. From there you will be able to isolate any gaps or opportunities in the organizational plan.

Creating a simple grid that builds on your earlier one (developed in chapter 4) will allow you to explore the various benefits expected from your proposed organizational changes. Any unknown areas should be flagged and followed up on. After completing this process, you will have a much better idea about the costs for your program, ensuring you don't over- or underspend.

Returning to the example of Company C (the household appliances manufacturer) and the organizational analysis we undertook to determine its degree of customer centricity (see table 4.1), we can apply the following gap and opportunity analysis:

TABLE 6.1: GAP AND OPPORTUNITY ANALYSIS—ORGANIZATIONAL INITIATIVES

LEADERSHIP

Problem Areas	Initiative	Expected End Benefit	New Cost Items	Estimated Cost	Estimated Financial Benefit	% of CX Budget	Gap/Opportunity
It may be difficult to get the business case for the CX program through the board. Without proper implementation, financial sustainability will not be achieved.	Convince the CEO of the plan, and ensure he/she sponsors the program at board level.	CX program will be approved.	No new resources required.	$0	Without sign-off there will be no plan to execute.	0%	
Without effective prioritization around customer-centricity objectives, the program will not meet objectives within the set time frames.	Once ideal customer experiences at each touch point have been designed, deploy a structured communication plan to all staff and departments.	CX objectives will be met within the set time frames.	Consulting firm or specialist resources required.	Unknown	Expertise will ensure a higher probability of success.	Unknown	Identify estimated cost of consulting company or resources.
Misaligned incentives will shape the behavior of staff and undermine the shift toward the desired customer-centricity behaviors.	After designing KPIs, require the CEO, CFO, and HR director to sign off on new KPIs and incentives plan.	Employee behaviors will change toward achieving greater customer centricity.	Current incentives are insufficient to meet the transformation goals of the plan.	$1,000,000	Employees are the enablers of the program, so without this, the program is unlikely to be properly executed.	14%	Create additional incentive budget to help achieve desired changes within time frame.

COLLABORATION

Problem Areas	Initiative	Expected End Benefit	New Cost Items	Estimated Cost	Estimated Financial Benefit	% of CX Budget	Gap/ Opportunity
Without the cooperation of a number of department heads working toward achieving customer-centricity objectives, the financial objectives will not be met	In the short term, establish a CX task force to work on collectively achieving financial objectives. In the medium term, reevaluate the organizational structure to enable cross-functional teams.	Financial objectives of CX program will be met.	Task force will require new resources.	Unknown	Task force will be the driving force for the program in the organization and will track financial objectives.	Unknown	Create the driving engine behind the program, ensuring it does not stall.

IMPLEMENTATION

Problem Areas	Initiative	Expected End Benefit	New Cost Items	Estimated Cost	Estimated Financial Benefit	% of CX Budget	Gap/ Opportunity
Without CX design, the organization will be unable to deliver on its brand promise or to provide customers with the products and services they value most.	After designing a CX program, ensure a structured training and mentoring program exists to communicate the desired employee behaviors and outputs required to achieve the program's objectives.	Employees will have a clear understanding of what is expected of them and will be trained in new behaviors.	External trainers are required, as current trainers do not have capacity for additional workload.	Unknown	Training and mentoring is a critical aspect of achieving the customer-centricity objectives.	Unknown	Determine cost of trainers and the program, and identify opportunities to ensure greater employee engagement.
Without meaningful customer insights, the CX program will not enable the organization to track and monitor progress.	Design an easy-to-understand dashboard for new customer metrics, organizational KPIs, and tracking against targets.	Measuring and tracking progress will ensure focus on important metrics.	Current dashboard application needs to be modified to meet tracking objectives.	$500,000	Clarity about performance compared with set targets over time.	7%	
Customer acquisition, retention, and CLV targets will not be achieved unless the organization is able to modify its products and services to more accurately deliver customer values.	Gather customer research to identify (1) key pain points along customer touch points, and (2) feedback on products and services. Design a new process to ensure customer input is gathered prior to manufacture or release of any products or services.	Products and services will more accurately meet customer values and enable organization to meet sales targets.	Research organization or consulting firm is required to undertake customer research.	$1,500,000	Customer research is required to pinpoint customer initiatives.	21%	Identify from research whether certain products and services should be eliminated.

Total CX budget: $10 million
Analysis and design phase budget allocation: $3 million
Implementation phase budget allocation: $7 million
Organizational initiatives cost: $3 million
Percentage of total implementation budget: 43%
The total cost of the organizational initiatives amounts to 43 percent of the total implementation budget for this program.

The Gaps

Now we know the additional tasks needed to complete the cost estimate for the organizational program. The analysis showed us that a number of our initiatives require specialist resources such as consultants that have yet to be incorporated into the plan. The first gap in our plan requires us to gather costing for some of the resources we have identified. In addition, we need to allocate an incentive budget to help motivate employees to achieve our desired objectives, and we also need to form a task force to help drive our CX program throughout the organization.

The Opportunities

The analysis has also shown further opportunities that could save the organization money and help achieve our objectives. For example, we now realize the customer research organization can serve a dual purpose: identifying pain points and customer values, and identifying any current product or service not valued by customers. Our household goods manufacturer can now consider retaining the services of a single vendor as opposed to two. This presents an opportunity to expand the scope of the research while also reducing the cost of duplication. Evidence collected on products or services not considered important by customers could help product managers stop production on certain items. This rationalization of product lines will contribute toward improving our gross margin targets.

The process of discovery is the primary objective of this stage, and our discoveries will permit us to take appropriate action to either fill a gap or capitalize on an opportunity. The end goal of this stage is to have a complete business case for your CX program, with cost and initiatives clearly outlined and empirical evidence to support why the initiatives are important to the organization.

REVIEWING YOUR CUSTOMER INITIATIVES

Thanks to the customer journey mapping process, by now you have identified a number of CX initiatives for your own organization that, if implemented correctly, will achieve some of your financial targets. The organizational changes you have designed will ensure the sustainability of your customer experience changes, although they may be more difficult to quantify in terms of providing direct correlations between changing some of the low-performing aspects that cause poor customer centricity and your desired financial gains. The customer initiatives, however, will seek a more immediate result, and it is easier to predict their financial outcomes by readily correlating an interaction at some point in the customer journey and its impact on the financials.

For our manufacturer's CX program (see table 6.1), and following the same analysis as for the organizational initiatives, we will now review the customer initiatives for gaps and opportunities, focusing on initiatives that have an impact on various stages in the customer life cycle, such as the customer research, purchase, and usage stages. Our goal is to identify the estimated financial gain and the percentage of the specific financial target to which the initiative relates. Be sure to include the basis for your calculation in order to help validate your numbers.

TABLE 6.2: GAP AND OPPORTUNITY ANALYSIS—CUSTOMER INITIATIVES

Initiative: Customer Awareness and Research Stages	Expected End Benefit	New Cost Items	Estimated Cost	Estimated Financial Benefit	Estimate % of Target	Financial Targets	Basis for Financial Calculation	Gap/ Opportunity
Engage with influential bloggers to write about the new and unique features of the latest-model ovens, dishwashers, and fridges.	Improved market awareness and validation of the product.	Social media agency service contract	Unknown	New prospects to website increased by 10%.	50%	Increase website traffic of genuine prospects by 20%.	Social media agency	Add more initiatives to reach the 20% target (currently only 75% of targets would be achieved).
Establish Instagram page adding new pictures of latest products to engage with online community.	Increased engagement with prospects.	Social media agency service contract	Unknown	New prospects to website increased by 2%.	10%	Increase website traffic of genuine prospects by 20%.	Social media agency	
Post recipes and pictures of dishes created using the new features of the latest oven on Facebook and Instagram to raise awareness.	Increased awareness of the new features of stove and oven product lines.	Social media agency service contract	Unknown	New prospects to website increased by 3%.	15%	Increase website traffic of genuine prospects by 20%.	Social media agency	Hire a single agency to perform the work, and reduce the cost of multiple agencies.
Engage with popular review websites to ensure products are reviewed, to help customers during the research stage.	Shortened time frame for research and selection.	Social media agency service contract	Unknown	Sales volume increased by 5%.	33%	Increase sales volume by 15%.	Social media agency	

Initiative: Customer Selection and Purchase Stages	Expected End Benefit	New Cost Items	Estimated Cost	Estimated Financial Benefit	Estimate % of Target	Financial Targets	Basis for Financial Calculation	Gap/Opportunity
Introduce a zero-interest-rate financing option to facilitate sales of new products.	Increase volume of sales	10 new resources required to design a finance product and manage process with finance company.	$1,200,000	Revenues increased by 5%.	50%	Increase revenues by 10%.	Estimate provided by HR director	Bundle the zero-interest option with the extended warranty offer.
Extend the warranty period without additional cost, to help customers make a decision during the selection stage.	Increased volume of sales and extended customer life cycle.	1 year extended warranty cost.	$950,000	Sales volume increased by 2%.	13%	Increase sales volume by 15%.	Internal regression analysis	Add an initiative to increase revenues by 3% to reach target.
				Revenues increased by 3%.	25%	Increase revenues by 10%.		
				Life cycle extended by 6 months.	67%	Extend life cycle by 9 months.		

Initiative: Product Usage, Maintenance, and Support Stages	Expected End Benefit	New Cost Items	Estimated Cost	Estimated Financial Benefit	Estimate % of Target	Financial Targets	Basis for Financial Calculation	Gap/Opportunity
Provide an application for customers to track delivery day and time of product, provide online videos of how to use the product, provide tips on maintenance, and establish one-click access to support center.	Increased retention and brand loyalty as customers experience more convenience during the buying and ownership stage and less effort to access maintenance and support information.	Mobile application development company contact.	Unknown	Retention increased by 10% for next sale purchases as loyalty increases.	67%	Increase retention by 15%.	Internal regression analysis	Add a retention initiative and increase a sales volume initiative to reach respective targets.
				Sales volume increased by 2% due to word-of-mouth referrals.	10%	Increase sales volume by 20%.		Add an initiative to reduce cost of sale by another 2%.
				Cost of sale reduced and repeat purchases increased by 3%.	60%	Reduce cost of sale by 5%.		

Customer initiatives cost: $2,150,000
Percentage of total implementation budget: 31%

The Gaps

The customer initiatives gap and opportunity analysis reveals that some of the financial targets are not going to be met unless new ones are added or existing initiatives are modified. For example, from the analysis above we have determined that the three key initiatives designed to increase web traffic to our site achieve only 75 percent of our financial target. This gap needs to be addressed by adding a new initiative. Similar gaps are identified for the revenue, retention, sales volume, and cost reduction targets.

The Opportunities

Our analysis identified some overlap in the agencies used to help our household appliances manufacturer implement our CX initiatives. This presents us with the opportunity to potentially save some of our cost budget by rationalizing the work with a single agency. Another opportunity identified in the analysis is the possibility of bundling the two offers—zero-interest financing and extended warranty—to make it more attractive for customers to purchase. These opportunities need to be explored further to maximize your program's results.

Interpreting Opportunities and Gaps

The gap and opportunity analyses for the organizational and customer components of our CX program offer us a clearer idea of what additional work needs to be completed, how much of our implementation budget we have spent, and how likely the plan is to achieve the financial targets. The household goods manufacturer and retailer can now conclude the following:

- 43 percent of the implementation budget has been allocated for organizational initiatives.

- 31 percent of the implementation budget has been allocated for customer initiatives.
- 26 percent of the budget remains to be allocated to unknown cost items.

Some of the financial targets are not going to be met unless new ones are added or existing initiatives are modified. There are a few options available to us at this stage:

- Reduce our financial targets to meet our budget.
- Scale back the proposed initiatives to make more funds available for new initiatives.
- Increase our budget.

Pros and cons exist for each of these options. To determine which option is best for your own organization, you will need to revisit the reasons your organization wishes to elevate its customers' experiences and become more customer centric, as discussed in chapter 3. This review will need to include the financial targets set at the beginning of the project (see table 2.3). Your objective for the gap and opportunity analysis is to align the targets, budgets, and initiatives so they meet your desired objectives within the time frames required. The alignment of all these components will give you the necessary information about the best course of action to take to finalize your CX program.

Determining the Cost of Your Proposed Initiatives

Next you will need to identify the costs associated with your initiatives. This step will normally require you to define a scope of work and then request proposals from external organizations such as social media companies or consultants. Often it is best to ask for high-level estimates from companies because a detailed scope may be premature, especially if one of your initiatives requires an application to be built. Most vendors will be able to give you a ballpark figure or a range of costs. These will suffice because your goals right now are simply ensuring that you are within your budget and that your initiatives are likely to achieve their financial objectives. A cost and benefit analysis will help identify any initiatives that need revision or can be discarded.

DETERMINING THE COST OF ORGANIZATIONAL INITIATIVES

As outlined previously, organizational initiatives are designed to achieve greater customer centricity that enables long-term sustainability. This understanding provides us with the two main metrics that will help you allocate your budget based on the area of value creation:

- Organizational customer centricity
- Sustainability of customer experience changes

Although it's not an exact science, allocating a percentage for each initiative and its likely contribution toward achieving one of these metrics is a valuable way to estimate the initiative's possible costs and benefits. Use your organizational customer-centricity scores (chapter 3) and the potential financial impact to your program (chapter 4) as your guide to proportion your budget. For example, if an aspect of the organization appears to have a significant negative impact on your CX results, then allocate a higher percentage of the budget to the initiative designed to overcome that weakness.

Not all the initiatives will have the same impact on your targets. Take, for example, the issue of getting the CEO of the household appliances company on board to sponsor our program and convince the board to move forward. We identified this as a potential problem because the organization scored Low in the area of openness to new ideas (see table 4.1). Allocating 50 percent of the organizational sustainability target to this initiative highlights its importance; without CEO sponsorship, we are unlikely to get the program to achieve its objectives. Yet there isn't always a correlation between the impact and the budget. Getting the CEO on board to sponsor the program will consume zero percent of our budget.

For your own CX program, you will also need to estimate the approximate time frame for completing each organizational initiative and beginning to realize the desired benefits. By identifying the impact of each initiative and its estimated allocation of the organizational budget, you will be able to flag which ones to keep or revise.

TABLE 6.3: COST AND BENEFIT ANALYSIS—ORGANIZATIONAL INITIATIVES

Organizational Initiative	% of Budget	% of Targets	Metric	Estimated Time Frame to Complete	Action
Convince the CEO of the plan, and ensure he/she sponsors the program at board level.	0%	50%	Organizational sustainability	2 months	Keep
Once ideal customer experiences at each touch point have been defined, deploy a structured communication plan to all staff and departments.	14%	10%	Organizational customer centricity	6 months	Revise
After designing KPIs, the CEO, CFO, and HR director to sign off on new KPIs and incentives plan.	14%	10%	Organizational customer centricity	8 months	Revise
In the short term, establish a CX task force to work on collectively achieving financial objectives. In the medium term, reevaluate the organizational structure to enable cross-functional teams.	0%	30%	Organizational customer centricity	12 months	Keep
After designing a CX program, ensure a structured training and mentoring program exists to communicate the desired employee behaviors and outputs required to achieve the program's objectives.	6%	30%	Organizational customer centricity	18 months	Keep
Design an easy-to-understand dashboard for new customer metrics, organizational KPIs, and tracking against targets.	7%	20%	Organizational sustainability	8 months	Keep
Gather customer research to identify (1) key pain points along customer touch points, and (2) feedback on products and services. Design a new process to ensure customer input is gathered prior to manufacture or release of any products or services.	21%	20%	Organizational customer centricity	24 months	Revise

DETERMINING THE COST OF CUSTOMER INITIATIVES

Because customer initiatives are easier to quantify than organizational initiatives, identifying the value each initiative will contribute to set financial objectives is a relatively straightforward task. The metrics used in your customer analysis need to reflect the key criteria that your initiative seeks to change.

TABLE 6.4: COST AND BENEFIT ANALYSIS—CUSTOMER INITIATIVES

Customer Initiatives	% of Budget	% of Targets	Metric	Estimated Time Frame to Complete	Action
Engage with influential bloggers to write about the new features of the latest-model ovens, dishwashers, and fridges.	2%	50%	Web traffic of genuine prospects	8 months	Keep
Establish Instagram page, adding new pictures of latest products to engage with online community.	3%	10%	Web traffic of genuine prospects	8 months	Discard
Post recipes and pictures of dishes created using the new features of the latest oven on Facebook and Instagram to raise awareness.	2%	15%	Web traffic of genuine prospects	8 months	Keep
Engage with popular review websites to ensure products are reviewed, to help customers during the research stage.	2%	33%	Sales volume	8 months	Keep
Introduce a zero-interest-rate financing option to facilitate sales of new products.	17%	50%	Revenues	9 months	Keep
Extend the warranty period without additional cost, to help customers make a decision during the selection stage.	14%	13%	Sales volume	12 months	Keep
		25%	Revenues		
		67%	Customer life cycle		
Provide an application for customers to track delivery of product, provide online videos of how to use the product, provide tips on maintenance, and establish one-click access to support center.	18%	67%	Customer retention	12 months	Keep
		10%	Sales volume		
		60%	Cost of sale		

Reviewing the Financials of Your CX Program

After your cost and benefit analysis has identified high-level costs of organizational and customer initiatives, the first thing to note is whether you are over- or under budget. Next note any deficits to your original performance targets by allocating the estimated percentages against the targets you set earlier. From there you will be able to review all your initiatives and see the complete plan. Only when you are able to examine the full picture will you be able to determine whether it needs any tweaking.

REVISING YOUR CX PROGRAM TO FIT THE BUDGET

A summary like the one below (table 6.5) captures the essential components of your financial analysis. In the customer and organizational analyses for our household appliances company, we determined that from the $7 million allocated for the implementation of our CX program, the current cost for all the initiatives exceeded the budget by 20 percent. We also identified, using the target percentages from tables 6.3 and 6.4, that the following percentages of the company's original performance targets are achievable from the metric.

TABLE 6.5: SUMMARY FINANCIAL ANALYSIS

Metric	Total of Performance Targets	% of Implementation Budget
Organizational Initiatives		62%
Customer centricity	100%	
Sustainability	70%	
Customer Initiatives		58%
Web traffic of genuine prospects	75%	
Sales volume increase	56%	
Revenue increase	75%	
Customer life cycle increase	67%	

Metric	Total of Performance Targets	% of Implementation Budget
Customer retention increase	67%	
Cost of sale reduction	60%	
	Total % of Implementation Budget	120%

In this example, there are two main areas to address. First, we need to reallocate 20 percent of the costs to ensure the CX program does not go over 100 percent of its budget. Second, we need to determine whether to add or modify any initiatives to achieve the original targets, by weighing up the likely return on investment and the time frames expected to achieve them. In the customer initiative analysis (table 6.4), the Instagram initiative was discarded because it would cost 3 percent of the implementation budget but would help achieve only 10 percent of the web traffic metric. Compared with the initiative of engaging with influential bloggers (2 percent of budget and 50 percent of our target), the Instagram initiative was more dispensable.

Normally a brainstorming approach is required during this stage to determine which initiatives should stay, which should be modified, and which should be discarded altogether. The brainstorming session should focus on the initiatives addressing existing customer pain points and the percentage of the performance targets to be achieved. Funds should be allocated to initiatives based on merit and their overall importance to your program. For example, it may be that increasing revenues is more important than spending 21 percent of the budget on the customer research company. So customer research could be reduced to 10 percent of the implementation budget, and 7 percent could be added to the new initiative focused on increasing revenues by creating a new value proposition for customers. This reduces the budget deficit by 4 percent, leaving us only 16 percent over budget. Discarding the Instagram initiative will reduce the deficit by a further 3 percent, still leaving us 13 percent over budget.

You should continue brainstorming, critically evaluating your program in this fashion, until the stakeholders involved are in general agreement about the program's priorities and the allocation of funds fits the predetermined budget. Avoid allocating funds to tactical initiatives unless they contribute to your overarching goal of creating a branded customer experience.

REVISING YOUR INITIAL FINANCIAL TARGETS

Once you have locked down your initiatives and your budget allocation, a final step is required: revising your initial financial targets to reflect what is most likely achievable given your budget, the time frames for achieving your objectives, and any other limitations.

Leaving targets unchanged would not be prudent given your goal of creating a realistic, measurable, and achievable plan. You should align the final set of initiatives with targets that more accurately reflect what your project is specifically aiming to achieve financially. Use this final orientation to ensure the original strategic objectives—the reasons you began this process in the first place—are accurately reflected in the design of your CX program. This necessary and important step will make certain the case for your CX program is able to withstand scrutiny and will address any questions about its conclusions.

Creating a Convincing Executive Summary of Your CX Program

To articulate the components of your CX program and what you expect it would achieve for the organization, you'll need to create an executive summary. The strength of the case you present for change will ensure the longevity of the program and reinforce the importance of its implementation. Without a convincing case, the program is likely to become derailed during implementation as other more appealing and convincing cases shift focus and resources to other compelling projects.

The logical case for your CX program, and for the importance in general of creating a branded experience for customers, should be easily understood and convincing for any stakeholder. It should highlight the fact that the methodology you use, as outlined in this book, has been designed around a robust scientific and empirically based foundation. In your executive summary, include the current situation the company is in and the negative outcome if the company does nothing to address its customer-centricity problems. Here is an example:

> We began an analysis to determine our organization's competitiveness in the marketplace, with a particular focus around customer behavior. This analysis extended to our immediate competitors and emerging competitors that are largely using technology to disrupt traditional business models in our industry.
>
> From the analysis, we determined that our organization had lost 3 percent market share in the past twelve months in the home appliances sector. This has resulted in a 12 percent reduction in company revenues, a 15 percent decline in profits, and a 10 percent increase in our cost of sale. Our reduced competitiveness is caused by our reduced focus on what our customers value most, and as a result, our prospects and customers have chosen new competitors over us. If we make no changes, we would expect further declines in profitability and market share.
>
> We undertook an extensive review using scientific and empirically based methodologies and created a customer experience (CX) program to achieve the following strategic objectives:
>
> - Deliver a better customer experience than our competitors by providing products and services that more accurately reflect what our customers value most, thereby making our organization more customer centric.
> - Increase customer centricity to ensure long-term, sustainable results generated from a branded experience to differentiate our organization.
>
> We established achievable financial targets and designed a CX program that will enable us to attain our strategic objectives. The program has seven organizational and seven customer initiatives. A rigorous process was undertaken during the design process to ensure we had the highest probability of achieving our financial targets and strategic objectives.

The budget to implement these initiatives will be $7 million. The expected return on investment at the end of the first twelve months is estimated to generate an additional estimated profit of $10 million for the organization. If all initiatives are implemented according to the design, we expect they will sustain the same level of profitability over the next five years. The additional profit will increase the value of the organization by an estimated additional $60 million.

Budget to implement initiatives	$7,000,000
Expected ROI at the end of 12 months	$10,000,000
Expected increase in the organization's value over 5 years	$60,000,000

The initiatives and their expected results are summarized here:

Organizational Initiatives
- **Obtain CEO sponsorship and board approval.** Without this, there is no way to move forward.
- **Develop structured communication about the CX program.** This will ensure organizational focus and adherence to time frames.
- **Establish new KPIs and incentives.** These are the organizational behaviors that must change to improve our customer centricity.
- **Establish a new task force.** This team will ensure the program achieves its objectives.
- **Establish a training and mentoring program.** This ensures employees know what is expected and are capable of delivering it.
- **Create a new dashboard.** This will ensure organizational focus on customer-centric metrics.

- **Create a process to incorporate customers into product design.** This process will ensure that products and services will more accurately meet customer values, allowing us to meet sales targets.

Customer Initiatives
- **Engage with influential bloggers.** This outreach is projected to increase website traffic by 10 percent.
- **Establish a program to increase Facebook and Instagram postings.** This program is estimated to increase website traffic by 3 percent.
- **Engage product review websites to increase reviews.** This outreach will likely increase web traffic by 5 percent.
- **Introduce a zero-interest financing package.** This package is estimated to increase revenues by 5 percent.
- **Extend the warranty period by one year.** This extension is projected to increase revenues by 3 percent, increase sales volume by 2 percent, and extend the customer life cycle by six months.
- **Introduce package deals.** These deals are estimated to increase revenues by 3 percent and increase profitability by 3 percent.
- **Create a mobile application that facilitates access, purchase, usage, and support information.** This application is project to increase retention by 10 percent, increase sales volume by 2 percent, and reduce the cost of sale by 3 percent.

We are confident the enclosed case for our CX program will be convincing and will secure the sponsorship and support of the entire board and leadership team. Once the program is approved, the team will immediately begin implementing the initiatives outlined.

This summary creates an effective case for the CX program by compiling the team's most important financial findings and providing empirical evidence for what the program will achieve. The fact-based approach taken, and the direct correlation between the initiatives and expected commercial benefits, provides the CEO approving the program with the necessary information to make an informed decision to sponsor the program.

You have now completed and presented the convincing case for your CX program. Presuming you receive sign-off on your project, the next stage will be implementation—which is what part two of the book will cover.

KEY LESSONS

- By stepping back and aligning your CX program to your objectives, you can begin to finalize your business case.
- Creating a simple grid allows you to explore the various benefits of your proposed organizational changes.
- Performing a gaps and opportunities analysis of your organizational and customer initiatives will allow you to make adjustments in order to capitalize on previously unidentified opportunities and further research any gaps, such as unknown costs.
- In preparing to finalize and present your CX program proposal, align the final initiatives with previous financial targets.
- By allocating time frames for each initiative, you can determine breakeven points, the percentage of the cost budget, and the percentage of the financial targets each initiative will take up.
- It is essential to create a convincing and thorough executive summary that succinctly communicates the value of your CX program to senior stakeholders. This is the final step in the initial process; once leadership has signed off on your proposal, the next phase is implementation.

CHAPTER 7

Review: Ten Rules for CX Excellence

Before moving to part two of this book, which is focused on implementation of your initiatives, let's review the ten major rules you learned in part one. These rules, if upheld, will help you navigate through the research and analysis stages and the designing of your customer experience program. They act as a reference point to help you determine what you should or shouldn't be doing throughout the entire process.

Rule 1: Have a Deep Understanding of Your Customer and Your Organization *Before* You Design or Implement Any CX Program

This may sound like an obvious rule, but one of the fundamental errors in customer experience management programs is that they are based on flawed assumptions about what customers actually want. The most important insights about your customers will form the foundation of your program, so getting an in-depth understanding of them is critical.

It doesn't matter how well you think you know your customers; it is still imperative that you undertake a detailed analysis of their unique characteristics. Customers are people, and people will regularly change their priorities based on what is happening in their environment. Their behavior and emotional states require a deeper analysis than simple customer segmentation. Having a multidimensional understanding of your customers means that you can identify their emotions, desires, and dislikes. Knowing how they feel during any specific time is as important as knowing what they value most. Customer research is an essential aspect of any customer experience initiative. The analysis of your research results will shape the design of your CX program, ensuring that it specifically addresses the important issues influencing your customers throughout their life cycle with your company.

Similarly, no customer experience program will be effective without understanding how customer centric your organization is and uncovering any fundamental problem areas that may prevent you from achieving desired financial results. An organizational analysis provides the insights about how aspects of the organization currently affect the customer.

After performing organizational and customer research, you will be able to draw correlations between organizational influences and customer outcomes. Unearthing the cause and effect of the relationships between organization and customer will afford you a more detailed understanding of the issues and empower you to better design solutions to address both aspects of the equation.

Rule 2: Fix Customer Pain Points First

There is no use implementing a "delight our customer" program when you have obvious customer pain points. In my view, any customer experience program that does not first address the obvious pain points articulated by customers is wasting company money.

The key is to identify the pain points by speaking to a broad section of your customer base. Don't assume you know the pain points. Listening to your customers is the most important aspect of achieving CX excellence. Find out from them what they find painful when doing business with your company. Then, fix these pain points first.

For example, you could make efforts to improve communication with your customers by personalizing calls or emails, but these efforts are wasted if your customers are upset that your billing process is broken or that they have to wait thirty minutes at a retail outlet to get basic customer support. Fix the obvious first before you move on to your next step.

Rule 3: Get Input from Within Your Organization *and* from External Parties

Don't allow your program to be driven purely by marketing or by customer support. CX initiatives need to have the buy-in of the whole organization. Your internal members should contribute to the design of a well-planned program that considers all customer interactions with your company.

Involving a broad mix of internal people is the first step toward achieving excellence, but it's shortsighted to think you can achieve greatness without assistance from external professionals. By getting external people involved, you will be securing different perspectives and insights and drawing on inspiration and ideas from other industries and companies. Use the diversity of staff as the basis to create your differentiated service.

Rule 4: Innovate and Disrupt to Reduce Effort for Customers

The effort required to do business with your organization contributes significantly to how customers feel about your company. This rule is closely tied in with rule 2. Often the pain points for customers are linked to unacceptable levels of effort.

When you undertake a customer journey mapping exercise, focus on measuring the effort required by your customers to complete a certain transaction or inquire about a particular service. Your priority should be reducing customers' efforts and making the process more convenient. Innovation should play an important role in designing solutions that reduce effort for your customers. Creatively addressing and rethinking current processes will propel you beyond just fixing problem areas to the potential redesign of entire customer interactions.

Without the benefit of disruptive thinking and innovation throughout the process, the program you design is unlikely to win your organization any marked differentiation from your competitors. The fact is, your future competition is likely to come from organizations that have applied disruptive thinking to your existing industry sector, so the only way to remain relevant is to apply the same thinking to your customers' experience today.

Rule 5: Align Your Customers' Experience with What They Value Most about Your Brand

I would expect to get a different level of service from a Porsche dealership than from a used car dealership. There is no use providing a level of service if it is not in line with what your customers expect or are willing to pay for. For example, if you are a budget airline and your positioning is based on providing low-cost airfares, then your passengers are not going to expect the same standard of service as they would get from a premium airline. Attempting to change the customer experience to the level of a premium airline could be detrimental to your primary value proposition of providing low-cost air travel.

There is a real cost to "delighting" customers, so be careful not to fall into the trap of trying to deliver, for example, a luxury customer experience when all your customers actually care about is how low your costs are. As a low-cost provider, you can still provide differentiated customer experiences, but they have to be carefully constructed and in proportion to the payback you can expect from the marketplace. It would be more prudent to design a CX program that achieves better experiences than your rival low-cost provider than to go up against a premium provider's customer experiences.

Rule 6: Benchmark Your Products and Services against Your Direct and Emerging Competitors'

The direction you take with your CX program should always focus primarily on beating your direct competitors. Delivering a better overall customer experience than your competitors is the key to gaining greater market share and generating more profits. Keeping abreast of what emerging competitors are doing is another important aspect of planning for the future. Be vigilant, so your market share is not eroded through digital disruption and emerging competitors challenging the status quo in your industry sector.

Globalization has created a playing field that is getting harder to define by geographic territories and protectionist laws. Even in industries such as telecommunications, with laws protecting the number of entrants in the marketplace, competition from global players such as Skype and Viber cannot be avoided. Technology-based competitors are in every industry sector. They disrupt accepted business models, creating new value propositions for customers by providing a product or service in a faster, better, or cheaper way.

A critical aspect of designing a branded CX program that will differentiate the organization in the marketplace is knowing what trends exist in your industry and what changes are likely over the next five years. You don't want to design a program that soon becomes obsolete because you didn't consider an emerging trend in your industry. Knowing what digital disruption looks like in your industry, and designing an effective strategy to capitalize on or defend your position, is an essential step on your journey toward customer experience and achieving sustainable market differentiation.

Rule 7: Make Consistency, Value, and Quality the Pillars of Your Strategy

Achieving excellence in customer experience requires having a solid strategy for delivering greater value to customers on a consistent basis. Standards organization ISO defines a quality organization as one that can deliver products and services that meet or exceed customers' expectations with minimal deviation. Quality has now become synonymous with customer centricity. In the future, no organization will be associated with quality unless it has demonstrated true customer centricity.

Consistency plays a crucial role in any customer experience strategy because of what consumers value most about a brand. Loyalty to a brand happens over a period of time, with a series of experiences that convey powerful psychological emotions such as reliability, trust, and loyalty. Psychologically, customers who experience consistency become loyal to an organization and form relationships with brands because reliability and trust are the foundations of any relationship. The inability to deliver consistency to customers will prevent you from achieving your CX objectives.

Consistency cannot lead to an emotional relationship without the delivery of value to the customer. Value is not a constant; it changes. Value is constantly evolving for customers because its meaning is continuously being rewritten by organizations.

Innovation shapes how customers perceive value. New business models, services, and products are always reshaping the customer's benchmark for value. Maintaining a finger on the pulse of your customers is necessary for any organization to remain relevant. Expectations change, and not all customers perceive the same definition of value, so knowing your customer segments and what they consider as valuable is an integral component of excelling at customer experience. Delivering real and perceived value to customers consistently is a vital aspect of achieving long-term customer loyalty.

Rule 8: Create a Work Environment That Supports Customer Centricity

For a customer-centric organization to achieve its financial objectives, employees must consider at all times what is best for their customers. Only in a specific work environment can employees translate customer centricity from design to daily execution. This environment extends beyond the physical work space. A number of components need to be aligned to support any customer-centricity objectives.

Shaping employee behavior to deliver a branded experience to the customer requires aligned KPIs and incentives. In addition, only a collaborative environment can enable employees from a large cross section of the organization to work together to solve complex customer problems or reinvent a differentiating customer moment.

The leadership needs to also confer a high level of empowerment on employees so they can be flexible enough to resolve various customer issues effectively. Traditional, rigid, rules-based practices usually do not work well to support customer centricity, because they tend to prevent an employee from applying common sense to circumstances outside of defined parameters.

Together, all the components defining how employees work together and behave toward customers must be aligned to encourage and foster customer centricity. Following through on this rule, and not letting internal obstacles hamper customer centricity, will help safeguard customer-centric practices in the organization.

Rule 9: Focus on Fixing Root Causes, Not Just CX Scores

Measurement and reporting, though important, can be a trap for many organizations. Using a single score such as NPS to measure your customer experience results can keep a company's practices from evolving if relevant customer touch points are not cultivated back into the system for further analysis. Companies that achieve CX excellence support a robust process for collecting customer feedback and using it to make real changes. These organizations also use this information to resolve any customer issues immediately before they manifest into something larger and lead to customer loss.

Underlying every customer issue or pain point is a business process, a piece of technology, or a person. Only when you remedy the root causes that inflict the customer pain points can you ensure they do not recur. Any scores measuring customer loyalty and satisfaction will end up naturally increasing to reflect the positive changes you have made for customers.

Rule 10: Make CX Excellence Part of Your Corporate DNA

To achieve a branded customer experience, you will need highly engaged employees willing to go the extra mile without being provoked. To develop a highly engaged workforce that truly understands the value of customer experience is no easy task. This rule is by far the hardest to accomplish.

Many companies still maintain that employees owe them a debt for their jobs. Organizations operating under this guise have employees who perform because they *have to*—they don't want to pay the consequences of nonperformance. Customer-centric organizations, on the other hand, have employees who *want to* work there because it inspires them and they get more than just a paycheck. A customer-centric organization effectively changes the servitude relationship between a company and its employees to a collaborative relationship based on mutual respect, ownership, and reward.

Organizations with traditional servitude cultures find it difficult to embed customer centricity into their DNA. Customer centricity at these organizations does not reach its full potential because the culture is based on fear of noncompliance with company directives as opposed to on proactive thinking and behavior. A compliance-based culture is not sustainable for the long term, as true customer centricity requires people to reflect a genuine desire to better service customers. Empowering employees to always think about the customer shifts their thinking away from their own needs. This is best achieved when an organization creates a culture based on values and beliefs that align with customer-centric behaviors and thinking, and supports that culture with a performance management system that rewards staff for positive behavior rather than simply punishing them for noncompliance.

This rule is difficult to accomplish, but certainly not impossible. Some basic elements will set you on the right path:

- **CEO and board sponsorship** of customer centricity and a branded customer experience
- **Clear, regular internal communication and branding** of your customer experience initiatives
- **Change management practices** deployed to achieve behavioral changes across the organization
- **Training and coaching resources** continuously available across the organization to embed desired new behaviors in employees
- **A measurement and reward program** that ensures continual positive reinforcement of desired behaviors
- **An organizational culture** that encourages innovation and adaptation, and removes the fear of failure

Changing human behavior is by far the most challenging task in business. Old habits are hard to break, but they can be changed with time and the right mix of training and positive reinforcement.

The ten rules are a reminder to you about the important aspects of delivering a strategic CX project in your organization. By no means is this a definitive, immutable list. Throughout the process of designing and implementing your programs, you may wish to add some rules of your own that have particular relevance for your organization.

The next part of the book provides a detailed approach to implementing your CX program and provides some tools and insights on how to deliver on your chosen customer experience outcomes.

Part 2

MASTERING IMPLEMENTATION OF CX INITIATIVES

CHAPTER 8

CX *Implementation Planning*

By now you should have a well-designed, researched, and approved set of program plans to achieve your strategic CX objectives. Companies that achieve the greatest commercial rewards from branded customer experience are the ones able to execute their plans. The key to achieving commercial rewards is your company's ability to implement. The fact is, your program is still "worthless" unless you can successfully convert the design elements of your plan into a reality. Before you implement these plans, you will need to identify a number of aspects about your program to ensure the success of your implementation.

This chapter covers the stages required to prepare properly for implementation, including stages 21 through 25 of the CX management process:

Stage	Desired Output
21. Allocate time frames and resources for your sustainability initiatives.	Detailed time frames and resources for each initiative
22. Identify stakeholders for initiatives, and note the ones that may pose risks in completing your tasks.	A list of stakeholders for each initiative, and possible risks in completing your tasks
23. Select a change methodology best suited to transform the organization.	A suitable method for managing changes that result from the CX program
24. Position customer experience management as a strategic imperative in the organization.	Direct accountability of customer experience management to C-level (reports directly to the CEO)
25. Plan customer implementations using appropriate methods.	An implementation plan with tasks following practices of a suitable methodology

Structuring Your Implementation Team— with Some of Your Design Team

Often the people involved in the analysis and design phases of the customer experience program are not the same people who implement it. This is because implementation requires particular skill sets not normally found in members of the design team, such as project planning and change management. Although such skill sets are required for some members of the implementation team, I strongly recommend that people from the design team also remain throughout the entire implementation phase. Just as architects oversee the construction of their buildings, the project's designers should oversee the implementation of its various design aspects according to your plan.

The size of the organization will normally dictate how many employees can be allocated from the design team during implementation, but at least two people from the design phase should remain to guarantee consistency and to address redundancy in the event one leaves the project or is absent for a period of time. These two design people will act as subject matter experts throughout the rollout and ensure that the implementation team executes plans to meet the objectives as they were originally conceived. The people selected need to have designated expertise in a particular area, such as the organizational changes, the customer initiatives, or the overarching leadership of the entire program. The master architect of the CX program should be the person who has ultimate responsibility for the success of the program and its desired objectives. Typically, this is the person who champions and leads the CX program within the company.

The Three Primary Implementations

Once the team members have been selected, you need to identify the implementation strategy you will follow. Again, the size of your organization or business will normally dictate how, when, and who will implement the customer experience plans. However, some important considerations are relevant for companies of all sizes. The plan should acknowledge that more than one implementation needs to be executed in order to deliver the customer experience program in its entirety. In your quest to ensure CX excellence, there are three implementations to consider: organizational changes, customer experience initiatives, and the governance model.

ORGANIZATIONAL CHANGES

Traditional approaches to customer experience normally ignore or fail to address organizational issues. The typical approach is to head straight into customer-related issues. Yet internal dynamics within your company, such as the company's inability to collaborate before releasing a new product or service, may threaten to prevent employees from becoming customer centric and thus from delivering a branded experience that is highly valued by customers and can be maintained on a long-term basis.

My methodology places the organizational changes ahead of customer ones, to focus on creating a long-term strategic change in the customer's journey with the organization rather than simply a short-term tactical change in how a customer experiences *part* of the organization. Implementation of the organizational plan needs to begin first to help the CEO communicate the messages and vision for your CX program. These messages provide the necessary catalyst for the change process to start and head in the right direction.

CUSTOMER EXPERIENCE INITIATIVES

Shortly after commencement, the organizational plan will typically be implemented in parallel to your customer experience initiatives. These initiatives are the ones addressing the problem areas in your customers' journey that prevent them from purchasing your goods or services and thus from establishing long-term loyalty through repeat purchases. As an example, one of these CX initiatives (as described in chapter 5) may be the redesign of a process for notifying customers when they are late paying their bill.

GOVERNANCE MODEL

A governance model is the operating methodology that will govern your customer experience program on an ongoing basis after it is implemented. A team of people will be assigned the responsibility of applying this methodology to ensure the CX program is properly governed—a process similar to a board of directors steering a company in the right direction. Assuming there is no structure already in place, this third primary implementation should ensure changes are properly maintained and keep achieving sustainable results over the long term.

Establishing a team to oversee the CX program and direct the company on the most appropriate path plays an important role in the overall success of the strategic program. The governing unit will need to incorporate any third parties, such as service providers, directly involved in the ongoing success of your program. Most organizations will outsource partners to deliver business processes throughout the customer journey, and being able to control the outcomes of those interactions is a critical aspect of being a truly customer-centric organization. Effective management of third-party vendors for consistency across the entire customer journey means your customers will receive a uniquely branded experience even if they interact with multiple outsource providers. The responsibility of any vendor's impact on customers should reside with the same team governing the CX program. Later (in chapter 12) I will outline this governance model in greater detail.

Collectively, the three types of primary implementations are designed to achieve the transformation you desire in your organization. Supplemental implementations at various points on your timeline boost the effectiveness of the primary implementations. Different components of your CX program may be designed to either accelerate or optimize customer outcomes, but collectively any successful strategic implementation will further the organization's goal of becoming more customer centric.

Planning the Organizational Implementation

The organizational implementation of your initiative will require you to address specific aspects of your company that prevent full and proper customer centricity. To effect change in these areas, employees will be asked to change their workplace attitudes and behaviors—one of the most difficult tasks to achieve. To manage this transformation, you will need an appropriate methodology that effectively deals with the psychology of change.

SELECT A METHOD TO MANAGE CHANGES

As your team implements organizational changes, you will encounter resistance from certain stakeholders, often in reaction to the disruption of familiar work practices. Any person directly affected by the program initiatives is considered a stakeholder. The billing manager, for example, may feel uncomfortable with proposed changes for how late-paying customers are managed. The transformative objective of your customer experience program guides us toward the best methodology to use for it. Standard project management will not suffice in this situation; because the objective of your CX program is transformative in nature, you need a change management methodology.

Change management is the discipline best suited for any program that requires people in a company to change attitudes, behaviors, and work practices from the familiar to the unfamiliar. This methodology equips you with the necessary tactics required to deal with resistance, aid people in accepting and adapting, and ultimately minimize the impact on your project.

One such method to ensure that the organizational initiatives achieve their objectives is the Prosci ADKAR® model, a research-based, individual change model that represents five milestones an individual must surpass in order to change successfully:

- **A**wareness of the need for change
- **D**esire to support the change
- **K**nowledge of how to change
- **A**bility to demonstrate new skills and behaviors
- **R**einforcement to make the change stick

ADKAR creates a powerful internal language that gives leaders a framework for helping people embrace and adopt changes.

In addition to the type of change management methodology you use, there are a number of other success factors. Without these elements, the change methodology will not be effective because it will not receive the support necessary to make a permanent change in the organization. These five essential factors will help fuel your change program and propel it in the desired direction until its successful completion.

The Five Essential Factors of Change Management Programs

These success factors will determine how well you can implement your organizational changes.

1. High-Exposure Sponsorship from the CEO

Strong backing from the CEO throughout implementation is instrumental in elevating the importance of the CX program to all stakeholders. Without the CEO's sponsorship, the program is likely to be perceived as a tactical project and will never achieve any transformational outcomes.

2. The Proper Positioning of Customer Experience within the Organization

How customer experience is positioned within an organization will determine the level of influence required to change the people, processes, and technologies currently influencing your customers. For example, if customer experience is positioned within a marketing department, it will be perceived as a marketing initiative. When the customer experience team from marketing makes or suggests organizational changes, they are likely to be met with resistance. However, if customer experience belongs to an autonomous unit with leadership at the C-level, then guiding change will become a lot easier.

Progressive, customer-centric organizations will normally position customer experience at their highest levels and allocate responsibility to a chief of customer, on the same level as a chief operating officer or chief commercial officer. Departments such as marketing and customer care would report to the chief of customer, promising consistency in messaging and the customer experience. Having senior-level accountability focused on the customer elevates the customer experience platform within an organization and contributes toward greater customer centricity.

3. Stakeholder Engagement and Communication

Stakeholder communication and engagement must be maintained at the highest levels throughout the entire implementation process. Stakeholders can become quickly disenfranchised if changes are occurring without their input or knowledge. Properly engaging senior stakeholders in the design stage smooths the way for procuring their support during implementation. Collaboration with stakeholders is equally important as regular communication with them. They need to feel they are actively involved in the change process so they are voluntary, not involuntary, participants.

4. Selection of Influential and Capable Change Agents within Your Organization

Change agents play a multifaceted role. They are influential ambassadors of your customer experience program—often identified as "champions" of the cause because they take on the responsibility of leading the transformation within a particular department. The ability to change behaviors within the organization depends on how effectively change agents influence and demonstrate the changed behaviors. Identifying and selecting change agents requires careful consideration of what role the agent will perform.

To be successful, change agents need to possess certain characteristics. They need to be influential in their department, have a high level of enthusiasm for the proposed customer-centricity objectives, and be able to coach others. The change agent should be someone who can take instructions and follow through. The role of the change agent is voluntary and often not directly compensated for the work required. Instead, the change agent takes on the additional workload because of future positioning within the organization and the potential for promotion. Compensation may be provided as time off or a bonus for completing tasks.

Here are some of the tasks normally performed by the change agent:

- Explaining the *need and value* of the change to the impacted employees
- Outlining the reward plan that *encourages the change*
- Outlining the process for change and *what is expected* from the impacted employees
- *Providing coaching and training* on the new behaviors required

A change manager may be appointed as part of the CX implementation team, to support the change agent(s) and to determine the actions to take according to the change methodology used. Change agents work closely with the change manager to monitor behavior and seek evidence of demonstrated behavioral changes in real-life work situations, to confirm whether employees have adopted the change. A cycle of coaching and evaluation will continue until the desired results are achieved and reinforced.

Occasionally, the change manager will intervene when there is evidence of persistent resistance. The role of the change manager is to provide the direction and mentoring required for the change agents to perform the necessary functions of their role. The change manager ensures the program receives the necessary focus to achieve its objectives on time.

5. Leadership by Example

The final success factor for a change management program is the visual displays of new behavior in organizational leaders. Change is easier when subordinates can see demonstrations of the desired behavior by their managers. Encountering displays of acceptance by senior staff makes it easier for others to accept the proposed changes. Conversely, if leaders are not practicing new behaviors, then staff are likely to resist making changes for a longer period. Leadership by demonstrated example is a powerful influencing factor for the adoption of new behaviors.

THE ROLE OF HUMAN RESOURCES

The implementation of organizational initiatives requires significant support and involvement from the human resources (HR) or people and culture department. In any customer-centricity project, employees must change some sort of behavior with the aim of achieving a new performance outcome. To ensure that new expectations and existing performance reviews align, the HR director will need to be actively involved and championing any required changes in existing processes. Often KPIs, targets, and job descriptions will need to be altered. Employees cannot be expected to demonstrate changed behavior if their performance reviews evaluate them on outdated criteria. The alignment of KPIs, targets, and performance reviews to the new behaviors will often trigger the need for ancillary implementations. These supplementary implementations should be controlled by the impacted departments, but must include reports directly to the change manager.

Planning the Customer Implementation

Once you have planned the organizational implementation of your program, it is time to develop strategies for implementing the customer initiatives. To do this, you will need to evaluate the impact each customer initiative will have on both the organization and the customer.

Most customer initiatives require changes to existing business processes and the technologies used in them. By identifying all the areas touched by the new customer initiative, you will be able to determine whether one of the outcomes is a change in behavior by either customer or employee. Once you determine this, you will have a better idea about how to implement the initiative.

In some cases you may need to apply two different implementation methodologies for an initiative. In our continuing example, we identified that the household appliance manufacturer would create a new mobile application to provide a range of relevant information about household appliances to customers. To accomplish this task, we can comfortably apply a methodology, such as Agile, suited for building software applications. Agile helps teams respond to unpredictability through incremental, iterative work cadences known as *sprints*. This gives teams the flexibility to build a feature in the application, test it with users, and then modify it based on feedback before they move on to other components. With this methodology, the household appliance application can be built efficiently and in line with the overall desired customer experience.

During this planning stage, we may note that this new application would mean a number of departments will require employees to change the way they process new orders and support customers with warranty claims. Having identified this probable outcome, we can now apply a change management methodology, such as ADKAR, to the rollout of the application.

Planning the CX Governance Model

The final implementation that needs to be planned is the rollout of the operating structure that will govern your ongoing customer experience program. Properly governing the changes you implement will ensure the longevity of results and financial rewards. If such a structure already exists in your organization, then you need to review this structure and its ability to govern. The review may create an opportunity to add new resources, create positions, or change reporting lines so this governing structure fits your organization's needs and accommodates its unique characteristics.

With the proper governance model, customer experience will be properly positioned within the organization, with the leadership role of the CX program at the most senior organizational level. The appropriate reporting lines will also determine the effectiveness of the unit in governing the organizational changes. For example, a governing unit that reports to operations would create a potential conflict of interest; if the operational manager had final say, it could be difficult to remedy any operational issues identified by the CX unit. The best practice in CX management is to have a separate and autonomous unit overseeing all aspects of customer experience across the entire organization. The autonomy of the unit enables the department to audit other departments without a conflict of interest that would hamper communication to the most senior levels about root cause problems.

Ensuring proper analysis and remedy of customer issues is pivotal to ensuring the proper governance of organizational customer centricity and customer experience issues. However, this unit should not only audit. The unit will also need to monitor trends and practices by competitors and identify new opportunities your organization can capitalize on to elevate its customer experience.

Once you have rolled out your new program, the governing unit should constantly be seeking out areas for improvement, by adopting a number of different methodologies. Lean Six Sigma and Process Excellence are particularly valuable for a unit focused on ensuring customer experience excellence, because they address the underlying problem areas associated with most customer issues.

Business processes and the effort made by a customer to conduct business with an organization are the most common causes of substandard customer moments. A team of skilled experts able to isolate such problems and uncover their root causes will help you not only remedy issues, but design new processes that deliver better outcomes for customers and your company, by assuming the following responsibilities:

- Monitor, measure, and report on customer experience.
- Educate the organization.
- Identify root cause problems with customer issues.
- Identify organizational remedy initiatives to elevate customer centricity.
- Propose new customer experience initiatives to ensure market differentiation.

The functions performed by the CX governing unit are necessary and instrumental to the longevity and success of your program. Without these functions, the delivery of uniquely branded customer experiences will be inconsistent, and the program results are likely to be short-lived and unsustainable.

Planning for the implementation of the governance unit should take into consideration existing people and departments currently performing aspects of its functions. You may be required to integrate team members from other departments and modify existing processes to align the operating model of the new unit. The resources required for the business unit should include the following:

- Chief of customer (or chief of customer experience)
- Customer experience manager
- Customer care manager
- Customer complaints manager
- Process Excellence/Lean Six Sigma managers
- Business analyst/performance analyst/MIS analyst

This list of important personnel is not definitive, but it provides a guideline for the resources you may require. The number of members in your unit will depend on the size and complexity of your organization. In some progressive organizations, sales and marketing also will report to this department. Streamlining the number of departments can create greater unity and focus for team members within the organization. Reducing the number of compartmentalized units can accelerate customer centricity by giving team members a clear direction that does not compete or conflict with other directions from leaders of other departments. The singular focus leads to team members executing their work more consistently, thus accelerating the desired CX transformation.

Planning for the governance unit must be considered at this early stage because the members of the team will also contribute to the success of the overall implementation by *demonstrating* the expected behaviors to others. When selecting the team members, consider not just their competencies but also their ability to influence and lead by example.

Collaborative Software and Mitigating Risk

Once you have identified the best methodology to apply for your implementations and the people who will lead them, you can begin allocating tasks to people, working through timelines, and defining success criteria. You should consider the tools you will use in the planning. Noncollaborative tools can be restrictive and prevent the necessary visibility and input from multiple stakeholders. Online solutions from software providers like Atlassian and Wrike enable collaboration using cloud-based applications, so users can easily interact and communicate, ensuring support and transparency throughout the project. These tools streamline the implementation process and provide participants with important information about their tasks and how others are tracking.

Once you have selected the preferred project applications, you will be ready to input the data for each implementation. As you do so, think about the associated risks for each task. Identifying risks is an essential aspect of sound project planning. There are numerous levels of risk in a project. The ones worthy of addressing are uncertain events or conditions that could affect at least one project objective. For example, if you are building a new software application and relying on a single programmer to complete a component, then you face the risk of delaying the project should the programmer become ill for an extended time.

After you identify the risk and its potential impact, you can determine the best action to take to mitigate it. On some occasions, it may not be possible to fully mitigate the risk, as there may not be enough funding in the budget. Continuing the previous example, it may be too costly to mitigate the risk by hiring a secondary programmer. Instead, you may decide that partial mitigation is acceptable, and require that the programmer document progress in greater detail to ensure a replacement programmer could be inserted with minimal disruption.

I recommend using a pragmatic approach when deciding how to mitigate project risks. All known risks should have a time frame and a person allocated to address the risk. The project manager or change manager should confirm that the risks have been reviewed and the necessary action taken within the set deadlines. You can use a simple matrix to complete the risk analysis:

RISKS

Source of Risk	Risk Description	Impact	Actions to Address Risks	Responsibility	Deadline	Evaluation Date	Evaluation Results

Setting Implementation KPIs

Once the risks are identified and the necessary mitigating actions are taken, you need to ascertain the performance measures for the different stages of the implementation. Unlike a normal project based around people completing tasks within a given time frame, the implementation of your entire CX program—both the organizational and the customer sides—will involve a number of tasks without a clear definition for their successful completion. These tasks are related to changes in employee or customer behaviors. It's important to identify performance targets for these tasks to measure their effectiveness. Certified change management professionals are well qualified in selecting the performance measures for such a program. Research undertaken by Prosci[5] identifies the best-practice KPIs used by change management practitioners, including in the areas of project performance, individual changes, and change management effectiveness.

PROJECT PERFORMANCE

Project performance seeks to measure the quality of the change management project's implementation. It reflects the overall execution of the project according to parameters such as time frames, KPIs, and benefit realization. You can apply the following measures to either an organizational or a customer change management project:

- Performance improvements
- Progress and adherence to plan
- Business and change readiness
- Project KPI measurements
- Benefit realization and ROI
- Adherence to timeline
- Speed of execution

INDIVIDUAL CHANGES

Once the project is implemented, you need to be able to measure individual changes witnessed in employees and customers alike, using the following measures:

....

5   Prosci, *Best Practices in Change Management–2016*, www.prosci.com.

- Adoption metrics
- Usage and utilization reports
- Compliance reports
- Proficiency measures
- Employee/customer engagement, buy-in, and participation measures
- Employee/customer feedback
- Issue, compliance, and error logs
- Help desk calls and requests for support
- Awareness and understanding of the change
- Observations of behavioral change
- Employee/customer readiness assessment results
- Employee/customer satisfaction survey results

CHANGE MANAGEMENT EFFECTIVENESS

Change management is a process that needs to follow a defined plan. The effectiveness of the program can be achieved only when the tasks, such as staff training, are properly delivered and measured, using the following metrics:

- Tracking of change management activities conducted according to plan
- Training tests and effectiveness measures
- Training participation and attendance numbers
- Communication deliveries
- Communication effectiveness

Take a pragmatic approach to setting KPIs, rather than selecting a number of KPIs that do not add value to your project stakeholders. The KPIs should be based on the important *outcomes* you expect from your customer experience program. For example, to achieve greater customer centricity and align employee actions to customer values, imagine your program contained a task for training employees on new behaviors and expectations. Because this is an important aspect of achieving sustainable customer experience outcomes, we need to set KPIs based on this specific task and to measure its effectiveness.

In this example, let's say the project manager or change manager—after consulting with the head of the CX program—selects three KPIs: proficiency measures, employee engagement, and observations of behavioral change. It is important to allocate measurable and realistic targets to each KPI. The task is then reflected as follows:

TABLE 8.I: THREE IMPLEMENTATION KPIS

Task	KPIs	Targets
Training of the new employee behaviors and outputs	Proficiency measures Employee engagement Observations of behavioral change	90% of all employee assessments achieve a result of 80% or higher Employee engagement for training is measured at 80% or greater via survey Change agents confirm changed behavior when they observe at least 3 examples of change over 3 consecutive months

The allocation of KPIs ensures accountability and clear deliverables. Whether these tasks were successfully completed can often be open to a wide range of interpretation, so it's important to agree on the final set of measures prior to commencing implementation. This will ensure the implementation team has a good understanding of which tasks are important for the success of the program and what the definition of success is for each of these tasks. Adding clarity around these aspects of the program will help contribute toward the desired objectives and the program's successful implementation.

Tracking Overall Financial Targets

The implementation KPIs set at this stage should also support the financial objectives set during earlier phases. Achieving the financial targets is the ultimate objective of any customer experience program. Everything contained in your implementation plan needs to relate back to this primary goal. Failing to incorporate the financial targets into your planning means you will be unable to prioritize and set the task-based KPIs and respective targets. The financial targets for the program should be visible to all stakeholders and easily track performance of each initiative—an outcome that may require input from your organization's technology people.

CREATE A DIGITAL CUSTOMER DASHBOARD

Your implementation plan should incorporate a digital customer dashboard to provide the organization with meaningful, real-time customer metrics. Making the program's financial performance easily traceable and visible to a larger audience will help foster a customer-centric culture. As soon as you have completed the implementation phase, you will need to begin monitoring and reporting on the performance of your program, so for a seamless transition to the governance phase, establish the dashboard before you complete implementation. Having the digital dashboard operational by the time the main projects are implemented will keep your CX program's momentum and focus.

Once you have planned the implementation of your program and engaged with the stakeholders directly involved, the next steps will be to solidify leadership and communicate with the entire organization about the program and its objectives—all of which is covered in the next chapter.

KEY LESSONS

- Before beginning implementation, you will need to identify a number of aspects about your CX program, such as the best methodology to apply for implementation (project or change management) and the skill sets required in the people implementing.
- At least two team members from the design phase should be included throughout the entire implementation stage to act as subject matter experts and ensure consistency.
- There are three primary implementations to plan for:
  » Organizational changes
  » Customer experience initiatives
  » Governance model

- Collectively, the three implementations achieve transformational change in the organization.
- The transformative objective of the program guides us toward the best methodology to use for implementation: a change management methodology, such as the Prosci ADKAR, which is well suited for any implementations involving behavioral changes.
- Success factors in a CX change program include the following:
  » High-exposure sponsorship from the CEO
  » Proper positioning of customer experience within the organization
  » Stakeholder engagement and communication
  » Selection of influential and capable change agents
  » Leadership by example

- Progressive organizations will normally position customer experience at the highest level.
- For stakeholders to voluntarily participate, they need to feel they are actively involved in the change process.
- Change agents take on the responsibility of leading the change within a particular department.
- The alignment of KPIs, targets, and performance reviews to the new behaviors will often trigger the need for a secondary implementation with HR.
- Best practice in CX management is to have a separate and autonomous unit overseeing all aspects of customer experience across the organization.
- Collaborative tools help streamline the implementation process and provide participants with information about tasks and tracking.
- Identifying and mitigating risks is an important aspect of managing any project.
- Setting KPIs and targets for individual tasks can help alleviate uncertainty about what constitutes effective completion of the task.
- A digital customer dashboard should be incorporated into the implementation plan to provide meaningful, real-time customer metrics.

CHAPTER 9

Leadership for CX Excellence

This chapter explores two of the most critical ingredients in achieving customer experience excellence in any organization: leadership and communication. Among multiple leadership roles in any CX program, the most critical is the CEO or president. The top person in whatever organization you are working with—business, company, or government organization—must provide unequivocal support and commitment to elevating customer experience. This person must be convinced about the benefits your program will deliver and be able to convince others of the same.

The CEO also helps ensure the organization has the necessary discipline to undergo the transformational changes that will achieve benefits. His or her ability to communicate the virtues of the program and inspire others to become believers will play a major role in determining your CX program's success.

This chapter covers stage 26 in the CX management process:

Stage	Desired Output
26. C-level sponsored communication to all staff prior to the launch of the program.	CEO-sponsored communication that clearly explains the journey of change and rationale

Recognizing Leadership Qualities and Values

According to the 2016 Prosci change management survey mentioned in chapter 8, change leaders in nine benchmarking studies commented on the greatest contributor to their success. These leaders identified a significant correlation between strong sponsorship and successful project implementations, attributing 72 percent of change management projects that had met or exceeded their objectives to having extremely effective sponsors. Active and visible sponsorship beat the second contributor to success by a 3:1 margin.

CEO sponsorship is unquestionably the single most influential component in any transformational customer experience program. However, not all CEOs make great customer experience sponsors. Identifying the essential requirements of effective leadership can help leaders adapt their thinking and behavior before launching a strategic and transformational CX program.

We can begin to isolate the elements of an effective customer experience leader by first understanding what leadership is and isn't. Leadership is the process that motivates people to exercise their creative abilities and produce superior goods and services. Leaders recognize how important people are to an organization's success. Leaders also identify and remove impediments to individual performance.

Leaders of companies that successfully deliver branded customer experiences are able to achieve results by displaying a number of uniquely identifiable core values and behaviors. From experience and research, I have isolated eight different qualities that define the leadership required for a progressive customer experience organization—the qualities that are essential in order to achieve sustainable results from a transformative CX program.

I. LEADERS HAVE A VISION

Successful leaders have a vision: a picture of both the present and the future. They are able to articulate clearly the current state of their company, and then visualize their goals and the path toward achieving them in the future. The vision should appeal simultaneously to logic and feeling; first it makes sense, and then it inspires strong feelings of hope and pride in its accomplishment. Vision adds meaning to corporate life and provides the reasons things need to happen in a certain way.

2. LEADERS COMMUNICATE THEIR VISION

Successful leaders communicate their vision clearly so that it is shared throughout the organization and executed properly. They must communicate their customer-centricity vision to others so that the customer experience journey is as clear as a picture painted on canvas—not just among C-level executives, but at every level of the organization.

If a leader communicates well, employees will share his or her vision, which means they will commit and buy in to the vision. Even the most inspiring vision will not be realized without input from other team members in the organization. A vision with transformational objectives requires a high degree of emotional and cognitive output from a wide array of people. This output cannot be achieved unless employees are empowered to enact the necessary changes.

3. LEADERS ARE COMMITTED TO REALIZING THEIR VISION

Effective leaders are committed to the *journey* the organization needs to take to achieve the vision. A great leader of transformational change displays commitment throughout the change process in many ways:

- Setting personal examples of the expected new behaviors
- Embracing change and continual improvement
- Fostering individual and organizational learning and growth
- Encouraging risk taking to achieve innovation
- Inspiring enthusiasm

All these leadership qualities demonstrate to employees that the leader is committed to change and is willing to take the necessary risks to transform the organization. The leader tempers the difficulty of transformation by inspiring employees who are about to embark on the journey.

A leader with doubts will not be able to communicate with confidence the benefits of a transformation program. This lack of commitment will send an unconvincing message to employees, and they too will doubt the program's benefits and longevity. As a result, employees may not bother to put any effort into making the necessary changes, and the program will fail.

4. LEADERS CONVINCE OTHERS TO COMMIT TO THEIR VISION

Successful leaders effectively persuade people to commit to their vision. They are able to harness their employees' energies and direct them toward achieving organizational goals. Leaders can obtain employees' commitment by helping them grasp significant points about the vision:

- The message of the vision
- The need for the vision within the organization
- The rightness of the vision for each employee
- The role of each employee in realizing the vision

Successful leadership and sponsorship of a customer-centric culture requires having a set of core beliefs and values based on complete customer centricity, and upheld by the leaders and employees of a company. These values form the foundation for action throughout the transformational journey.

Achieving a truly customer-centric focus in a quality organization depends on leadership to uphold these beliefs and values, to model and teach them to the organization's people in both word and deed.

5. LEADERS FOSTER A CUSTOMER-CENTRIC BELIEF SYSTEM

The sustainability of an organization's customer centricity requires a belief system that forms a foundation for change and innovation, without which the organization is unlikely to adapt to a constantly evolving customer landscape. The organization must embrace change as the catalyst for continual improvement. There are four core beliefs associated with a commitment to this principle of continual improvement:

- You have to know the facts.
- You must reason and learn.
- There is always a better way.
- Keep trying for perfection, although you never will achieve it.

The first two beliefs focus on gaining the knowledge required for improvement; the second two focus on maintaining the spirit necessary to improve continually. Customer experience excellence is a continuous cycle of improvements based on fact-based evidence, so fostering learning and continual improvement are critical aspirations.

6. LEADERS ENCOURAGE EMPLOYEE EMPOWERMENT

A highly effective leader of a customer-centric organization understands the importance of removing constraints that bind employees to regimented work. A restrictive work environment stifles creativity and proactivity—two essential qualities for innovation. Empowerment, on the other hand, gives employees more responsibility and control over their individual work and teamwork. A high degree of empowerment enables employees to take the necessary actions required to identify and resolve customer issues quickly.

Empowerment gives an organization speed. Employees act when necessary rather than when institutional rules dictate. In any organization that wishes to stay ahead of the competition, speed is imperative. The ability to move and act quickly to address customer issues is a key differentiator for companies because it aligns with the customer's expectation of instantaneous results. For the leader of an organization to impart control and responsibility to employees, he or she has to adopt certain underlying values. Leaders of empowered employees who eagerly advance the customer-centric goals of the company hold and promote the following beliefs, which guide the actions of every member of the organization:

- Employees are people.
- People are basically good.
- Bureaucracy kills initiative and innovation.
- The manager's job is to provide training, tools, and support.

The concept of empowerment is a paradoxical one. It implies that leaders give something to employees (power, authority, or responsibility), when actually it is more a question of taking something away: the constraints and limitations imposed by unnecessary controls and bureaucracy.

7. LEADERS ACT WITH COURAGE

One of the qualities essential for leadership of a successful customer-centric organization is courage. Though it is not often spoken about in this context, courage is necessary in leadership because people tend to maintain the status quo rather than venture to new pathways. Navigating an existing path is much safer than risking unchartered waters. Successful change demands determination, persistence, and the willingness to take chances.

The commercial benefits achieved from a customer experience transformation are supported by numerous case studies and research. For many leaders, however, changing course and venturing into the unknown brings its own risk. Because changing an organization with a long tradition of hierarchical operations is more difficult than changing the course of a smaller and more nimble one, this risk plays a more significant role for leaders of larger organizations, often preventing them from making the necessary leap of faith. In any case, a leader changing course has to be courageous in pulling the trigger on the program, knowing full well there is no turning back.

Highly effective leaders in customer experience leave no room for doubt when they make a decision to change course. As I mentioned earlier in this chapter, a leader who does not exude confidence about the benefits of and need for the change will create an opening for doubt in the minds of employees. Successful transformation projects have highly supportive CEOs who eradicate any elements of doubt within the leadership team. They use all their influencing powers to create commitment and solidarity around the transformation. By throwing their full force behind a CX program, CEOs mortgage their reputation and credibility throughout the entire transformation process. Effective leaders understand the alternative—treading carefully and distancing themselves from sponsorship of the initiatives—would compromise the program's success. As this is not a viable option, they make the calculated and courageous step to wholeheartedly embrace the program as its primary sponsor.

8. LEADERS CHAMPION OWNERSHIP

Though ownership is often undervalued, the overwhelming evidence proves that it plays an important role in determining the actualization of a leader's vision. A sense of possession or ownership of the company appears to contribute to the level of enthusiasm, desire, and persistence present in leaders and employees alike.

Ownership can be a prime motivation for successful leadership and focused management. In some of the most successful organizations of our time, top leaders have also been part owners:

- Ray Kroc: McDonald's
- Sam Walton: Wal-Mart
- Bill Gates: Microsoft
- Sir Richard Branson: Virgin

Leaders of transformational CX programs can be as effective as the owners of organizations if they create a financial reward for employees, linked to the outcomes of the program. This creates a higher level of motivation only attributable to people who have a vested interest in making it a success.

Ownership is neither an attribute nor an action, but rather the psychological and financial relationship between an individual and an object. It helps an individual define his or her existence in relation to the rest of the world. Employee ownership affects job performance and the level of commitment to the company's vision. Wal-Mart and Microsoft have publicly claimed the positive effects of employee ownership through the various employee share schemes. These companies' levels of productivity, creativity, and profitability all exceed industry averages, while their staff turnover figures are below industry averages. Such facts and figures strongly suggest that ownership, whether directly or through stock options, plays a major role in determining the overall success of an organization.

By offering direct financial rewards for employees' work or activity, ownership also provides meaning. It creates a sense of belonging and becomes the driver for innovation, change, quality management, and excellence. Ownership may be seen as belonging to the wider context of the growth imperative, which psychologists theorize is the driving force responsible for the general direction of human activity. Theorists such as psychologist Klaus Riegel have argued that the natural order of development is not to remain in a state of equilibrium, but to constantly change toward a better state.

This perspective on the growth imperative illuminates the importance of ownership in determining successful leadership. In a sense, ownership satisfies a fundamental need for an individual to accumulate, grow, and develop. It offers the perception of growth for individuals and thus makes the work they perform meaningful within the realm of their existence.

Transformational customer experience requires people in an organization to do new things that are not always easy. Change from the status quo takes more mental and emotional energy than retaining what is normally practiced. Asking people to shift from their comfort zones and practice their work in an unfamiliar way requires a high degree of motivation. Not all organizations have ownership plans to motivate their staff, and not all organizations with ownership plans do well at effectively transforming to customer centricity. But ownership can play a key role in determining the effectiveness of your program's implementation and should be considered by the leaders of the program prior to implementation.

Regardless of whether your organization has a preexisting ownership plan, the CX program leaders should incorporate a direct incentive to reward employees for making the desired changes. Acknowledging what will motivate employees to make changes is an important aspect of laying the foundation for a successful implementation. Incentives don't always have to be cash payments. If you discover what will be more meaningful for key employees, you can tailor suitable incentives. For example, a monetary incentive can be in the form of a paid holiday or educational tuition for children. Just as you have prepared a plan to implement experiences that are regarded by customers as highly valuable, so should you develop a plan to identify what would motivate employees to adjust to your organization's new way of operating. Above all, the incentive plan needs to be easily understood, carefully administered, and realistically achievable for employees.

The philosophy adopted by great leaders centers around ideas about quality, commitment to continuous improvement, the customer as king, and the empowerment of people. These are the concepts leaders focus on and identify as the key contributors for successful leadership of an organization. Transformational change requires a few additional attributes to achieve implementation of the vision. Change can be difficult for anyone, so ownership plays an important role in satisfying a person's reasoning for the work and adding meaning to the changes requested of them. Including a purposeful incentive for employees directly related to the desired changes will improve the probability of a successful implementation.

KEY LESSONS

- The CEO must provide unequivocal support and commitment to elevating customer experience in an organization. He or she must be convinced about the benefits the CX program will deliver to the organization and be able to convince others of the same.
- Leaders must communicate the customer-centricity vision to others and set personal examples of what behaviors are expected.
- Sustainability of a customer-centricity organization also requires a belief system that forms the foundation for change and innovation.
- Empowerment gives the organization speed. It enables employees to act when necessary rather than when institutional rules dictate. In any organization wishing to stay ahead of the competition, speed is imperative.
- Successful transformation projects have highly supportive CEOs who are able to use their influencing powers to create commitment and solidarity around the transformation. They eradicate any elements of doubt within the leadership team.
- Ownership offers individuals the reasoning behind their work or activity. It creates a sense of belonging and becomes the driver for innovation, change, quality management, and customer experience excellence.

CHAPTER 10

Employee Engagement during CX Implementation

Way back in chapter 1, when I first outlined how to design a strategic CX program, I highlighted how employee engagement was necessary for achieving sustainable commercial rewards for an organization. As discussed in chapter 4, research on employee engagement has shown evidence of a solid correlation between organizations with above-average financial performance and highly engaged employees. Engagement during implementation of the customer experience program is important because most initiatives require a higher level of employee engagement to achieve their objectives of making an organization more customer-centric and delivering a branded experience.

This chapter provides guidance on managing and elevating employee engagement during implementation. It covers stage 27 of the CX management process:

Stage	Desired Output
27. Implement the plans for the organization and customer initiatives.	Progressively implemented organizational and customer initiatives, and engaged employees

How Transformative Programs Can Impact Engagement

Transformation projects can alienate and unsettle employees because an underlying current of distrust and insecurity exists with all these types of projects. A change program can arouse emotions that lead employees to ask the following types of questions:

- "What have I done wrong?"
- "Am I not valued for what I do?"
- "Am I going to lose my job?"
- "Is this change just for their benefit?"

Moving past these concerns should be a top priority for organizations going through a transformational process, and this should start with opening up the lines of discussion between C-level executives, management, and employees.

THE IMPORTANCE OF ENGAGING EMPLOYEES

The objective of any CX program implementation is to get employees actively participating in the change process. An engaged employee knows why the organization needs to transform, works with colleagues to implement the change, and works for the benefit of the organization.

Engagement involves a two-way relationship between employer and employee. An employee will give more positive mental and emotional energy to an organization only once the organization has provided him or her with a value proposition strong enough to warrant the additional effort. If we break down employee engagement to a single visible behavior, it would be going the extra mile without provocation to serve an altruistic purpose. Employees display this behavior because they are proud of their employer, have a genuine belief in the quality of the products and services, and feel they are respected and well rewarded for their work.

Consultants and workshops can be unsettling to employees, as they may seem to indicate a problem is being dealt with. Without engaging people through proper communication and consultation, the customer-centric transformation program can be perceived as an attempt to fix a problem created by the employees. There are definitely remedial objectives in the program, but employee perception needs to be adjusted if you wish to avoid creating a rift between employer and employee.

A transformation project requiring employees to change their behavior will immediately have a negative impact on engagement if the right levels of communication and collaboration are not delivered.

ADDRESS EXISTING PROBLEMS AND ESTABLISH TRUST

Before determining the best message to communicate to employees about a transformative program, it's important to recognize any existing issues in the organization that may be impacting employee engagement. A number of companies, including Decisionwise, Quantum, People Streme, Custom Insight, and Gallup, conduct periodical surveys of employee engagement levels and the areas that impact employee engagement. You can link these surveys directly to work-based outcomes to isolate those that have the greatest impact.

Any number of issues in an organization can reduce employees' trust in senior management and create a feeling of unfair treatment. For example, work-life balance is a primary issue when it comes to work performance. Employees may claim they are dissatisfied with amenities available in the office, but their more fundamental issue may really be how much time they are spending at work. Surveys such as the Gallup Q^{12}, produced by Gallup, use targeted questions to provide an organization with the areas directly impacting work performance. Gallup has been able to benchmark its results using a large database accumulated over time, pinpointing the issues likely to impact performance and comparing results with those of others in an organization's industry sector.

If your company's survey results indicate a below-average level of engagement, then embarking on a transformation program without addressing the primary issues first is likely to yield poor results. How can you expect your customer experience program to achieve transformation when employees are not fairly treated and thus are not motivated to better the organization? A customer-centricity program will not remedy a fundamental trust issue between employees and their employer.

Employers earn trust through consistent, reliable behavior that demonstrates a genuine interest in the health and well-being of their employees. Because trust requires time and repeated demonstration, it is hard to earn trust from employees quickly—and certainly not within the time frame required to implement a transformation program.

If any issues prevent your employees from trusting your organization, seek to establish a bridge toward future trust—a way of addressing, though not necessarily fixing, employees' issues in a constructive and time-bound manner. This bridge can create the necessary emotional and mental engagement required to achieve your program's transformational objectives. An employer has to demonstrate its openness and attention to complaints, and lay out a process to evaluate and potentially remedy the problems. This can buy the organization some time and also pave the way for the transformation project to commence. The time frame to resolve these issues has to be realistic and acceptable to employees, however, and any difficulty resolving an issue within that time frame has to be communicated to employees to secure their confidence in organizational leaders. The bridge toward trust will last for only a set period of time and will disappear quickly if promises are broken or time frames not met. The goal should always be to earn the trust of employees in order to achieve greater employee engagement. Remember, a higher degree of engagement leads to greater acceptance of your changes and greater appreciation for how they benefit all employees.

KNOW WHAT DETERMINES YOUR EMPLOYEES' ENGAGEMENT

To achieve the best outcomes from employees, transformational change programs must address two components of employee engagement: first, the removal of issues that might hamper the cooperation required so new behaviors are accepted and effective, and second, knowledge of the aspects of the employee–employer relationship that define an employee's engagement level.

A deep understanding of what determines engagement will enable you to implement your CX program using elements that are important to employees. Engaged employees are committed, passionate, and inspired, which makes it easier for them to also inspire others about the benefits of the changes you are advocating. Disengaged employees are reluctant to identify and accept the genuineness of the program. They remain skeptical and become unwilling participants in organizational change.

Employees' engagement drivers are very similar to those of customers. Insights gathered from research on employee engagement isolate a number of key drivers:[6]

---

6   Institute for Employment Studies, *The Drivers of Employee Engagement*, 2004, http://www.employment-studies.co.uk/report-summaries/report-summary-drivers-employee-engagement.

- Supportive and capable management
- Authentic and honest communication
- A happy and positive work culture
- Empowerment and individual autonomy
- Formal recognition and rewards
- Clear instructions to follow
- Clear communication of vision and values
- Work efforts that make an altruistic contribution

Increasing the engagement levels while you implement your CX program will require an evaluation of the areas you can influence to achieve uplifts in engagement. Some areas are more difficult to change, but an awareness of the issues will arm you with the necessary information for the change agents to address.

Take, for example, a scenario with a department of employees who are disengaged because they do not trust or respect their immediate manager. Changing the manager is an option, but it's unlikely to be a simple or timely one, particularly during your implementation. After investigating the root causes for the mistrust, you could discover it's a result of both poor communication and a lack of authority given to subordinates to perform their duties. Using this information, you can formulate a strategy to elevate engagement levels in the department. Communicating authentically and honestly with these employees will neutralize the poor communication from their manager. Giving them more authority to achieve positive results for customers will provide these disenfranchised employees with new hope that their situation could be short-lived.

Not addressing employees' issues merely preserves the barrier that prevents employees from engaging at the desired levels; it also implies they will not receive any benefits from the change program either. Providing a positive context instead for how the transformation program will address employees' issues and frustrations will encourage greater engagement during implementation.

Best Practices for Increasing Engagement

You can increase engagement among all employees, regardless of their current attitude and approach, by following a number of best practices during implementation. These best practices are closely linked to the drivers of employee engagement. During the analysis and design phase, you gathered insights on your business and the problem areas that inhibit customer centricity, by performing a root cause analysis (as in table 3.1). The employee engagement survey, mentioned earlier in this chapter, provides you with insights into employees' emotional relationship with your company. Reviewing the results of both surveys will help you define the approach and tactics you must take to engage effectively with employees and harness their emotional energy to achieve your desired objectives.

For example, your customer-centricity survey (discussed in chapter 3) may have uncovered low prioritization scores from a particular department. If the results from the employee engagement survey later uncover a problem with empowerment in the same department, it would be reasonable to argue that low empowerment causes employees to poorly prioritize their work. This knowledge enables you to target the problem area most likely affecting employee engagement and tailor your implementation accordingly. Each best practice should be customized to address the unique attributes identified during the analysis phase. Customizing each implementation step leaves you able to resonate more effectively with the rhythm of the organization and thus compose a more harmonious tune to be played throughout the change process.

In the following pages, I will list seven best practices for increasing employee engagement during implementation.

I. COMMUNICATE HONESTLY AND AUTHENTICALLY

The type of messages you write and how you deliver them to employees will play a major role in determining whether employees believe in the benefits of your CX change program. In the early stages, avoid jazzing up the communications going to employees with marketing methods. They won't be excited yet, so hold back on any flowery or hyped-up language. The danger of hyping the communications with marketing language is that you can create suspicion, leading employees to distrust your program's intentions. Communications that come across as having to sell you something are greeted with immediate mistrust.

Before the CEO announces the changes and pledges support for the transformation project, you should engage with smaller groups of senior-level people to outline your research findings and the need for any organizational changes. If you have been properly communicating and engaging with stakeholders throughout the analysis and design phase, there should be no surprises for anybody. The aims of this communication are to put everyone on the same page and to create desire for employees to change. Creating this desire helps support acceptance of the program when the CEO formally launches and pledges support. Your messaging should cover the following topics:

- How competitors and market forces impact on the organization
- Organizational areas influencing the customer experience
- The organization's future if nothing is done
- How change is necessary for the collective benefit of employees and the organization
- How the transformation program will help both employees and the organization achieve commercial success in the marketplace

Once the CEO has formerly launched the program, you can communicate the details and the changes to employees in messages that are clear, simple, and confident, but that do not exaggerate or distort any facts. If, for example, there are unknown elements regarding implementation, then you should communicate this fact. Employees are more likely to accept that you don't have all the answers and appreciate the honesty; if you present a makeshift fact, they may be suspicious. Maintaining honest and authentic language is an essential ingredient for a successful implementation.

2. DELIVER REGULAR CEO COMMUNICATION AND SUPPORT

Employees must receive confirmation on a regular basis that the transformation project and the changes themselves are strongly endorsed by the company's highest authority. The CEO must communicate frequently the virtues of the program and his or her deep commitment to the implementation. If the CEO is unconvincing, then throughout implementation employees are unlikely to impart the emotional energy required to change.

Any CEO communications should be addressed to different groups within the organization. Larger group presentations should be reserved for launching the implementation stage, while it seems best to communicate with smaller groups if they have a greater impact to the project's deliverables or if the group is known to resist change. Employees are more likely to remain engaged and keep momentum throughout implementation if the CEO is sending out regular messages about the program's progress. As these employees begin to demonstrate new and changed behavior, other employees within the organization will want to become part of the change rather than be left behind. As the CEO communicates any positive changes, momentum will build in the organization.

3. CUSTOMIZE THE IMPLEMENTATION FOR DIFFERENT TEAMS

Employees operate in team environments. Each team will have unique characteristics that define how best to engage them. Taking these unique characteristics into consideration and addressing them will enable teams to respond more receptively. Some teams may have time pressures and be committed to completing other projects. Respecting that team members have time-bound tasks to complete, and working around these commitments, will boost engagement from team members. If some of these constraints require you to hold a meeting afterhours, then work something out with their line manager to compensate team members for the additional time. This may be as simple as providing dinner on-site.

Customizing any meetings and presentations to team members based on their expectations as well as their seniority level is an important aspect of making sure the messages are relevant and absorbed more thoroughly. A presentation for contact center agents should not be the same as one given for accountants. Know your audience, and ensure the messages are delivered appropriately. Never assume you know the correct format to use in a meeting for a particular team. Asking the line manager what team members normally expect not only facilitates appropriate customization but also achieves greater engagement from the line manager for being asked.

4. EMPOWER TEAMS TO TAKE CONTROL OF CHANGES

Empowering teams to take control of the change process within their working groups is an excellent way to achieve greater employee engagement throughout implementation. Do this by leveraging trusted, respected people within each team. Influential team members acting as change agents are going to be more effective than untrusted outsiders trying to change a team's behaviors. Giving team members control over the change process also gives them a greater sense of self-worth, because any changes are a result of their efforts rather than because of an external influence. Acknowledging the accomplishment of achieving the desired changes and assuming accountability for performance gives participants a sense of control over their own destinies. Control is a common theme in this approach—an important dimension for employees and customer engagement levels.

You also can empower a team of employees by involving them in the problem-solving process. Let team members resolve the complicated issues of implementing a transformation program that strives to achieve a uniquely branded customer experience. Involving team members in the search for solutions will give them a sense of ownership and control over the outcome, giving them a vested interest in its success because people want to be recognized for wins rather than failures.

5. LEVERAGE YOUR ORGANIZATION'S VALUES AND BELIEFS

If your business or organization has well-grounded values and accepted cultural beliefs, use any of them that will support the change process and help justify any required actions. For example, one value widely adopted by employees might be respect, which you can use to support the need for your customer billing process to change: "to *respect* our customers' expectation of easily understood billing." This rationale corroborates that the change is consistent with the organization's long-held values; not completing the change would prolong a hypocritical practice of disrespecting customers.

Another example would be using a cultural practice—say, employees celebrating a new customer installation with an outing paid for by management—as a reward for the team once it achieves a target for changes. Leveraging accepted internal behaviors into your implementation practices will ensure greater acceptance of the program and its objectives.

In an organization where there are no widely accepted practices and values, you have the opportunity to create new ones that will motivate employees to achieve desired outcomes. Employees from a cross section of the organization should participate in workshops to identify values that represent the vision of your organization's future. Clear communication of the vision will conjure up for employees the values most applicable to achieving it.

It's imperative that values are not constructed by senior managers in isolation. Ownership of the values by employees is important to ensure acceptance and adoption of the values across the workplace. This can be achieved only when a cross section of employees choose the values that hold the strongest psychological connection and meaning for employees. Selecting the most relevant values will help ensure sustainable change is maintained over the long term, by giving employees a solid foundation for explaining to future employees why certain behaviors are more desirable than others.

6. TRAIN AND MENTOR TO WIN

The change process will be more effective if your program has a strong theme of winning and supports employees with training and mentoring. All individuals want to be successful at what they do. No individual seeks to fail or wants to be part of a losing team. Implementing a change program to transform the organization needs to be squarely rooted in the ideology of winning. Employees simply want to win. They are seeking the knowledge about how to win and be successful, but this knowledge is insufficient without the actions required to materialize a winning outcome.

Training and development are important aspects of winning and of adopting behavior that leads to the desired results in your organization. Without a proper training and mentoring program to help employees develop new behaviors, focus on customer centricity will diminish during implementation. Good coaches know their players well and can develop players' strengths; they encourage the team to overcome weaknesses and win the game. Likewise, employees need to be trained and mentored on what they need to do to win. The initiatives required to scale this across the organization are detailed in the next chapter.

Defining what it means for employees to win is as important as providing them the know-how. Your CX project should have clear and measurable objectives defining success. Employees need to have a solid understanding of how their actions will lead to the organization winning by becoming customer-centric and delivering a branded experience for customers.

Successful transformation projects provide employees with a new and better way to win. They are more engaged and embrace the change because there is clarity around what and why they need to change. The correlation between the changes and winning is made very clear. Highly motivated employees with a strong desire to win will lead the behavioral changes and provide inspirational examples for less motivated employees to imitate. The key to unlocking great transformational change is to arouse the desire to win in people and then support it with a well-structured program of training and mentoring.

7. RECOGNIZE AND REWARD NEW BEHAVIORS

Positive reinforcement with public recognition and rewards is a proven practice for shaping and cementing a particular type of desired behavior. Public recognition is a great way to let others know the type of behavior your organization values most. You can vary the level of recognition depending on the culture and seniority of team members. For example, it may be more appropriate to recognize senior managers among their peers than openly to all the organization. Conversely, less senior staff may relish being in the spotlight and appreciate the recognition by senior management. Public recognition should be encouraged throughout the implementation to motivate employees to change behaviors.

The worst approach would be to avoid recognizing people's accomplishments entirely because of the fear that it may be viewed as favoring certain employees. Higher-performing employees who are treated no differently from their lower-performing peers are going to be less motivated to go above and beyond. Failing to recognize or reward employees for displaying highly desirable behaviors is a weak spot for low-performing organizations.

During the implementation process, employees are constantly asked to change long-practiced behaviors they are comfortable with and to unlearn the old and familiar. The positive emotions generated from public recognition and rewards help condition employees to learn the new behaviors. Select the rewards based on what you know motivates employees. Be careful not to provide rewards that may be disdained or inappropriate. For a positive association with the new demonstrated behavior, employees need to genuinely desire the reward.

Collectively, these best practices for transformational implementations, when applied, achieve a superior outcome. The materialization of your customer experience program from design stage to completion is no easy task. Changing behaviors and sustaining them is difficult and complex. These seven best practices improve your chances for success by increasing employee engagement levels and eliminating obstacles likely to impede your CX project.

Next we will learn more about scaling customer experience excellence across the entire organization.

KEY LESSONS

- To work properly, most initiatives to change an organization's customer centricity require a high level of employee engagement.
- Transformation projects can potentially alienate and unsettle employees because an underlying current of distrust and insecurity exists with all these types of projects.
- Employee surveys will help isolate the areas that impact employee engagement levels prior to commencing a transformation project.
- A bridge toward trust can create the necessary emotional and mental engagement to achieve the program's transformational objectives.

- Knowledge of what determines engagement will enable you to implement your program using elements that are important to employees.
- Employees' engagement drivers are very similar to customers'.
- Increasing the engagement levels during implementation will require an evaluation of the areas you can influence to achieve uplifts in engagement.
- Providing a positive context for how the transformation program will address employees' issues and frustrations will encourage greater engagement during implementation.
- Increased engagement can be achieved by all employees, by ensuing seven best practices during the implementation stage:
  » Communicate honestly and authentically.
  » Deliver regular CEO communication and support.
  » Customize the implementation for different teams.
  » Empower teams to take control of changes.
  » Leverage your organization's values and beliefs.
  » Train and mentor to win.
  » Recognize and reward new behaviors.

CHAPTER 11

Scaling and Maintaining CX Excellence

How will you overcome the problem of partial or temporary results from your program after the initial rollout? When implementing a transformational program to create a branded experience, most organizations are challenged with effectively influencing the entire organization and maintaining momentum after the initial implementation. Retaining the new organizational behaviors ensures the investment made in the initial transformational project achieves maximum financial returns. Refocusing the organization toward customer centricity requires an implementation strategy that factors in how you will scale up CX excellence across the entire organization—and maintain it after the initial implementation tasks have been properly completed.

This chapter covers stage 28 of the CX management process:

Stage	Desired Output
28. Mentor and train staff in new work behaviors.	Staff's consistent demonstration of new behaviors

What to Do When Employees Resist Change

Often the largest challenge faced in any transformation program is how to embed new behaviors permanently in the organizational culture. Effecting successful change in parts of the organization may create pockets of excellence, but unless excellence can spread, mediocrity and behaviors preventing true customer centricity will keep the organization from achieving the rewards set in the design phase.

CONSIDER EMPLOYEES' PERSPECTIVE

Changing human behaviors and thinking patterns is challenging because the method that achieves permanent change differs from the one used at implementation. There is no one-size-fits-all when it comes to achieving long-lasting behavioral changes. Some employees come on board relatively quickly and display changed behavior right away. Others take longer and may not respond to the influence of the change agents—not necessarily to be difficult or resist change, but perhaps because they struggle with change or are disengaged and genuinely unhappy about their job or the company. The reluctance to adopt change or practice new behavior may be related to fundamental problems in employees' relationship with the organization or can simply be related to an ineffective change methodology. Either way, when implementing your transformational plan, it's important to consider things from the employee perspective.

Good decision making is based on facts and evidence. For some employees, acceptance of new methods of work depend on persuasive factual evidence. Why should they adopt this new behavior? The absence of an answer based on facts will create resistance toward change. To transform the entire organization and not just certain departments or employee groups, you will need a strategy for convincing resistant employees of the importance and value of the required changes. Failing to transform the entire organization opens the door for unconvinced staff to influence others to convert to old behaviors, which can undermine the financial and other long-lasting benefits from organizational transformation.

PRESENT PARTIAL RESULTS

Even though the foundation for your customer experience program was based on factual evidence, some employees may need evidence that is specifically sourced from within your organization. This evidence would be easily obtainable if all employees changed their behavior according to your program; however, the resistant employees want it before they agree to make the changes. In this case, one approach is to present partial results of your program to demonstrate benefits to the employees.

To gather these results, you'll start by identifying a department or group of employees who have demonstrated strong customer-centricity behaviors while implementing a component of your program. This component should be able to produce results quickly and convincingly. Select a business process that has a direct impact on a department that is resisting change, so employees will be able to relate to the benefits achieved.

For example, consider a finance department, whose employees are likely to rely heavily on facts as a reason to change their behavior. Maybe these employees will be directly affected by the number of daily adjustments they must make when refunding money to customers who complain. Assume the number of refunds is directly related to the length of time it takes the customer relations department to acknowledge and respond to simple complaints. Turning around this known problem area in the organization would provide convincing evidence to the fact-hungry employees in finance. Complaint acknowledgement and resolution may be one of the areas identified in the plan for our CX program, and also one with a high probability of generating quick results.

To demonstrate that our program is able to generate these positive results, we compare the partial results achieved since implementation against a control group. The control group should continue processing complaints in the traditional manner, while the test group should apply the changes according to the new program, including both process and behavioral changes toward managing customer complaints. Once we have implemented the changes in the test group and are able to generate measurable results against the control group, we will be in a position to present the facts to the finance department. The results should clearly demonstrate the direct benefits of the changes on the finance department's workload, the company, and the customer.

This mini case study of the benefits achieved from the implementation of a CX program will become important in overcoming resistance in departments and ensuring transformation is achieved across the entire organization. Building a convincing case from a smaller implementation test will give you the confidence to scale up and ensure your program has unquestionable credibility with all types of employees.

The Role of Organizational Culture

The universally accepted behaviors of an organization define its culture. An organization can be said to have a strong, well-defined culture if the majority of its employees have a clear and consistent understanding of what behavior defines how things get done. A strong culture helps determine the identity of a company and what it means to be working there; in organizations with a weak culture, employees do not have a distinct understanding of how they should behave or what makes their identity unique. A uniquely identifiable culture builds a brand that is prominent in the marketplace and that customers can distinguish from competitor brands. It tends to be consistent in its interactions with customers, who in turn appreciate that consistency.

Your organizational culture plays an important role in ensuring permanent change. Customer-centric organizations are able to achieve differentiated, long-lasting results by creating an organizational culture that inspires employees to give 110 percent and act in desired ways even when no one is monitoring them. Getting employees to display desired behaviors without provocation is the ultimate achievement of any transformational program and an indication of the organization's pervasive culture.

Well-defined and lasting behavior is linked to a deeply cherished set of values and beliefs. Values and beliefs have universal importance to individuals, but they vary based on culture, religious beliefs, and upbringing. It's important to identify what values and beliefs a group of individuals in an organization consider most important. An organization with employees who are predominately one type or from one group will place importance on certain values, whereas another company might characterize a different culture. Take, for example, millennials (generally defined as the generation born between late 1980 and 2000) and what they consider important, compared with what is important to baby boomers (generally defined as the generation born between 1946 and 1964). A survey by Pricewaterhouse-Coopers[7] identified that 82 percent of millennials are likely to seek employment at a company that has been publicly awarded for its ethics, compared with 68 percent of people from older generations who said the same.

Companies that have different groups of employees with different values need to embrace diversity and find a middle ground of shared values. The common ground may not be evident at first, but examining the language used by employees will provide the clues to building a unified culture. Baby boomers in your company, for example, may articulate the importance of mentoring, while millennials may express the importance of personal development. The common ground would be to a company value that stresses "continual learning and development."

When an organization's values and beliefs represent the majority of its staff, it can build a culture that is both strong and unique. Defining a culture of highly relevant and accepted values and beliefs requires the consistent behavior of many people over a period of time, so imitating another organization's culture is not a durable solution. Culture is not something that can be prescribed. It has to feel right for the people in the organization and properly reflect what they consider most inspiring. When it does, it motivates and inspires employees to behave in a particular way without provocation or instruction.

Strengthening Culture through Employee Training and Mentoring

Linking employee behavior to a set of values and beliefs associated with the delivery of CX excellence does entail some effort. Organizations often fail to achieve excellence because they don't align their behaviors with the values and beliefs of their employees. Training and mentoring employees on the desired behaviors is required, both to convey the types of behaviors that are considered representative of the organizational culture and to inform them about when to take action, what action to take, and why the

7   PricewaterhouseCoopers, "Millennials at Work: Reshaping the Workplace," accessed June 2, 2015, http://www.pwc.com/gx/en/managing-tomorrows-people/future-of-work/millennials-survey.jhtml.

action is necessary. Each employee must know he or she plays an equally important role in delivering an overall excellent experience to customers—and what every employee must do to perform this role properly.

It's best to scale up new behaviors across the organization using a multi-strategy approach to accommodate the complexity of changing human behavior. Enacting multiple strategies gives you the best chance of overcoming numerous variables to achieve your desired transformational outcome. Following is a description of the eight key culture-building strategies for scaling up CX excellence across the entire organization.

I. FIND EVANGELISTS WHO CAN SPREAD AND MAINTAIN NEW BEHAVIORS

Employees with a high energy level, the right attitude, and a certain competency level can, through their actions, coach others in the organization on how to deliver customer experience excellence. Their positive and infectious attitude will transmit new forms of behavior to others and accelerate the process of transformation. These "evangelists" need to be from diverse departments across the organization, and they need to represent the organization as a whole and not just the areas that they come from. Selected during the implementation process, these change agents effectively spread new lessons, influence colleagues, and transform behaviors because they are highly influential, enthusiastic, and able to lead properly—by modeling the desired behaviors themselves. They come in handy after the primary implementation too, to help the governance team maintain high levels of CX excellence.

2. ENCOURAGE EVANGELISTS TO EXCHANGE LESSONS

Evangelists can spread their knowledge by meeting and communicating on a regular basis to share ideas, lessons, and any obstacles they face. These regular meetings help maintain momentum and focus the team. Beyond the initial implementation, the role of the change agent should be not only to maintain behavior in the department, but also to ensure new employees entering the department are properly inducted and understand how the organizational values and beliefs translate into expected behaviors. So evangelists should develop their own support network, where they can meet with other evangelists to exchange lessons and discuss how to overcome challenges. The ongoing exchange of lessons inserts a structure for maintaining and rejuvenating new behaviors over the long term.

3. REMOVE OBSTACLES BETWEEN EMPLOYEES AND CX EXCELLENCE

Leaders need to recognize that processes, behaviors, and beliefs in their organization prevent their staff from achieving desired new behaviors. The plan for your customer experience program should have identified the obstacles between your organization and a branded experience for your customers, and eliminating these obstacles should be included in your implementation. After the initial rollout of your program, new obstacles will arise that prevent employees from being able to perform their roles as expected. Organizational leaders must take a continual improvement approach toward reviewing and changing elements in the business that no longer have relevance or that prevent employees from delivering excellence.

Obstacles in an organization can act like weeds and strangle the excellence employees could be delivering for customers. Appoint a specialized team—preferably the governance unit—to constantly review and enhance business processes within the company. Skilled employees who display a passion for change should identify obstacles, simplify processes, and uproot obstructive behaviors so employees can deliver CX excellence on an ongoing basis.

4. INCREASE EMPLOYEE EMPOWERMENT AND ACCOUNTABILITY

Leaders can't hope for widespread, sustained change without increasing the levels of both empowerment and accountability among their employees. Employees who are not empowered to perform their roles feel stifled and experience lower job satisfaction and engagement. If employees are trained to deliver great customer experiences but have rigid policies and procedures in place that prevent them from doing what their company asks of them, frustration will follow. Greater employee empowerment is necessary for any organization to achieve long-term transformational change and its economic benefits.

On the flip side of empowerment, a strong sense of employee accountability is another key behavioral change required to achieve transformation. All staff in the organization should feel not just able to deliver a uniquely branded experience, but highly accountable for doing so. No staff member should ever say that it's not their job to help a customer.

Together, empowerment and accountability create an environment where employees act quickly to resolve customer issues that, if not resolved properly, could create a negative experience for customers. The faster employees can resolve customer needs to a high level of customer satisfaction, the more likely they will be able to convert potentially negative customer experiences into emotionally positive ones. The proliferation of customers' reviews on social media about their experiences with organizations has further highlighted the importance of the empowerment/accountability factor in preventing brand damage. Any business processes that require multiple levels of escalation or create other delays in resolution of customer needs should be revised or eliminated, as they contradict any goals outlined in your CX program.

5. EVOLVE YOUR ORGANIZATION'S STANDARD HAPPINESS PROCEDURES (SHPs)

Most companies have standard operating procedures (SOPs) outlining the steps of a certain process according to the organization's practices, typically written from the organization's perspective. The SOPs describe how an employee should follow procedures to complete a workflow and achieve an operational outcome, but they often ignore the impact of processes on—and the happiness level of—customers.

Review your organization's SOPs, and either reengineer or eliminate them altogether based on their emotional impact on customers. Earlier, when you mapped the customer's journey (in chapter 5), you captured moments that elicited a heightened negative emotional response from customers. Now you must revise the processes behind these moments to remedy the root causes and prevent a recurrence of the negative experience.

To maintain longevity for your transformational program, you need to create a policy for achieving the desired outcome from future business processes. Some organizations may incorporate this into a quality policy or quality management system (QMS) document that outlines the company's philosophy on quality and customers and defines its customer-centric focus. The QMS guides the design of future business processes in delivering a branded experience, by specifically addressing the customer's emotional state. Any process unable to deliver a positive emotion, or at best a neutral one, should not be included in a customer-centric organization.

All business processes that have a direct impact on customers should have a clearly documented practice for quickly resolving issues when things don't go according to plan. Employee confusion over how to act when a customer is unhappy is one of the fundamental obstacles preventing an organization from achieving widespread customer experience excellence. Simply providing soft skills training on how to deal with complaining customers is insufficient. When employees don't act quickly to remedy an issue, problems can escalate for customers. Providing employees with clear direction on issue resolution empowers them to act effectively when they encounter an unsatisfactory event.

A standard happiness procedure (SHP) provides employees with instructions on how to act and what they need to do to achieve a positive outcome. The SHP is a structured process that ensures representatives of the organization are accountable for making the customer's experience a happy one. It takes the SOP one step further, because the desired end outcome of an SHP is not an internal business function, but customer happiness.

6. ALIGN KPIs TO CUSTOMER EMOTIONS

Scaling and maintaining the transformational goals of your CX program will require the organization to align and modify KPIs and other productivity markers so they are centered on customer emotions and feedback, not on traditional productivity goals. Misaligned or conflicting KPIs that draw employees' focus to productivity or administrative outcomes rather than to customer experience are a major hindrance in spreading and maintaining CX excellence across an entire organization. When the business has started telling employees that customer happiness is the new mantra, yet employees are still measured on how efficiently they perform a task, they can feel conflicted. Changing employee KPIs is as critical as coaching your staff on how to better serve your customers. Aligning KPIs to customer emotions ensures a sustainable long-term transformation.

7. LINK HIGH PERFORMANCE WITH A HIGHER PURPOSE

Employees will not go the extra mile simply because they get paid to do so. The real driver behind achieving more is the sense that employees are doing their work for a higher purpose than themselves. Often this higher purpose is linked to the greater good, a sense of achievement, and being part of a winning team, and it can motivate and convince employees who are resisting the changes from your transformational program. Change agents can sway even difficult or reluctant employees into accepting the new *modus operandi* and seeing the new behavior as achieving an outcome for the greater good of the team.

Being proud to work in an exceptional organization is a powerful motivator. Embedded deep in every individual's psyche is the need to identify his or her place in the universe. At some point every individual will ask fundamental questions about their identity, such as "Why am I here?" and "What is the meaning of life?" and "Does my life amount to anything special?" Organizations can help individuals find meaning and answers by providing the stage for realizing their potential, achieving excellence, and becoming extraordinary. Employees become proud to work for the organization because it gives them an opportunity to accomplish something special and add meaning to their lives.

Great leaders understand the grander role that an organization can play in an individual's life. Creating a platform for fulfillment feeds employees' desire to act unselfishly and drives them to go the extra mile. Leaders who tap in to the hidden potential of their employees can unleash a powerful driver for customer-centric organizations.

8. HELP EMPLOYEES FEEL THEY "OWN" THE ORGANIZATION

Organizations need to give their employees a sense of ownership in the business. This feeling can be accomplished by directly linking employee compensation with overall organizational performance and by constantly, clearly communicating performance expectations that help shape their mind-sets and behaviors. Linking the success or failure of the organization with employees' actions helps them accept an obligation to make the organization successful. Promising a reward for their efforts ensures that this sense of ownership and obligation is reciprocated. Employee ownership plays an important role in maintaining your transformational program over the long term, because employees understand that compensation is a direct result of their behaviors and actions. Any bonus or share option plan should reflect ownership and directly mirror the performance of the individual and team, so be sure to develop strong alignment between KPIs and the customer-centric behaviors that achieve the financial objectives of your CX program.

Recruiting the Right People for Long-Term Success

These eight strategies for scaling and maintaining a culture of customer experience excellence are only ever as good as the people implementing them. To support an enduring CX program, the organization must effectively recruit and induct new employees who are a good fit. If there is no discipline around the type of people recruited into the organization, over time the program will diminish in importance and eventually extinguish.

One by-product of the implementation of a strategic CX program is the ability to define the types of behaviors that the organization seeks from employees. Taken together, the behaviors your program has established amount to a profile of the employee you should recruit in the future. A large part of making customer experience excellence a widespread organizational success is matching the employees you hire with the mind-set and behaviors you desire. It's significantly easier to scale CX excellence when your employees naturally believe what you believe. When chosen behaviors evolve into a definable culture, new employees easily adopt and practice the customer-centric behavior defined in your CX program—and vice versa.

Knowing the characteristics of people you need to recruit ensures consistent behavior among employees. Only by maintaining this consistency will you achieve a definable organizational culture that is capable of delivering a differentiated and uniquely branded experience to customers.

Perhaps the ultimate in effective recruitment practices can be illustrated by the Taj Hotel in Mumbai, India, an organization with some of the most exceptional displays of customer experience excellence in the hospitality industry. In 2008, when a terrorist attack took place at the Taj, hotel staff spectacularly chose to stay and risk their own lives to protect guests. A review of the hotel's recruitment strategy highlights that hiring staff who have a natural tendency to serve others and put the customer first plays a key role in the Taj's success and in its recognition as a CX leader in the hospitality industry.

Scaling and maintaining customer experience across your organization over time is no easy feat, but it is an essential component in your implementation plan. An organization is a living and breathing organism that evolves, matures, and hits bumps on the road. The strategies deployed to transform it may need to be revised over time to reflect the evolving profiles of the organization and its customers. The constantly changing expectations of employees and customers alike require a dynamic approach to ensure the organization can deliver valuable experiences that are a step above what is offered by the competition, for both employee and customer.

Despite the many common themes and practices when it comes to achieving long-term transformational change, no single approach suits every organization. Each CX project should be customized to fit the goals of the individual company, business, or organization, based on the competency levels of the staff and the degree of remedy required to deliver the desired branded experience.

KEY LESSONS

- Striving for longevity of the CX excellence program ensures the investment made in the initial transformational project produces the maximum financial return for the organization.
- Changing human behaviors and thinking is challenging because there is no one-size-fits-all when it comes to achieving permanent change.
- Building a convincing case from a smaller implementation test will give you the confidence to scale up your program and ensure its credibility.
- Getting employees to display desired behaviors without provocation

is the ultimate achievement of any transformational customer-centricity program.

- When an organization has a clearly definable culture, it is more able to provide the consistency that customers seek.
- Every well-defined and lasting behavior is linked to a deeply cherished set of values and beliefs.
- Highly relevant and accepted values and beliefs will motivate and inspire employees to behave in particular ways without provocation or instruction.
- Training and mentoring help employees understand the types of behaviors that represent typical values and beliefs held by their colleagues.
- Scaling up demonstrated new behaviors across an organization is best achieved using a multi-strategy approach. The eight key strategies are as follows:
  » Find evangelists who can spread and maintain new behaviors.
  » Encourage evangelists to exchange lessons.
  » Remove obstacles between employees and excellence in customer experience.
  » Empower employees and increase their accountability.
  » Evolve your organization's standard operating procedures (SOPs) into standard happiness procedures (SHPs).
  » Align KPIs to customer emotions.
  » Link high performance with a higher purpose.
  » Help employees feel they "own" the organization.

- Recruiting the type of people who easily align with the beliefs and values established by the organization and display the right attitudes toward customer centricity ensures consistency in behavior over time.

CHAPTER 12

Building the Right Organizational Structure and Governance Model

Previous chapters touched on the importance of having an organizational structure that is capable of supporting organizational customer centricity. As I described in chapter 8, the governance unit that oversees and maintains desired customer-centricity outcomes is a particularly important aspect of ensuring the momentum of a customer experience program. This chapter will now explore both of these topics in more detail to provide guidance about the types of structures most suited for customer-centric organizations and the roles performed by the CX governance department.

This chapter covers stage 29 of the CX management process:

Stage	Desired Output
29. Establish a CX governance unit and the organizational structure to maintain and elevate the CX program after its implementation.	A CX business unit that maintains, fixes, and elevates the customer experience on an ongoing basis; customer-centricity behaviors that are embedded in the organizational culture

Redefining Structure in a Changing Marketplace

Consider how changes in the marketplace have impacted the operating structure of traditional organizations. The Internet has provided a platform for accessing and transmitting information at lightning speed. We now live in the age of hyperconnectivity—according to Collins Dictionary, "the state of being constantly connected to people and systems through devices such as smartphones, tablets and computers—and sometimes through software that enable and promote constant communication." Social media, smart mobile devices, the open source movement, and digitalization have together changed the global competitive landscape. The basis for this argument is evident in two key market characteristics:

1. Items sold by different companies offer minimal differentiation in the marketplace because competitors are able to mimic and quickly deploy similar offerings in equivalent markets using the Internet's global reach and easily developed software applications.
2. Consumers have changed the way they buy goods and services, thanks to the Internet (which enables customers to easily research a particular item before purchase and to influence others with their feedback) and mobile devices (which give consumers control over their buying decisions regardless of location or time zone).

These two key changes in behavior define the new competitive landscape. The primary shift is in *control*. Control over brand messages has shifted from organizations to consumers due to the increased accessibility, frequency, and usage of information.

THE RISE OF CUSTOMER CONTROL

Before the Internet age, in which people are globally connected to each other through smart technologies, the corporation had the upper hand. A company was largely in control of how and what it would sell to a consumer. Marketing was easier because the company could predict the number of sales it would make if it spent a certain amount on advertising and distribution. In the age of hyperconnectivity, however, with consumers able to connect and share their thoughts about a particular product or service, individuals have the same influencing power as a large corporation with a hefty marketing budget.

As I will discuss further in chapter 19, this shift of control to the consumer has disempowered the corporation. Choosing a different brand because of a poor customer experience or negative feedback from a network of peers has become as easy as point and click. Loyalty to brands now depends on the collective feedback of consumers on the Internet.

Research confirms that consumers no longer trust what a company says. As early as 2009, The Nielsen Company reported that 90 percent of respondents trust recommendations from people they know and 70 percent trust consumer opinions online.[8] Similar research by Forrester in 2013 confirmed that 70 percent of people surveyed trusted brand recommendations from friends.[9] A consumer is no longer a lone voice. The collective consumer voice has redefined how organizations need to operate and compete.

Corporations can no longer organize themselves in specialized structures that operate independently of each other, as they had done for many years with a trusted, predictable marketing formula and well-defined markets. The marketplace is now global, and choice is everywhere. Well-informed consumers can be loyal only if their experience with a company meets or exceeds their expectations relative to the price they paid for goods and services.

So far this book has outlined some key characteristics that define what companies, businesses, and organizations need to do to achieve sustainable market differentiation in customer experience:

- Become customer centric by considering the customer in everything they do.
- Deliver consistent experiences for customers.
- Deliver products and services that are highly valued by target customer segments.
- Provide an effortless and personalized customer journey.
- Overcome areas of pain in the customer journey.
- Innovate using technology and new business models to create new customer value propositions.
- Respond rapidly to resolve customer issues and meet customer needs.
- Embrace change and constantly seek to improve the customer experience.

....

8   The Nielsen Global Online Consumer Survey was conducted by Nielsen Consumer Research from March 19 through April 2, 2009, among 25,420 Internet consumers in fifty markets across Europe, Asia Pacific, North and Latin America, and the Middle East.

9   Forrester, "How to Build Your Brand with Branded Content," March 21, 2013, https://www. forrester.com/report/How+To+Build+Your+Brand+With+Branded+Content/-/E-RES92961.

To achieve these objectives, a customer experience–led organization needs to adopt an organizational structure or governance model that supports employees in their quest to better serve customers. Companies bound by a traditional structure do not enable employees to collaborate or act effectively toward customer-centric outcomes, and so they will struggle to embrace the new competitive traits of leading CX organizations.

THE PROBLEMS WITH OUTDATED ORGANIZATIONAL STRUCTURES

Organizations founded prior to the age of hyperconnectivity were structured based on the concept of specialization. The three main types of structures were first introduced in 1776 by Adam Smith, the father of economics, and built on the division of labor around specialist functions to speed up production. This guideline became the basis for many companies adopting one of the following structures:

- **Simple.** This structure has centralized control and minimal specialization, with minimal rules to govern the operation.
- **Functional.** This structure, often considered departmentalization, is focused on grouping similar occupational specialties that have a common function in the company. Occupations such as those in human resources, finance, and research and development are examples of such groupings.
- **Divisional.** In this structure, companies create highly specialized and autonomous divisions to address specific needs. The divisions usually have their own objectives to achieve.

These three structures are based on traditional hierarchical models where the CEO sits at the top and reporting lines are tiered. Smaller companies usually use a simple tiered structure because it has the flattest reporting lines. Larger companies mostly adopt functional or divisional structures. Supporting these structures are performance metrics and budgets, which are allocated to departments or divisions based on the company's growth plans. Each department is allocated a budget that depends on its overall contribution to the bottom line, as well as specific targets to reach based on its area of control.

While these structures worked well when the company had control over its markets and had the luxury of internal control over product design, manufacturing, and distribution, they no longer work in the age of hyperconnectivity. Larger organizations with a traditional structure lack the nimbleness and agility required to respond to hyperconnected consumers who have control at their fingertips and who demand a fast, effortless, emotionally enhancing experience when they interact with an organization. When the consumer has access to multiple channels using many different smart devices and can influence how a brand is perceived in the marketplace, an organization needs to be structured so its people have a holistic view of their customer and can access metrics that support consistently high-value customer experiences.

Organizations with an antiquated structure are at a disadvantage compared with younger companies whose structure is designed to deliver better customer experiences. Traditional structures are problematic today because they inhibit an organization's ability to compete for market share, particularly given these key problematic areas:

- **Staff work in silos.** When departments and employees are unable to share information with each other, it creates a myopic view of the customer.
- **Staff are given specific targets.** When performance metrics are specific to a department's area of control, this leads to self-interest and behavior that may be counterproductive. Too often, departments are competing against each other to demonstrate their worth to the company.
- **Company culture is focused on sales.** When praise and reward are based on how many items are sold, it leads to a product-centric culture that is counterproductive to the customer-centric environment required in today's service-oriented environment.
- **Staff do not have the right technology or data analytics.** Today's businesses need to keep up with technology and information in order to understand the changing needs of the hyperconnected consumer.
- **Budgets are misaligned based on poor information from management.** When the C-level fails to obtain useful, timely information about the changing marketplace and customer needs, budgets

are incorrectly proportioned around channels and areas that are no longer as relevant.

- **Companies are not able to innovate fast enough.** Today's companies need to deliver experiences that keep customers' long-term attention, engagement, and loyalty. Traditionally structured organizations are usually hampered by the bureaucracy inherent in the organizational structure.

- **Management fails to recognize the economic value in delivering differentiating customer experiences.** A lack of knowledge at the top level about the financial benefits of a strategic CX approach makes it difficult for CEOs to articulate to their board why it is important to make radical changes. As a result, change does not occur and inertia prevails.

Building a Suitable Organizational Structure in the Age of Connectivity

To overcome the challenges inherent in a traditional organizational structure, an organization striving toward customer centricity must rethink how employees should be organized so they can best meet new customer expectations and address today's competitive forces. The evolution of the competitive landscape requires traditionally structured organizations to make some potentially significant changes, by adapting their traditional structure and/or adopting an entirely new, more competitive structure.

ADAPT THE STRUCTURE OF TRADITIONAL COMPANIES

Leading customer-centric organizations are able to meet the key challenges described in the previous section and to compete for market share more effectively by making some internal changes to their structure and decision-making processes:

- **Break down silos.** Work in an open and collaborative manner, and not in isolation. This will enable staff to work toward common company goals as opposed to individual departmental ones.

- **Change the reporting and approval process.** Provide employees with meaningful and real-time reports about customer issues, and empower them to resolve issues without numerous escalations. This gives employees greater agility and nimbleness in responding to customer needs.
- **Increase data analytic capabilities.** This will give senior managers accurate and real-time information about the new landscape and its impact on the business.
- **Realign budgets toward growth channels.** This realignment will enable investments in the areas that can make the business a leader in its industry.
- **Create an environment that encourages innovative thinking.** Making the right investments in people, technology, or processes can ensure that innovation becomes a core component in the company.
- **Ensure metrics are changed to reflect quality of service, not sales.** This will ensure uniformity across the company and track the quality of service delivered as opposed to sales.

ADOPT A NEW, COMPETITIVE ORGANIZATIONAL STRUCTURE

An organization seeking to optimize its ability to compete in a hyperconnected age requires an alternative to traditional hierarchical and compartmentalized structures. There are a number of alternate structures better suited for contemporary organizations:

- **Matrix.** In this structure, employees are grouped by function and project. The matrix structure maximizes the use of cross-functional teams to get work done, so a project can be completed by utilizing the specialties of a number of different people across the organization.
- **Team.** This structure forms teams from different functional areas and harnesses the richness of diversity to solve larger complicated problems. Its aim is to break down functional barriers across the organization and strengthen working relationships with common objectives.
- **Network.** This structure acknowledges the limitations of trying

to become nimble and responsive as a larger organization. Speed, agility, and expertise are gained by outsourcing noncore functions to a network of providers and retaining only core functions, in order to give larger organizations the benefit of acting like a smaller and flatter company.

The key outcome from adopting one of these structures is the breakdown of silos of specialized groups and the formation of diverse teams that work toward a single goal. The team-oriented environment with the right customer-centric culture forms the foundation for building the organizational structure necessary to address the unique aspects of the new competitive landscape.

Changing organizational structures that have been in existence over long periods of time is not a quick process. Newly established organizations with an understanding of the competitive traits required to compete in the age of hyperconnected consumers, on the other hand, can form their teams around these structures without any legacy issues to contest with.

Adopting a CX Governance Model

Regardless of the structure in place, an organization that is serious about using customer experience as a differentiator will need to have a governance department. As discussed in chapter 8, this department will ensure the objectives of the organization's customer experience programs are achieved and the program continues to deliver measurable results over the long term.

A governance unit can take many forms and comprise a number of different roles—there is no one-size-fits-all model. The unit should properly reflect the objectives, size, and complexity of the organization. When the governance unit is formed, it should be clear to all employees that although there is a dedicated CX team, all employees of the company remain accountable for customer experience. A governance business unit is not about centralizing customer experience responsibility, but about monitoring, controlling, and advising on the organization's customer experience activity.

Several attributes are essential for the success of the governance unit:

- **A strategic objective to improve customer satisfaction across multiple customer touch points.** All customer-facing departments and their employees, including the contact center, any self-service platforms, and other key customer channels, must internalize and practice the primary CX objective in the following manner:
  » Maintain the highest standards of customer excellence in accordance with the organization's brand promises.
  » Remedy any areas that prevent customers from receiving a strategically branded experience.
  » Enhance the customer experience across the organization by designing and implementing innovative, leading solutions that are valued by customers.

- **Authority and sponsorship from the CEO and board.** Everyone in the organization, from the C-level down, must acknowledge the governance unit's license to make the necessary changes required to improve the customer experience.

After the governance unit's functions and objectives are agreed on by stakeholders, its structure and reporting lines—which will ensure that the business unit is able to perform its functions effectively—need to be designed. Often it's at this point that most of the debate occurs.

POSITIONING THE CX GOVERNANCE UNIT

Ideally, a governance unit for customer experience should be autonomous and report directly to the CEO. In my experience, and according to my research, the most successful customer-centric organizations make the governance unit autonomous and independent from other business units. Given this structure, the unit can accomplish the following tasks:

- Perform audits without conflicts of interest.
- Be powerful enough to make permanent changes that fix root causes of customer problems.

- Represent how important customer experience is throughout the entire organization.

By giving the governance unit independence and the authority to influence change, you can be certain that known problem areas are not hidden from senior managers and root cause problems are not left festering.

Some people may argue with this viewpoint and offer some good reasons why a customer experience unit should report to another department such as marketing or operations. But making the governance unit answerable to the marketing department immediately positions customer experience as a subset of marketing. This reduces the influence and auditing capability of the governance unit and ultimately makes customer experience a less important organizational imperative.

Having an independent structure and a direct CEO reporting line supports the objectives of the CX governance unit, and both features are pivotal for how customer centricity and customer experience will be viewed internally. If customer experience is a subset of another department, the strategic importance of what you are trying to achieve will diminish over time. A best-practice implementation of the governance model will ensure the organization is able to attain the following goals:

- **Reduce investment risk** for the initial organizational change implementation because the unit will be properly empowered to follow through on program objectives.
- **Elevate the importance of customer centricity** and experiences throughout the organization over time.
- **Focus on customers across all touch points** throughout their journey, and ensure experiences remain relevant or are remodeled to create new value propositions.
- **Fix root causes** and elevate the customer experience.

The CX governance unit plays an important role in presenting a branded experience to customers, by ensuring that all the moving parts are operating at optimal levels. The unit acts as a CX compass for the organization, constantly measuring performance and realigning focus to deliver on the brand promises and changing customer expectations.

STAFFING THE CX GOVERNANCE UNIT

Assuming you decide to adopt an independent governance model, the next consideration would be to determine the type of employees who will compose this department. Rather than cover every possible version of how you might compose your resources within this business unit, instead I will equip you with the knowledge required to identify the employees in your organization who are best suited for such a role:

- **Chief of customer or chief of customer experience.** In leading the unit and providing strategic direction for all of the organization's customer experience initiatives, the chief of customer has ultimate accountability for how the organization delivers its customer experience objectives. This person will report directly to the CEO.
- **Customer experience manager.** This person is responsible for the implementation of the transformational aspects of customer experience.
- **Customer innovation manager.** This person is responsible for designing innovative new ways to deliver better experiences for customers.
- **Process excellence manager.** This person is responsible for ensuring that business processes are optimized to meet both organizational requirements and CX objectives.
- **Quality assurance manager.** This person monitors and audits aspects of the organization and ensures the organization is delivering on its promises to customers.
- **Customer relations manager.** This person manages customer complaints, resolves them quickly, and identifies recurring customer pain points.
- **Business analyst.** This person collates CX data and presents reports to the unit, with a goal of helping determine the course of action.

This is not a definitive list of positions; some, all, or additional resources could belong in the governance unit. As an example, some organizations may place customer care in the same unit. Others may wish to include an innovation manager who can focus on creating new value propositions for customers. The finalized structure of the unit and its staff should empower the governance unit to achieve its objectives.

An organization's ability to maintain the momentum of its CX changes beyond the implementation phase will determine whether it can achieve strategic transformation and not simply temporary lifts in results. The governance unit plays a crucial role in ensuring the program achieves its strategic objectives. Market differentiation does not happen overnight. It can take three or even five years before an organization is recognized in the marketplace as having a uniquely branded customer experience that is better than the competition's. The journey toward differentiated services is not immediate or easy. Any organization seeking to master a branded customer experience needs to invest time and resources to doing so, and must be committed to a difficult but, ultimately, highly rewarding transformational journey.

KEY LESSONS

- The Internet, social media, smart mobile devices, the open source movement, and digitalization have together changed the competitive landscape on a global basis.
- The shift in control to the consumer has disempowered the corporation.
- Organizations with a traditional structure will struggle to achieve the competitive traits of leading customer-centric organizations, because they do not enable employees to collaborate or act effectively toward customer-centric outcomes.
- Organizations seeking to compete in our hyperconnected age and to position their customer experience offering as a competitive advantage require an alternative to the traditional hierarchical, compartmentalized organizational structures.

- The team-oriented environment with the right customer-centric culture forms the foundation for building an organizational structure that addresses the unique aspects of our new competitive landscape.
- Regardless of its structure, an organization that is serious about customer experience as a differentiator will need to build a governance department that ensures its CX program's objectives are achieved and deliver long-term results.
- The best practice is to make a governance unit autonomous and independent from other business units.
- An organization's ability to maintain the momentum of its CX changes after implementation will determine whether it can achieve strategic transformation.

How to Innovate in

Customer Experience

Any strategic customer experience program seeking to remain relevant and achieve long-term commercial benefits will need a continual cycle of improvement that helps an organization adapt to customers' changing expectations. The final stage of the transformational CX management process is covered in the remaining chapters of part two:

Stage	Desired Output
Implement a continual cycle of improvement by measuring, monitoring, and innovating customers' experiences to maintain differentiation in the marketplace.	Identification and prioritization of CX innovations to ensure ongoing market differentiation; operational delivery adapted to changing customer expectations

Stage 30 is an ongoing cycle of measuring, monitoring, and innovating customer experience components to retain your market differentiation and competitive position. This process involves three primary components:

- Employees
- Customers
- Outsource partners

This chapter focuses on the first and second components—namely, how an organization can build an effective innovation engine that helps employees adapt to customers' changing needs.

The Importance of Innovation

As we discovered during the analysis and design process, you can't turn around poor customer moments in the customer life cycle without innovative thinking. Innovation lies at the very heart of every successful branded customer experience strategy. It provides your customers the uniqueness that will define why your brand is better than your competitor's.

The ability to innovate in customer experience after the initial implementation of your CX program is an asset to your organization because it delivers relevance and differentiation over the long term. An organization can win the loyalty of its customers, successfully shaping how they experience its products and services, by continually innovating in areas that excite them. Innovation is the gauge that measures whether a company will be able to deliver a branded experience and reap the financial rewards from repeat purchases and referrals.

Innovation is all about how an organization can adapt, evolve, and leap ahead of the pack. Look at businesses such as Google and Amazon, and you can quickly appreciate the commercial value of innovation. These companies entered the marketplace focusing on a single product offering, but have innovated to create new products and services that offer different value solutions for their existing customers and continually attract new ones. Innovation was also the key to IBM's survival. IBM was rapidly becoming obsolete and faced economic decline, but has managed to remain relevant by bravely shedding old business models and reinventing itself to deliver new and more compelling solutions for customers.

There are numerous such examples in the business world, of companies that have used innovation to propel their business forward. Customer experience innovation stimulates growth and creates economic value when it can achieve the following four outcomes:

1. Acquire new customers.
2. Retain existing customers.
3. Increase the spend of existing customers through voluntary loyalty.
4. Reduce the cost of acquiring or retaining customers.

Companies need to innovate in customer experience to achieve their long-term vision and to keep or exceed their desired position in the marketplace. Any organization adopting the methodology outlined in this book will need to create an innovation engine capable of designing customer solutions throughout the customer journey and delivering more value than competitors do.

How to Build a Customer Experience Innovation Engine

A CX innovation engine has a number of characteristics and functions. When I refer to the creation of an "engine," I am interested in the output generated by the members of the innovation machine. To achieve a functioning innovation engine, you need to have the means to measure internal performance, understand how customer expectations are changing, and be able to identify the opportunities to capitalize on—all leading to the creation of new value for customers. Only when your company is able to apply the necessary creative thinking and master the processes to execute an innovation is the innovation engine functioning properly. To achieve this requires people with the right skill sets and processes to progress new ideas and execute them. To leverage existing employees and information, the people responsible for your CX innovation should also be part of the CX governance team.

Five key steps are required in order to make your CX innovation engine generate the types of outputs that will uphold your brand's enduring value among customers.

STEP I: CAPTURE AND MEASURE EMOTIONAL STATES
THROUGHOUT THE CUSTOMER JOURNEY

During the analysis stage, I outlined the importance of knowing what your customers value most. You will need to reference these values when designing an innovative solution, to ensure that it meets your organization's brand-specific promises. Periodically checking in with your customers' emotional state is the only way to know whether your organization is continuing to deliver on that promise.

For example, if your primary customer is over the age of sixty-five, there is no use designing a digital solution simply because "everyone else is doing it." Coming up with innovative solutions without properly considering your current customers' habits, likes, and dislikes could potentially alienate them. What you may consider an innovation may be viewed as a hindrance by your customers—and may have them searching for competitors that offer more familiar services.

Any new CX innovation should answer the question "How will this benefit existing customers?" If your team cannot answer this question, then the innovation needs further evaluation.

Analyzing what customers value is simply the first requirement of innovation. Over time these values will change, and you will need to remain current by continually measuring emotional responses and expectations.

STEP 2: UNDERSTAND HOW FUTURE TRENDS AND SOCIOECONOMIC CONDITIONS WILL CHANGE EXPECTATIONS

Innovation must be forward-thinking, not just based on the current situation. Innovation also requires you to forecast what your customer segments are likely to expect in the future. The innovation team must develop a process to anticipate these expectations and a mechanism to address them through well-thought-out innovations. Capturing evolving customer expectations and values is an important component of your innovation engine.

The final part of the book takes a look at the future of customer experience and explores how evolutions in technology might lead to a possible paradigm shift. Considering both current and future customer expectations is an important aspect of ensuring your innovations are relevant.

STEP 3: TEST YOUR SOLUTION

The third step for ensuring your innovation engine is able to produce value-creating solutions is to test your solutions with one question in mind: Are they accepted by customers?

During the testing step, you may discover that customers like your product conceptually but are reluctant to purchase it. Google, when testing its new self-driving cars, discovered that a target audience of physically challenged elderly people were frightened (understandably!) by the concept of a driverless car. Getting into a car without a driver requires the passenger to place enormous faith in an organization's technology. Google specifically addressed this customer concern by designing the car to appear nonthreatening and safe. Airplane passengers probably had a similar fear in the early days of the aviation industry. Having flight attendants casually serve food and beverages helped passengers take their mind off the dangers of being in a gigantic steel capsule flying at fast speeds over land and sea. These examples show that the adoption of any new innovative solution needs to address customer concerns properly if the solution is to achieve widespread acceptance.

STEP 4: CHANGE YOUR TEAM'S THINKING PROCESSES

The fourth step for creating an innovation unit capable of producing workable creative solutions is to change the thinking processes of the team. Ideally, this change in thinking will later be applied across the entire organization, but start with the people entrusted to create innovative CX solutions. The challenge of creating multiple innovative solutions is capturing a thinking process capable of replicating great innovative ideas. Changing how people think requires a structured approach to achieve the desired outcome. Practicing a structured way of innovative thinking is the means to achieve the types of outcomes that lead to sustainable economic growth. By following a series of proven steps, you can help the CX team think beyond the status quo.

Sometimes an organization must completely destroy its business model to reinvent itself. You may have to be willing to overhaul your business model even when business is booming, because your analysis has identified that its relevance is near an end. Restaurant owner Ferran Adrià of el Bulli in Spain, rated by *Restaurant* magazine as the best restaurant in the world year after year, clearly wrestled with this question. Despite a six-month waiting list and a constantly full restaurant, Adrià decided to close the restaurant in 2010. "Part of my job is to see into the future, and I could see that our old model is finished," he told *Time* magazine. "It's time to figure out what comes next." Five years later the Adrià brothers built a successful foodie empire in a mostly unremarkable part of Barcelona, Poble-sec, where they serve cuisine that ranges from affordable and approachable to expensive and innovative.

It takes a lot of courage to shelve your successful business model and make way for something new and unproven. The enormity of this type of action is tempered by applying structured thinking that will help you innovate.

The thinking required to achieve innovative solutions is different from traditional "outside the box" thinking, which often leads to ideas that do nothing to differentiate your company or add minimal value for customers, because it is unstructured, limited, and erratic. To achieve new value creation for customers, a more structured process of thinking is required.

Two types of thinking processes form the basis of any innovation process:

- **Creative thinking** (also identified as divergent thinking or inductive reasoning)
- **Logical thinking** (also identified as convergent thinking or deductive reasoning)

To develop a systematic process of thinking that arrives at innovative customer experiences that can be delivered quickly and achieve desired outcomes, both creative and logical thinking are required.

Business creativity is not a new concept, and numerous authors—including DeBono, Wertheimer, Osborne, Parnes, and Koestle—have written about how to think creatively. Brabandere and Iny, in *Thinking in New Boxes*,[10] outlined a practical methodology well suited for innovative thinking. Their process aims to break down our preconceived ideas of a company and its products and services. They rightly highlight that the human brain quickly categorizes what it perceives into tightly constructed "boxes." This enables humans to process information quickly and has greatly contributed to our survival as a species. In business, however, these boxes can prevent us from thinking differently. Brabandere and Iny's process teaches us to create new boxes that enable the type of thinking our brains are more accustomed to. Identifying these new boxes is a critical process during which you ensure you are not blind to risks and opportunities in the marketplace.

This five-phase process is described here.

....

10   Luc De Brabandere and Alan Iny, *Thinking in New Boxes: A New Paradigm for Business Creativity* (New York: Random House, 2013).

1. Doubt Everything

The first phase is designed to make you ask questions, to challenge rigid rules and tired frameworks. The primary goal of doubting is to take you out of your comfort zone of cognitive thinking. An example would be an exercise in which you describe what line of business you are in—without using all the normal descriptive words associated with your business. This first phase of the creative process required for innovation will help you identify the tightly held beliefs that form your current boxes. Once you identify these beliefs, you will need to determine how the categories should be challenged, revised, enhanced, or replaced. The creation of new boxes that outline the types of issues you wish to investigate and the outcomes you want to achieve will drive you to the second phase.

2. Probe the Possible

Phase two is designed to explore possibilities by investigating three dimensions:

- » Consumer insights
- » Competitive intelligence
- » Exploring megatrends

This phase focuses on prospective thinking. You need to examine the three dimensions around a series of "what and how" questions. For example:

- "What experiences are your customers seeking now, and how is that likely to change in the future?"
- "In what way will the megatrend of wearable technology affect how your customers interact with you?"
- "What can my competitors do to provide a better customer experience in the future, and how can they achieve that?"

These first two phases are designed to create the new boxes that will provide structure for the third phase: divergence.

3. Diverge

During this phase, you are asking people not simply to "think outside the box" but to break the rules around their thinking, transcend the past, and shatter existing assumptions. The hope is that you will arrive at new, creative, more focused ways to identify your business, by asking, "What line of business am I in?"

A good example is McDonald's. The company does not sit back and accept its "fast food" identity, but instead sees its core business as providing consistency and convenience. More recently, McDonald's has added a healthier, more natural option for customers. This is considered divergent thinking because now McDonald's has to create new value for its health-conscious customers by ensuring it can still make the food with consistency and deliver it with convenience. If the food cannot be made according to the company's core values, then it won't meet customer expectations. Divergent thinking enables McDonald's to rethink how to deliver new value propositions for its customers while retaining its core brand values.

4. Converge

This critical phase reintroduces deductive thinking to help you determine which box you should focus on. During convergence, you will need to take each idea and see how well it fits the following criteria:

- » **Alignment.** How well is the idea aligned to your company's vision, goals, competence, values, and culture?
- » **Feasibility.** What do your company's resources, time frames, financial returns, and regulatory environment reveal about the feasibility of the idea?
- » **Impact.** Will this idea enhance the brand, give you a competitive advantage, or affect your customers, and what risks are associated with it?

In the case of the McDonald's health food options, convergent thinking would require that the team explore how the new menu items are aligned to the company's vision and goals. The team would also consider how the new food items would be incorporated into daily production, and finally what the impact these items would have on the brand image of McDonald's as a "hamburger restaurant."

5. Reevaluate

The final phase involves reevaluating your ideas. No idea is great forever. As the world changes, so will your customers' expectations, so you must constantly change boxes and create new ones. Technology, economic upheaval, natural disaster, political changes, and cultural shifts all assure us that what happens today will change tomorrow. This never-ending cycle takes you back to phase 1, where you regularly doubt everything.

Some key signals will help you determine whether you need to innovate:

- A changing value proposition
- Unmet consumer or customer needs
- New competitors or suppliers, or changing offers from business partners
- New breakthrough technologies, products, or service offerings
- Changes in your organization's core performance metrics
- Unfulfilled business and other potential opportunities
- Disruptive events
- Intuitions and/or anxieties

One example of widespread disruption comes from the advent of smartphones and the service applications later developed for them: Uber, and what it has done to the taxi business worldwide. In 2009, Uber created a business model that leveraged the technology inherent in smartphones (mapping, GPS tracking, Internet access) to disrupt how people could get a ride. By 2016, the company was valued at around $18 billion. CEO Travis Kalanick described how his company aimed to make getting a car to pick you up "like turning a tap to get running water."[11] Uber used disruptive ideas to transform how people get ground transportation.

....

11   "Uber CEO: We'll run your errands," CNN, September 14, 2014, http://cnnpressroom.blogs.cnn .com/2014/09/14/uber-ceo-fareed-zakaria-gps/.

STEP 5: SELECT WHICH CUSTOMER EXPERIENCE
YOUR ENGINE WILL INNOVATE

You should prioritize customer experience innovation on the basis of how advanced your organization is in eliminating customer pain paints. If the organization is struggling to deliver its core services, it makes no sense to pursue an innovation designed to acquire new customers from referrals. An investment in the innovation makes sense only if it will deliver new, important value to customers, and the value of an innovation will always be relative to what the customer is currently experiencing with the organization's goods and services. An organization that is unable to deliver fundamental products and services should focus its innovative thinking on how to remedy this first.

Consider a telecommunications provider that sells airtime on a mobile network that is unable to deliver reliable coverage for its customers. Any effort to create new, innovative products or services would be a wasted investment if there was a problem with a core service or function provided for customers. An organization incapable of delivering quality core services reliably will greatly damage its brand reputation. Customers are much less forgiving when a company cannot deliver a core service or product with a high degree of quality on a consistent basis. A lack of access to basic services will immediately negate any initiative designed to elevate the customer experience throughout the customer life cycle.

Not delivering on core services is the equivalent of an organization flat-lining. The organization ceases to have any relevance for the customer, and regardless of the strength of the relationship, eventually customers will seek a competitor capable of delivering. This was dramatically illustrated in Australia in 2013, when Vodafone suffered ongoing mobile network outages. Customers left the carrier in a mass exodus. Vodafone lost 8.4 percent of its customers in six months,[12] highlighting how quickly people will leave an organization if it cannot deliver on the most basic of services. The road to recovery for Vodafone has been a slow and costly one.

....

12   Renai LeMay, "Massive Customer Outage Increasing: Vodafone Loses 8.4% in Six Months,"
Delimiter, July 22, 2013, https://delimiter.com.au/2013/07/22/massive-customer-outage-increasing
-vodafone-loses-8-4-in-six-months/.

Winning back customers after such a significant public failure of services requires time, not to mention targeted marketing, to address the failure and assure customers it will not happen again. Often a business will need to provide financial offers guaranteeing reliability and quality. Before any future innovations, Vodafone should prioritize the robust delivery of its core services to customers with the highest level of quality and reliability. Only then should Vodafone consider innovating to win back the customers it lost during the mass outages.

Your innovation engine can take many forms. Some organizations will have units dedicated to specifically innovating and incubating any new ideas until they become commercialized. These dedicated units tend to be focused on product innovation rather than service innovation. Ideally, the innovation role will be placed within the organization's CX governance unit. However, innovation requires a high degree of creative thinking. To ensure you gain rich and diverse input, use the same team structure from the customer journey mapping stage, procuring employees from a cross section of the organization as well as external subject matter experts. The team members chosen should demonstrate not just creative thinking but also openness to new ideas. The team should meet to specifically brainstorm customer issues targeted for innovation. The customer innovation manager will lead the team through the structured thinking process to resolve problem areas identified by the governance unit.

Organizational Culture and Innovation

An organization's ability to innovate may be hampered if the company culture includes impediments that prevent new ideas from being explored or accepted. The essence of innovation is closely linked to organizational culture. Organizations able to encourage and foster innovation build a culture that cultivates creative thinking and acceptance of trying new things without negative consequences. A culture of innovation provides employees with assurance that it's OK to fail and that trying new things is valuable.

A true embodiment of this culture is Apple during the early reign of Steve Jobs. The whole purpose of his company was summed up in its slogan:

"Think different." Apple's brand was directly linked to challenging the status quo and delivering new, simpler, and different ways to perform everyday functions. When Steve Jobs took over in 1997, he streamlined the organization's products and services and gave the business a strong, clear focus. The fusion of innovation with Apple's culture affected all aspects of the organization, from product design right through to supply chain. Similarly, Tesla has also made innovative thinking a core cultural trait of the company, by innovating every aspect of the automotive manufacturing and supply chain. In 2016, *Forbes* ranked Tesla as the most innovative company in the world.[13]

Without an environment that encourages innovation, organizations will struggle to achieve a fully functioning and productive innovation engine. The key impediments to an organization's innovation engine are as follows:

- The CEO does not value or raise awareness of innovation.
- The importance of innovation is not understood or articulated throughout the organization.
- There is no strong link between innovation and cultural beliefs or values.
- There is an inadequate level of understanding about current customer values and experiences.
- There is no adequate allocation of time and resources to cultivate innovative thinking and develop prototypes for testing.

For an innovation engine to operate properly, these components need to be addressed. Without them, the process of innovation will stall, and the business will be unable to think of new ways to deliver better products and services than their competitors do. The organization will become less competitive as companies with better and more focused innovation engines introduce disruptive solutions. Having a healthy pro-innovation culture with a properly functioning innovation engine, on the other hand, provides an organization with the mechanism to retain and increase market differentiation over the long term.

A company culture of innovation stems from external social, economic, and political influences. Countries with limited resources, incentive,

---

13   "The World's Most Innovative Companies," 2016 Ranking, *Forbes*, accessed November 17, 2016, http://www.forbes.com/innovative-companies/list/.

or historical context for innovation will have fewer organizations producing innovative solutions in the marketplace. The onus is on governments and the private sector to drive the innovation mandate in a country so this creative approach can be adopted and more widely practiced. An innovative culture is essential if a country and its economy are to reap the financial rewards from prosperous, innovative corporations.

KEY LESSONS

- The ability to innovate in customer experience after the initial implementation of your CX program is an asset to the organization because it delivers long-term relevance and brand differentiation.
- Innovation is all about how an organization can adapt, evolve, and keep ahead of the pack.
- Building an effective innovation engine for customer experience requires the following components:
  » A deep understanding of your customer segments and the various emotional states currently experienced throughout their customer journey
  » A solid grasp of how future trends and socioeconomic conditions will change your customers' expectations
  » A prototype to test your solution and determine if it's accepted by customers
  » A change in the thinking processes of the innovation team
  » A system of prioritizing customer experience innovations based on the organization's proficiency at eliminating customer pain paints
  » The input of people from a cross section of the organization as well as external subject matter experts
  » A culture that encourages creative thinking and trying new things without negative consequences

CHAPTER 14

CX *for the On-Demand Generation*

This chapter explores how customer expectations have changed in recent years, and what leading practices can ensure your organization meets these new expectations and continually delivers richer, more relevant experiences. The focus here is on the "on-demand generation," which represents the largest proportion of modern-day consumers.

Understanding the On-Demand Generation

The on-demand generation is typically associated with people born from the mid-1980s onward, but for our purposes this category is not age-specific. Anyone who has embraced technology and uses it to receive either goods, services, or emotional gratification on demand can be deemed a member of this generation. These are people who post their lives on Facebook, book cars using Uber, get their facts via Google, entertain using Netflix, and track pizza deliveries in real time on the Domino's website. Yes, this generation has an app for everything. It's a generation of people who can't be separated from their mobile phone. Most important, it's a generation that expects to receive most things immediately.

Members of the on-demand generation exhibit the following key characteristics:

- Intolerance toward anything that fails to just work or be simply intuitive
- Intolerance toward delivery delays
- An expectation of gratification from the use of technology
- An expectation that there will be no compromise in quality
- An expectation of getting anything online, at any time

These characteristics have evolved as businesses have introduced new, technologically innovative ways to deliver products and services faster and better. The on-demand generation has been conditioned by today's high-tech environment to respond in particular ways. For example, Facebook has provided the platform for this generation to realize a sense of social belonging and self-esteem though "likes." In fact, digital interactions now satisfy many of Maslow's hierarchy of needs required by people across all cultures (see figure 13.1).[14]

Maslow's theory—a five-stage model based on basic human deficiencies—attempts to explain how people are motivated. The deficiencies are needs that, when they are unmet, motivate us into action. The original model was divided into five categories covering need (physiological, safety, love, and esteem) and growth (self-actualization). The model was later expanded to include cognitive, aesthetic, and transcendence needs. Maslow states that the motivation necessary to fulfill such needs increases the longer they are denied. For example, the longer a person goes without food, the hungrier he or she will become.

14   Saul McLeod, "Maslow's Hierarchy of Needs," *Simply Psychology*, published 2007, updated 2016, http://www.simplypsychology.org/maslow.html.

Research conducted by Cornell University psychology professor Dr. Thomas Gilovich in 2015 identified that adaptation is the "enemy of happiness since we adapt to most things." For example, a new material purchase makes us happy initially, but very quickly we adapt to it and soon it doesn't bring us all that much joy. Other kinds of expenditures, such as experiential purchases, don't seem as susceptible to adaptation. Gilovich's earlier studies found people get more enduring happiness from their experiences than from their possessions.[15]

If we take Maslow's basic theory on what motivates people and temper it with Gilovich's research on our overpowering ability to constantly adapt, then we can begin to develop a better understanding of what will motivate the on-demand generation.

As members of the on-demand generation adapt to the instantaneous satisfaction from ordering anything from food to a car, or from having access to encyclopedic knowledge, the logical evolution is toward satisfying needs yet unmet, such as the following:

- **Cognitive:** Knowledge and a deeper meaning of the world and the things in it
- **Aesthetic:** Beauty
- **Self-actualization:** Realizing your full potential as a person
- **Transcendence:** Helping others achieve self-actualization

Based on this theory, a shift appears likely—from having quantifiable needs being met to yearning for the fulfillment of more abstract, qualitative needs. This change is reflected in the types of products and services that motivate the on-demand generation. This generation is no longer interested in just the utilitarian purpose of goods or service, but is motivated by the following:

- Beautifully crafted technology that is considered fashionable (i.e., technological function contributes only 50 percent of the buying decision)

15   Susan Kelley, "To Feel Happier, Talk about Experiences, Not Things," *Cornell Chronicle* (Cornell University), January 29, 2013, http://www.news.cornell.edu/stories/2013/01/feel-happier-talk-about-experiences-not-things.

- Services that further reduce effort, increase control, and improve quality of life (e.g., a service that reduces the effort of managing social media, which has become a daily chore for many consumers)
- Experiences that provide opportunities for greater social belonging
- Products and services that enhance body image or fast-track a career or financial standing
- Smart machines that were once dumb (e.g., fridges that can order your food when you run low on essential supplies)
- Customer service that is personal, provides positive reinforcement, and elevates consumers to a higher sense of worth (beyond unappealing loyalty programs in their current form)
- Companies and government bodies that can demonstrate they use a portion of revenues to actively help others (i.e., it will no longer be sufficient to be a silent donor)

In other words, the drivers motivating the on-demand generation are more heavily weighted towards abstract, qualitative attributes capable of elevating social standing.

Redefining *Cool*

If you provide branded customer experiences for the on-demand generation, you need to understand the latest definition of being *cool* and how your organization can deliver cool experiences. *Cool* in the context of customer experience can best be defined as a product or service that is at the forefront of the latest trends or developments, is fashionable but unlikely to go out of style, and performs better than other products and services in its category. Using this definition of *cool,* and considering the needs likely to motivate the on-demand generation, you can begin to imagine the different designs of products and services needed to deliver experiences that will appeal to these customers.

Delivering cool experiences has become arduous because the on-demand generation has high expectations as they work their way up the hierarchy of Maslow's unmet needs. Having had to compete with unprecedented social chatter through social media and self-publishing, this generation consumes anything that helps make them relevant. The noise created by social media, along with its global reach, has led many people to struggle with personal insecurities. Overcoming these insecurities requires individuals to receive constant affirmations of their worth in social, family, and work groups. Consuming cool products and services helps members of this generation confirm their relevance among social groups and satisfy a number of needs. So the motivation to own cool products and services is more than just a current trend; for some it has become a necessity.

Providing cool products and services to satisfy new needs and expectations of the on-demand generation is insufficient on its own to achieve market differentiation. Organizations cannot rely solely on having cool products and services as a path to greater customer acquisition and retention. Customer loyalty and advocacy will be achieved only once an organization has carefully considered the impact of all possible interactions with the customer. Careful design of customer interactions is essential to ensure the entirety of the customer's experience with the organization delivers an overall image that it is cool. As long as this cool image is perpetuated, customers will keep coming back. An organization with a cool persona ensures customers spread the word to their social groups. Telling others of their association with a cool organization elevates their standing in their social group and further justifies the value the brand offers the individual.

Yet it's important not to try and be too cool, as this strategy is likely to backfire. When Virgin Australia first launched its airline, passengers boarding their plane were greeted with sassy crew members trying really hard to be cool. Not all passengers were in the mood for a sassy crew. I remember being on flights and hearing the moans of weary business travelers when they were subjected to overly upbeat air stewards. Before long, Virgin realized this was not a sustainable strategy and stopped the try-hard behavior.

The difficulty of being cool is that you can't be seen as *trying* to be cool. You can only achieve the status of being cool if you are not *visibly* seen by your customers to be trying. It's the ultimate catch-22!

Mastering Physical Customer Experiences

Face-to-face retail interactions play an interesting role for the on-demand generation, which has largely resorted to self-service via the web and mobile phones. This gravitation toward digital channels reduces the amount of human interaction this generation experiences. Paradoxically, despite near-constant Internet connectivity, people often feel isolated. Eventually their need for human contact increases, and they seek out face-to-face interaction, the most powerful means to satisfy the need for belonging and affection.

As outlined earlier, the desire to fulfill a need increases the longer the need is unmet. Based on this equation, it is my belief that face-to-face interactions will become a key differentiator for customer experience in the future. Digital channels may currently be the hero for organizations, but the saturation of all things digital is beginning to create a yearning for physical connection. Implementing an effective face-to-face experience for the on-demand generation requires an organization to pay particular attention to elements that will create the ideal interaction experience.

Face-to-face interactions have the potential to yield a key point of difference in the marketplace and place a brand ahead of its competition. Successfully mastering these interactions is difficult. Many organizations are still unable to deliver great retail experiences, and instead they simply waste resources and damage their brands, leaving us with some fundamental dos and don'ts for avoiding mistakes with face-to-face interactions.

THE DOS OF FACE-TO-FACE INTERACTION

Getting customers to feel good about themselves is key, regardless of whether a sale is made or not. To accomplish this, train your staff to reach for the following goals:

- Have a strategy based on the mood of the customer.
- Read body language and people's moods.
- Be pleasant.

- Use customer names instead of issuing a numbered ticket for service.
- Be authentic instead of sarcastic.
- Have conversations with customers.
- Accept that it's OK not to make a sale if the customer is unsure about a product or service.
- Lift customers to positive energy levels.
- Understand cultural and gender differences instead of relying on stereotypes.

THE DON'TS OF FACE-TO-FACE INTERACTION

If you are a business owner or executive, strive (and instruct your staff) not to make the following mistakes:

- Don't have a strict uniform policy.
- Don't hire employees who are not genuine advocates of your product or service.
- Don't hire employees whose cultural or sociological differences are not in sync with your brand and may create a barrier to your customers.
- Don't overwork your staff (face-to-face work can be emotionally and physically draining).
- Don't use a script when talking to customers.
- Don't fake a smile.
- Don't focus only on selling a product or service.

The on-demand generation has learned to live though mobile phones, social media, and microblogging sites. For them, long lines and "fake" scripted services in a face-to-face interaction are less tolerable; they crave authentic interactions without hidden agendas, because this is what they have become used to online.

Organizations that are able to deliver pleasant, personal moments of authenticity without pressuring customers into purchasing an item will gain an edge in face-to-face interactions.

Case Study: Pressing the Flesh for Success

It's not surprising to know that Apple has a better brand image than Google.[16] The experience Apple provides to customers at its stores is cool. Customers can walk into the store and ask someone about how to use their device, or can play with other devices just lying on tables. These storefronts give customers a "face" with which to identify Apple.

Google does not have a store. It's a 100 percent pure online brand with no retail presence. As such, its brand remains faceless. The customer's inability to "press the flesh" of Google will always place Google at a disadvantage to its competitor brands with comparable products and services.

Meanwhile, Microsoft recently launched branded stores to display and sell its products, marking a key deviation from the company's previous strategy that relied on strong partners and online sales. Microsoft's entry into physical retail space as a channel is designed to directly compete with Apple and acknowledges the importance of creating an environment for customers to physically interact with the brand's products and services.

UNDERSTANDING MOOD AND ENERGY LEVELS

A person's mood is a reflection of how he or she feels. A tired or hungry person will be in a different mood compared with a person who has just received a bonus or had that first cup of coffee in the morning. Mood is often reflected in body language, facial expressions, and tone of voice. Teaching employees of your organization how to read another person's mood is an essential element of mastering face-to-face interactions.

A person in a negative mood will be less responsive to positive information and more critical of any information he or she is presented with. Conversely, a person in a positive mood will absorb positive information and be more responsive to the value a product or service may offer.

Research on how moods impact information processing (Trope, Ferguson, & Raghunathan, 2000; Trope & Fishbach, 2000; Trope & Neter, 1994) confirms that a positive mood enhances people's ability to act according to their long-term goals rather than according to competing

....

16   Patrick Kulp, "Apple Passes Google as the World's Most Valuable Brand, Ranking Says," Mashable, May 27, 2015, http://mashable.com/2015/05/27/most-valuable-brands/.

short-term outcomes.[17] A positive mood presumably facilitates elaborate processing of such emotionally aversive but potentially useful information. When people are in a positive mood, they feel more confident coping with the emotional impact of negative information.

Klaus R. Scherer provides some insights[18] into how you can map emotional states into a dimensional graph to help identify those states associated with positive and negative energy levels. He grouped emotional states such as frustration and boredom together as negative energy levels and emotional states such as happiness and interested as positive. The grouping of emotional states with positive and negative energy levels provides us a reference for the energy levels of customers based on their moods. This reference can be used to train staff on different approaches to take in face-to-face interactions based on customer moods.

Customer-facing employees need to be trained to read moods of people and to apply the appropriate strategy for effectively managing interactions. Their aim is for the interaction to achieve an emotional state associated with positive energy, to ensure the information regarding the product or service is processed favorably. Furthermore, employees need to be encouraged to do what is required to ensure the customer does not, in any way, leave with a negative mood, even if it requires them to simply leave the customer alone.

Earlier, in chapter 4, we discussed how positive energy influences optimal performance. We also have identified the importance of creating continual positive energy within the organization in order to inspire thorough engagement in the new strategic CX excellence program. Creating positive energy at a face-to-face interaction achieves similar high-level engagement with customers. Once you have been able to fully engage with a customer, you can hope he or she develops a positive emotional link to your brand and its products and services. Just as highly engaged employees are willing to go the extra mile for their company, so are highly

....

17   R. Raghunathan and Y. Trope, "Walking the Tightrope Between Feeling Good and Being Accurate: Mood as a Resource in Processing Persuasive Messages," *Journal of Personality and Social Psychology*, American Psychological Association, Inc. (2002).

18   Klaus Scherer, "Trends and Developments: Research on Emotions—What Are Emotions? And How Can They Be Measured?" *Social Science Information* 44. no. 4. (2005): 720.

engaged customers. They will likely promote the organization to their friends and family without provocation.

USING THE SENSES TO SHAPE CUSTOMER EXPERIENCES

The on-demand generation has become accustomed to carefully crafted technology applications that deliver effortless and intuitive interfaces for the user. Organizations that have used online applications to win over this generation have done so by meticulously analyzing every line, color, box, and font in the user interface. Their goal has been to deliver the right experience for the user based on the function of the application. When they speak of *function*, they refer no longer to utilitarian outcomes but to subconscious emotional sculpting. The aim of such organizations is to get customers using their application or device on a repeated basis for as long as possible, which can be achieved only when the vehicle's design and function trigger a pleasurable emotional exchange. Digital engagement can be difficult because of its limited access to our senses. Its shaping of our senses is largely restricted to sight and sound.

The advantage of face-to-face interaction is its full access to our human senses. Used in tandem, all five senses can deliver a memorable, pleasurable experience for a person. As soon as a person enters your store, he or she should instantly feel the uniqueness of your brand and why they want to own or belong to it. Your setting needs to send out a clear message for the person entering your store or office: "This is my brand, and this is what it stands for." It needs to be cool and appropriate, and it must embody the brand.

For example, think of the no-thrills warehouse layout when you enter a Costco store compared with the deep, all-encompassing engagement of entering a Hollister store that is set up like an upscale, dreamlike island surf shop. Both experiences represent their brands well. The Costco store portrays its low-cost, bulk purchase advantage, while the Hollister experience takes you to a fantasy experience full of summer delight and the beautiful bodies that go with it.

Each of these settings is an appropriate embodiment of its brand. Each creates the perfect environment for its customers to experience the brand persona. Customers receive reinforced messages about the brand image, which increases their grasp of and confidence about what that brand stands for. If the environmental setting evokes emotions or ideas that the customer values, he or she experiences a moment of pleasure. In the Costco warehouse, the environment evokes the idea of getting goods at wholesale prices, so customers feel they are getting a bargain—their primary association with the brand. On the other hand, the Hollister experience evokes a relaxed seaside vacation with all the smells that go with it, so customers can momentarily escape their stressful work and feel joy through this simple physical experience.

Setting the appropriate retail scene for your brand experience requires you to design a strategy for several elements of your environment:

- Physical settings
  - » Lighting
  - » Background music and volume
  - » Flooring colors and covering
  - » Wall colors and covering
  - » Smells
  - » Displays
  - » Available stock

- Staff and customer experiences
  - » Floor design and line management
  - » Customer amenities
  - » Number of staff members
  - » Staff tasks and schedule
  - » Style of checkout and customer service

Other considerations can help set the right scene, but these are the key ones. The on-demand generation is impatient with face-to-face interactions that lack attention to detail. By evoking all the senses, your organization can provide a rich experience and satisfy a fundamental need for immersive social interaction not available online or through self-service channels.

Creating Memorable and Positive Customer Interactions

For members of the on-demand generation, the sale is all about having control over their world and choosing to purchase anything by themselves. If you take this trait and apply it in a face-to-face interaction, the worst thing you can do is be all over a customer when he or she enters your store. Members of the on-demand generation want to experience your product and service, but prefer to approach you when they need assistance. This requires your organization to have a strategy that carefully balances the experience of your product and service with that of the face-to-face interaction. Remember, ultimately customers go to a retail environment not only to "press the flesh" but also to obtain a deeper human interaction that is missing from today's digital channels. Your goal is always to focus on giving your customers a positive brand experience, regardless of the sale.

Deeper social interaction is the key to creating moments of pleasure and has the desired strategic impact on your customer. If a social interaction fulfills a fundamental need, even momentarily, customers are likely to overlook any flaws in your setting. Some common aspects to a pleasurable interaction, however, apply regardless of the product or service. These ingredients are powerful because they cut to the heart of what the on-demand generation seeks in a great experience:

- Remember to use your customer's name in the interaction.
- Remember and acknowledge an important date such as a birthday, anniversary, or loss of a loved one.
- Remember the name of the customer's child, partner, or favorite pet.
- Listen equally to what the customer is saying and how he or she is saying it.
- Be empathetic if the conversation leads to a complaint, and acknowledge the problem.
- Speak at the same rhythmic tone of your customer, but never use an angry tone.
- Never use sarcasm or emphasize a point on which you disagree from your customer.
- Take the conversation to a place where the customer feels comfortable expressing his or her feelings.

- Always end the conversation pleasantly.

Author Alexander Lowen sums up the type of pleasurable conversation you should be creating for customers:

> We enjoy a conversation when there is a communication of feeling. We have pleasure in expressing our feelings, and we respond pleasurably to another person's expression of feeling. The voice, like the body, is a medium through which feeling flows, and when this flow occurs in an easy and rhythmic manner, it is a pleasure both to the speaker and [to the] listener.[19]

However, many plans ignore the trade-off occurring when digital and self-service are designed as exclusive channels for the on-demand generation. Today, for example, it has become possible to go to the supermarket and buy your week's groceries, all without having spoken or interacted with a single human being. This reduction in social interaction needs to be evaluated when engineering the relationship you want customers to have with your brand. Retail settings, if developed with care, can compensate for the loss of emotional engagement inherent in the digital environment. Creating physical personas of the brand that are considered by customers to be cool builds engagement and satisfies unmet emotional needs. The creation of moments of pleasure in retail settings can build brand loyalty when all the senses are engaged to offer customers a reflection of what they value most about the brand.

Still, the on-demand generation enjoys the freedom and control offered by digital solutions. These solutions deliver efficiency and lower costs, and empower them to make better decisions. The use of digital applications to achieve greater employee and customer engagement should never be ignored in the plans for your customer experience program. The next chapter covers how you can capitalize on the unique attributes of digital to create rewarding experiences for your customers.

....

19   Alexander Lowen, *Pleasure: A Creative Approach to Life* (Alachua, Florida: Bioenergetics Press, 2006). First published 1970 by Coward-McCann.

·················· **KEY LESSONS** ··················

- The on-demand generation includes anyone who embraces technology and uses it to receive goods, services, or emotional gratification on demand.
- Digital interactions now satisfy many of the needs in Maslow's hierarchy.
- Maslow highlights that the motivation necessary to fulfill needs increases the longer they are denied.
- As the on-demand generation adapts to instantaneous satisfaction from ordering anything from food to a car, or from having access to encyclopedic knowledge, the logical evolution is toward satisfying needs yet unmet.
- A shift is likely toward yearning to fulfill more abstract and qualitative needs.
- If organizations want to provide market-differentiating customer experiences for the on-demand generation, they need to understand what being *cool* means and how they can deliver cool experiences.
- Careful design around customer interactions ensures their experiences with an organization deliver an overall cool image.
- Digital channels may currently be the hero for organizations, but the saturation of all things digital will create a yearning for human physical connection.
- The advantage of face-to-face interactions is access to all our senses, whereas other channels are usually limited to one or two senses (typically sight and sound).
- If the environmental setting evokes emotions or ideas that the customer values, it creates a moment of pleasure for them.
- Creating cool physical personas of your brand builds customer engagement and satisfies customers' unmet emotional needs.

CHAPTER 15

Redefining CX for the Digital Age

Technology has become personal. It is a companion in our everyday life, a tool that entertains us and keeps us connected to anyone and everyone. Technology also offers an excellent opportunity to differentiate your business by delivering great customized experiences for your customers that are uniquely reflective of your brand. This chapter focuses on the unique attributes of digital solutions and provides guidance on how organizations can capitalize on digital to build better branded experiences.

Tracking the Digital Revolution

Moore's law is the observation that the number of transistors in a dense integrated circuit doubles approximately every two years. This observation by Intel cofounder Gordon Moore in 1965 provides us with the framework to understand why technology is evolving at such a rapid pace. That was the year the digital revolution began, when the concentration of semiconductors on a circuit board increased computing capacity. The introduction of the Internet in 1983 paved the way for electronic transfer and storage of digital information from one machine to another. These improvements unleashed a true technological paradigm shift that changed how people live—including how customers buy things.

Then, suddenly, devices no longer needed to be fixed to a wire. Wireless technology was no longer bound to a fixed position in our homes or offices. It could go with us wherever we went. The ability to take smart computing with us transformed our relationship with technology. It was no longer a box we turned on to do work. And since 2008, a plethora of applications have been released into the marketplace, marking the end of technical restraints as a hurdle for creativity: If you can think it, we can build it.

Many analysts consider 2014 the year of the mobile revolution. It is the year that access to the Internet via mobile devices such as smartphones and tablets exceeded the computing capability of desktop computers. Smart mobile devices have penetrated the global marketplace at rates previously unseen. Their adoption rate has surpassed most technologies over the past fifty years, taking less time to penetrate households than most other technologies. According to research by Statista, the top four countries for smartphone penetration in 2016 were United Arab Emirates, South Korea, Saudi Arabia, and Singapore—all in the Middle East or Asia. The US ranked thirteenth according to the Statista report on smartphone penetration.[20] And according to BI Intelligence, there are 6.2 billion mobile connections globally, of which 1.2 billion use mobile web. This figure is estimated to grow to two billion by the end of 2017.

This mobile revolution has given organizations an opportunity and a mandate to reinvent themselves in their customers' eyes. The high adoption rate and usage of mobile devices have simultaneously created opportunities and threats for organizations, and have changed consumer behavior and expectations in ways we are just beginning to understand.

What Mobile Domination Means for the Marketplace

Why is mobile dominating the marketplace? What makes mobile different from other technologies? What has led to this phenomenon in the global uptake of devices? And how has it transformed our behavior as human beings and as consumers? The answer to these questions lies primarily in what mobile offers the customer—its unique attributes and the value it offers, both in its usage and in how it's distributed.

WHY CUSTOMERS—AND ORGANIZATIONS—ARE ATTRACTED TO MOBILE

Smartphones and tablets have provided customers with unique value propositions:

....

20   "Number of smartphone users in the United States from 2010 to 2021," Statista, accessed November 22, 2016, https://www.statista.com/.

- A dramatically more personal experience when communicating, shopping, gaming, or researching
- A unique, individual personal space that can be customized in any way
- A tool to access a multitude of services
- A fully portable medium that is accessible anytime, anywhere

These high-value propositions offered by mobile devices are accelerated by the declining prices of these devices and the ease of their distribution. Device manufacturers and telecom companies have helped the adoption rate of these devices by reducing the barrier of up-front costs and amortizing it over the term of a contract for voice and data services. The convergence of easy distribution, low up-front costs, and high value offering has delivered a compelling buying proposition for consumers.

Customer behavior and expectations are evolving because these devices have given them a new way to access information and control their world. These devices are portable and have a growing number of applications, empowering the customer unlike ever before. Consumers are attracted to mobile devices because of the wide range of uses they offer—not only multiple utilitarian functions, such as the ability to become a flashlight, GPS navigator, and record of daily exercise, but also educational and entertainment ones. The ease of switching from one use to another through a simple swipe of the finger has made mobile the fastest adopted consumer technology in history.

Furthermore, mobile capability presents a unique characteristic with significant potential: Unlike the desktop, mobile devices enable the convergence of time, place, and content. This makes mobile devices powerful, game-changing pieces of technology. Smartphones using telecom carrier smart networks and GPS can geo-locate the user at any given point in time and potentially offer content that is relevant at that given moment and place. The contextualization capabilities of mobile have the potential to create an even more highly personalized experience for the user.

Mobile devices are unique for all these reasons. They have given consumers new ways to interact with their world and changed their expectations about interacting with organizations to research, acquire, and seek support for products and services. This unique, interactive capability has created a new ecosystem where businesses interact and exchange information with their customers.

This ecosystem is becoming the primary environment for organizations to differentiate themselves by delivering new and better customer experiences. Industries such as banking and finance have leveraged the inherent security features of mobile devices to streamline how consumers can access their accounts. For example, most banking apps have a second authentication requirement that is invisible because each smartphone has its own unique, inherent identifier. Banking applications are therefore easier to use on smartphones than on desktops. The convenience and ease of Apple and Android applications has enabled banks such as Chase in the US and ANZ in Australia to differentiate their services and create a branded experience through their mobile apps. Organizations able to capitalize on the ability of this ecosystem's features to increase the value to customers are the ones positioned to flourish. Others unable to adapt will decline as their market share erodes.

HOW MOBILE DEVICES HAVE CHANGED CONSUMER BEHAVIOR

Look around, and you will see the number of people staring into their devices while walking down the street, sitting in restaurants, shopping at the mall, and doing just about anything at just about any place you can think of. The fixation with mobile devices is everywhere. No country seems to be immune.

The degree of obsession is closely aligned with a person's age and gender. Each generation uses a certain group of applications more frequently than others. This preference for particular apps provides valuable insights into what is considered appealing in the digital world.

A thorough analysis of each generation and its customer segments enables an organization to better understand the how, what, and why of a particular consumer. Insights from the analysis should reveal the types of applications customers prefer and how they use those apps on a daily basis. This can help your organization isolate the differences and commonalities between customer segments and thus better understand how to deliver value for each segment.

For example, we know that millennials—the first generation to have grown up with the Internet—are more frequent users, and that female millennials are on the higher end of usage because of their social media practices. Following is an example of this analysis:

US Female, Millennial
- **Applications:** Snapchat, YouTube, Tumblr, Instagram, WhatsApp, Candy Crush
- **Primary purpose:** To share experiences with others, socialize, be entertained, and learn how to do things not taught at school or home
- **Daily usage:** High—any spare moment, while traveling and at work

US Male, Generation X
- **Applications:** Banking apps, LinkedIn, Google Maps, CNN, Twitter, Evernote, Call of Duty
- **Primary purpose:** To reduce the time required to locate things or shop, and to remain abreast of breaking news
- **Daily usage:** Moderate—mostly when relaxing, spending time in coffee shops, or waiting to meet someone

From the analysis, we can determine that female millennials are more likely to respond favorably to applications that permit self-publication and sharing postings with friends. Meanwhile, the Generation X male is time-poor and more likely to respond to applications that are uncluttered, quick, and easy to interact with. At the same time, we note the common theme of entertainment and control for both segments.

While each generation has a slightly different focus for how its members use their mobile devices, some common behavioral changes across all consumer types have defined the digital landscape. Understanding these unique characteristics and customer expectations, as described here, helps companies build better apps for their target consumers:

- **Shorter attention span.** According to the National Center for Biotechnology Information, the average attention span dropped 33 percent in recent years, from twelve seconds in 2000 to eight seconds in 2013. This figure is now even lower in 2017.
- **Single-click onboarding of applications.** Customers no longer have the patience for entering their personal details multiple times. Customers are drawn to a single Facebook or Twitter registration that affords them entry to other apps.
- **Visual based.** Mobile's rich visual display lends itself to creating attractive pictures and graphics. Consumers are drawn to applications that are easier to navigate and that offer more visuals than text.
- **Richer and quicker control.** Mobile devices' portability has enabled developers to offer a diverse range of applications that allow consumers to have a richer, quicker means to control their environment. This improved interface has enabled self-service to become the new preferred method for consumers to receive goods and services.
- **Digital personal space.** Mobile users have a unique, personal, private relationship with their devices. Sending mass marketing to your customer's mobile device is a sure way to lose that customer. If you are sending content through mobile, make sure it's highly personalized. A recent survey[21] found that a whopping 90 percent of users keep their phones next to their bedside table; it's the last thing they use at night and the first thing in the morning. The intimacy created by these devices and their apps has motivated consumers to adopt them as the preferred way to access, control, and connect with their world.
- **Review of websites to make buying decisions.** A plethora of review websites that rate products and services of all sizes and shapes have helped shape consumers' purchasing behavior. The vast majority of customers now research their desired category of product or service on the Internet before making a purchase.

....

21　Amanda Lenhart, Rich Ling, Scott Campbell, Kristen Purcell, "Teens and Mobile Phones," Pew Research Center, April 20, 2010, http://www.pewinternet.org/2010/04/20/teens-and-mobile-phones.

The unique attributes of mobile devices provide companies with an opportunity to build a digital relationship with their customers. Organizations can create a branded experience for their target customer segments by leveraging the unique characteristics of digital.

Customers' Expectations for Digital Solutions

The high reliance on mobile devices has defined what consumers now expect and value most from their mobile applications. Knowing these expectations and creating digital solutions for consumers that adhere to them helps organizations design segment-appropriate applications. To be successful in function and form, the application design should meet a number of important customer expectations.

SELF-SERVICE

Empowering customers to perform different types of common transactions is a key benefit derived from digital solutions. Surveys have outlined consumers' preference to serve themselves rather than wait in a line. For the value to be realized, digital solutions need to be shorter than the length of a transaction using alternate channels such as a retail outlet or call center. The speed at which mobile applications deliver transactions has naturally reduced users' attention span and tolerance for waiting. The convenience of transacting using a smartphone application obviates wasting time in a retail outlet or contact center. Consumers are all about point-and-click, download, or home delivery options. This has driven the self-service movement.

MINIMAL EFFORT

The hyperconnected consumer has become accustomed to using services online that require very little effort. For many members of the millennial generation, performing a task that is not linked to online services is simply unheard of. A positive customer experience has now become a function of the amount of effort required by a customer to do business with an organization. To meet today's customer expectations, your organization needs to measure this effort beyond the first sale and through all touch points of the entire customer life cycle. Make sure you incorporate research and service phase interactions, too. The less effort required by a customer to do business, the better the customer's experience.

OMNICHANNEL ACCESS

Hyperconnected consumers want to reach a company anytime using any device or application they choose. They require 24/7 access and a comparable experience to other channels, such as retail, whether they are contacting the company via phone or tablet. Customers reasonably expect retail outlets to have limited operating hours, but they will not accept limited functionality online or a difficult online experience. Customers want to choose how and when they contact a company.

PERSONALIZATION

In our hyperconnected age, social media shapes how individuals view themselves. The Internet and social media create a platform for people to self-publish anything and everything about themselves and their likes and dislikes. The responses their postings get from their network of friends and associates create a barometer of how a person feels about the world and about himself or herself. The instantaneous nature of receiving feedback on a self-portrait digital photograph shared over the Internet—the ubiquitous *selfie*—has created an important emotional link between social media networks and the way a person feels. This bond is stronger among growing young adults in the process of forming their adult identity. Mobile applications offering a high degree of personalization achieve a greater level of importance for consumers.

CONTROL

The sense of control offered by mobile applications plays an important role in how confident an individual feels. Being in control gives people a sense of self-gratification. The emotional association of control with online interactions has shifted customers' preferred style of interaction from assistance to self-service. Performing self-service tasks gives consumers the sense of control they require to feel good about themselves. They choose what they want and when they want it. Companies able to provide this emotionally gratifying experience for their customers can deliver a branded experience that is valued by the hyperconnected customer.

AUTHENTICITY AND TRANSPARENCY

The hyperconnected consumer seeks to build a relationship with organizations that are authentic in their approach and transparent in their dealings. Because time is of the essence and less effort is optimal, consumers are looking to deal with companies that don't use fine print in their agreements. They don't have time to deal with complicated rules and procedures, and they are wary of business dealings that seem constructed to "catch them out." They prefer digital applications that offer simple commercial arrangements and a service model that can address their problems without asking numerous questions or making them go through red tape.

GUARANTEE OF RETURNS

Purchasing products and services using digital applications can be risky if the consumer is unable to try the product first. Organizations that offer a risk-free return policy successfully overcome this barrier to purchase. Consumers prefer organizations that stand behind their products and services. For example, the company Sleeping Duck offers mattresses online with an innovative 100-night comfort guarantee. Customers unhappy with their online purchase can return the mattress for free within the 100 nights. By de-risking the purchase for consumers, Sleeping Duck has removed the barrier associated with purchasing a mattress online, and the 100-night comfort guarantee also differentiates the company from brick-and-mortar competitors that offer no such guarantee.

GAMIFICATION

Psychologically, consumers are always looking for ways to feel good about themselves. Through social interactions and gamification—engaging users in solving problems through game thinking and game mechanics in non-game contexts—mobile applications provide customers with instant gratification. Applications offering recognition for consumers as they achieve targets or advance through different levels, primarily for entertainment purposes, provide positive reinforcement that builds self-worth. The emotional gratification increases repeat usage of the application.

Designing a Successful Digital Application

To achieve an optimal digital experience, organizations need to recognize these new consumer behaviors and incorporate all these expectations in their application designs. A digital application that translates into a rewarding experience for consumers should feature the following characteristics:

- Personal
- Contextual
- Intimate
- Informative
- Able to be used anytime, anywhere
- Social
- Frictionless
- Effortless

SIMPLICITY IS COOL

What defines a good application is how simple yet functional it is. The digital world is ruled by minimalism. Keeping the application simple so any user can benefit from using it should be an objective for any digital designer. The focus on simplicity has to encompass all aspects of the application, including the terms and conditions and the return policy. Simplicity is valued because it reduces the time it takes customers to think and act to achieve a desired transaction.

More organizations are now innovating further simplified experiences to create a better customer experience. Amazon, for example, has designed a single-click option for common repeat-usage items such as laundry detergent. Consumers can order goods and have them delivered to their door by clicking on just one icon. Future innovations around reducing effort and increasing simplicity will enable organizations to differentiate their brand using digital and mobile solutions.

Offering a digital solution that works faultlessly, is simple, and delivers contextual and rich information better than competitors makes an application cool. As discussed in chapter 14, customers talk about cool applications on social media and freely recommend them to others. If the application is widely considered cool, its adoption rate increases.

The paradigm shift brought on by mobile has put consumers in control, a position to which they have grown accustomed. Any experience that detracts from their ability to control their world is going to deliver a subpar experience for them. This evolving nature of consumer expectations requires organizations to align their channel strategy with experiences delivered by the digital channel.

AVOID DESIGN ERRORS

Your organization can focus all its energies on creating a really cool digital experience for customers, but ignoring your other channels is a mistake. These alternate channels have a purpose, though their importance may vary based on the business model and the customer segments serviced.

Many organizations wrongly design digital solutions from their internal perspective and not the customer's. Some companies show complete disregard for customers by purposely frustrating access to simple information such as the contact details to force customers to use self-service or crowd-based support. In fact, minimizing the effectiveness of certain channels to shift customers from expensive channels (such as retail) to lower-cost channels (such as digital) is a growing trend. Contact center interactive menus become more complicated, making it harder for callers to access a live agent. Companies bury the customer support phone number deep in a website to force customers to use self-service or digital solutions. These tactics, though they potentially bring immediate cost savings for the organization, can often backfire in the long run by frustrating customers and forcing them to choose more accessible competitors.

A customer-centric organization would not purposely seek to alienate a segment of its customers in this way. Rather than frustrate customers for using a more costly channel, an organization should address costly, high-volume support calls in more intelligent ways: by examining the root causes of the high volume of customer inquiries to isolate and then remedy the underlying problem areas.

It's also important to understand the unique characteristics of each channel and why a customer may choose one over the other. Some customer segments simply will not use a digital service because it is out of their comfort zone. These customers may expect to easily call someone if a problem arises, because this is the most comfortable means of communication for them. Ignoring or over-automating this channel will only alienate these customers further. Some organizations that serve a large, mature-age customer segment have identified the value of customer helplines and have made investments in differentiating their contact centers by placing them onshore and making them more accessible. This makes great sense strategically because it goes against the tide, creating a point of differentiation that can be used in marketing.

The key message is: Do not ignore traditional channels when trying to cater to the hyperconnected on-demand generation. Delivering cool and valued experiences through any channel should be your ultimate goal.

The mobile ecosystem is an exciting and interesting space. The unique attributes of mobile devices have created the ideal platform for disruption in many industries. This disruption is occurring at a historically fast pace and affects numerous industries, especially banking and retail. This pace of change may seem frightening to organizations that are not structured to deal with innovation and change. But adapting quickly is imperative in today's market. Otherwise, slowly but surely, your organization will suffer the consequences of digital disruption.

If your organization is vulnerable to disruption, the last thing you should do is rush into developing technological solutions without proper analysis of what your customers expect and the types of experiences they value most (which we covered extensively in part one). Properly understanding strategic customer experience and learning to master it will ensure your business grows and flourishes in our transformational digital world.

KEY LESSONS

- The ability to take smart computing with us has transformed our relationship with technology.
- Smartphones and tablets have provided customers with unique value propositions that differ greatly from desktop offerings.
- Mobile devices have given consumers new ways to interact with their world and have changed expectations about how they interact with organizations to research, acquire, and seek support for products and services.
- The mobile ecosystem is becoming the primary environment for organizations to differentiate themselves by delivering new and better customer experiences.
- While each generation has a slightly different focus for how its members use their mobile devices, some common behavioral changes indicate new preferences for an application's design.
- To be successful in function and form, an application should be designed to do the following:
  - » Provide the option for self-service.
  - » Minimalize effort.
  - » Allow omnichannel access.
  - » Allow personalization.
  - » Help customers be in control of their world.
  - » Be authentic and transparent.
  - » Guarantee returns.
  - » Gamify the customer's experience.

- Keeping the application simple so any user can benefit from using it should be an objective for any digital designer.
- The evolving nature of consumer expectations requires

organizations to align their channel strategy with experiences delivered by the digital channel.

- Don't ignore traditional channels when trying to cater to the hyperconnected on-demand generation.
- It is imperative today to adapt quickly or, slowly but surely, suffer the consequences of digital disruption.

CHAPTER 16

Outsourcing and
Other Implementation Options

The remaining three chapters of this section address outsourcing relationships, the impact of outsource providers, and how to incorporate outsourced functions into your customer experience program. In these chapters, I will examine why outsourcing needs to be a consideration of your implementation plan, and I will explore other options that you may find are better suited for an effective implementation of your CX program.

Outsourcing is the final consideration required to achieve stage 30 in the transformational CX management process.

Why Choose Outsourcing?

Outsourcing a business process is related to the delivery (or partial delivery) of a business process by a third party *not* owned by the legal entity that requires the services. Almost all organizations have to make a decision about using external business providers to deliver their products and services. The question of outsourcing a component of the operation is a common yet critical consideration for any organization aiming to implement a strategic CX program. Your organization may have already entered into multiple relationships with vendors to deliver services, and these relationships may have met one of the following business needs:

- Scaling up the business offering
- Increasing speed to market
- Delivering a noncore service
- Cost saving
- Leveraging intellectual property

Outsourcing of services plays a major role in the operation of a modern organization. It normally acts as an accelerator, by helping organizations reach customers faster and deliver better products and services than if they had attempted to perform the function on their own. Outsourcing can play a pivotal role in an organization's ability to compete, by making it more agile in responding to customers' changing demands.

When building a customer experience program, your company needs to consider the increasing importance of outsourcing and the role it plays in growing organizations. This is especially important when outsourcing providers are utilized to deliver part or all of a customer touch point within the customer journey.

Throughout this book I have highlighted the importance of ensuring consistency and reliability of services. From the customer's perspective, only once this consistency is delivered can an experience be considered unique to the brand. The introduction of a third-party vendor into the equation can undermine the objectives of your CX program if the provider is unable to deliver the same consistency and standards you require to achieve that branded experience for your customers. To protect your brand against this risk, your organization must perform a complete evaluation to determine the best methodology to evaluate and manage outsourcing vendors.

Even before this step, however, you need to ask two important questions: "Should my organization use outsourcing at all?" and "If we don't outsource, what other options are available?"

Outsourcing decisions are normally strategic and therefore are made at the C-level of an organization. At some point in every CEO's and CFO's career, the question will arise regarding the best path to adopt for a particular business process that is a cost item on the profit and loss statement. The options available to the leadership team extend beyond whether to simply retain the function internally or outsource it, to include options such as having a co-sourcing arrangement with a vendor, creating an internal shared services department, or even carving out a business function and converting this into a business in its own right. An organization can also form a joint venture with a vendor to deliver a component of its business, or the organization could sell an internal business unit to a third party as an asset in exchange for a committed period of servicing. These multiple options have their own pros and cons, and deliver different value propositions. A four-step evaluation process may help you determine which outsourcing solution works for your organization.

Evaluating Potential Outsourcing Solutions

As the importance of customer experience becomes better understood at senior levels, so has the criteria for evaluating the best option. Executives with a deeper understanding of CX now consider the implications beyond the short-term financial benefits of outsourcing.

Executives with a mature understanding of the relationship between outsourcing and effective CX implementation will consider a multitude of variables to reach a decision, including the organization's ability to successfully manage a relationship with the outsource partners and to transfer the essence of its organizational culture that is necessary to deliver a branded experience to customers. Executives should also determine whether there are vendors capable of mirroring their brand.

Often executives will emphasize the difficulties of outsourcing, by focusing on the vendor side of the operational delivery equation, but then fail to acknowledge the limitations within their own organization that could hinder a unified, seamless extension of their brand with the third-party provider. Several aspects should help you determine the best option for your organization, such as considering the balance between immediate financial gain and long-term brand consequences.

To reach the decision most aligned with your CX objectives, you will need to answer several questions regarding the business process your organization may outsource. Your responses will enable you to evaluate and narrow your options as you decide whether to outsource or take an alternate route.

I. IS THIS BUSINESS PROCESS A
CORE FUNCTION OF YOUR ORGANIZATION?

The first question you need to answer is whether the business process considered for outsourcing is a core function of the organization. One of the key characteristics of leading customer experience organizations is clarity of vision. This clarity translates into knowing specifically what is defined as *core business*. The answer to this question is not necessarily related to a particular product or service sold by the organization. As the competitive landscape has shifted toward consumer control of brands, so has the organization's positioning of what is considered core business.

More leading organizations are aligning their core business with their key differentiators. For example, McDonald's makes burgers and fries, but so do a lot of its competitors. Its core business, as identified in chapter 13, is its ability to deliver fast food *consistently* and *conveniently*. McDonald's has been successful in a heavily commoditized industry because of its relentless efforts to ensure consistency and convenience in the delivery of quality fast food anywhere in the world. Consumers go to a McDonald's restaurant because they know what they are getting and know it will be delivered quickly. Similarly Zappos, an online shoe retailer also operating in a heavily commoditized industry sector, has identified its core business as "delivering happiness" to customers.[22] More organizations are shifting their definition to what is considered a core function as they correctly reposition their organizations to better compete in this landscape dominated by consumer reviews and opinions.

The identification of core competencies with customer experience outcomes is linked to an organization's level of customer centricity. Customer-centric organizations able to clearly articulate their core business in terms of the value they deliver for customers have the foundation to determine properly whether the business process should be retained in-house, delivered by a third party, or performed using some form of other hybrid solution. Meanwhile, organizations still identifying their core business as simply the delivery of easily imitated products and services will be driven to make operational decisions based on cost. These same organizations will inevitably compete on price in the marketplace and will drive margins lower and lower in their respective markets. In the end, they will only survive and prosper if their markets are large enough to compensate their low margins through sufficient sales volume.

....

22   Tony Hsieh, *Delivering Happiness: A Path to Profits, Passion, and Purpose* (New York: Grand Central Publishing, 2010).

Some organizations operating in different markets may need to apply different strategies to define their core business and properly compete. An organization competing in an emerging market may determine that its core business for that market is delivering low prices, because it's the only thing valued by the customer in *that particular market*. Low prices in an emerging market may be considered delivering happiness for customers. In the case of Zappos, delivering happiness in a mature market like the US is associated with different values: convenience, no-cost returns, and high-quality customer service. The key is to ensure the core business is what uniquely differentiates your organization in the marketplace *and* enables it to compete better than its rivals.

Case Study: Apple and Its Shifting Core Business

During his tenure, Apple CEO Steve Jobs turned a failing business into a leading, highly profitable organization. He achieved this by correctly identifying the core function of Apple—not being a hardware provider, but instead being an organization that challenged the status quo to deliver customers amazing products. The "Think different" slogan of the late 1990s became publicly identified as the core of the Apple brand.

Today, Apple faces new challenges. The company has mistakenly redefined its core business in terms of hardware and services rather than innovation, creativity, and delivering awesome products. Apple's differentiator was its ability to compete in its own space, not in the shadow of competitors. Unfortunately, now competing as a hardware and services business beside strong competitors such as Samsung and Google, Apple has seen dwindling market share as it struggles to redefine its core business to differentiate itself. Still, Steve Jobs's management of Apple serves as an example of the benefits to an organization with a clear focus on delivering unique customer value.

---

2. WHAT IS THE IMPACT OF THIS PROCESS ON YOUR BRAND PROMISE AND YOUR CUSTOMERS' EXPERIENCE?

Once you have articulated your core competency, you need to evaluate the impact of the business process on your customer and the delivery of your brand promise. For example, if you are an online retailer with no brick-and-mortar shops and you identify delivering happiness as a core business function, then the outsourcing to a third party would have a major impact on customers.

Let's go back to our Zappos example, where the only touch points are the website and the contact center. Zappos' ability to deliver happiness is predicated on its ability to build and maintain an internal culture that can keep this promise. So for Zappos, deciding to transfer its core competency to a third party would be problematic. Regardless of how well the outsource partner could be trained in the Zappos way of doing business, its employees would never be able to match the uniqueness of experiences within an internally managed contact center. That's not to say that the third party is *incapable* of delivering a service that is equivalent to or even better than the function Zappos provides. But it is very difficult to precisely transfer a uniquely branded customer experience to a third party.

Unlike organizational culture, other business processes could yield a positive impact on customers if outsourced. For example, Zappos uses UPS as an outsource partner for the process of delivering its packages to customers anywhere in the world. An online business incapable of delivering purchased items reliably and conveniently is unlikely to fulfill its promise of delivering happiness. Logistics and supply chain management are important aspects of delivering a great customer experience, but are rarely considered core functions in any business. In this case, the outsourcing of logistics to a competent third-party organization improves the impact on the customer.

Determining the customer impact of the business process in relation to your core competencies is a critical component when evaluating whether some form of outsourcing is right for your organization. Once you have determined the impact on customers, the next step is to determine the organization's ability to operationally deliver the business process according to the standards set in your CX program.

3. IS YOUR BUSINESS OPERATIONALLY READY?

The decisions around outsourcing are often purely pragmatic. Your organization may have a timeline for delivering a product or service to the marketplace and may not have the internal operational capability to meet its deadline. Out of necessity, the organization is likely to engage with specialist providers to execute the plan, whether on a temporary or a permanent basis.

Even if your organization has the financial capacity to establish a business unit to deliver business processes, doing so may not meet the schedule of the business plan. Delaying launch of a product or service because your operations are not ready is not a desired outcome. In this instance, even if the business process is considered a core function, the organization may decide that an outsource partner should be involved temporarily. Or perhaps your organization simply does not have the capital to fund a new operational unit and so, out of financial necessity, decides to adopt an outsourcing model with transactional costing. Timing and financial capacity will largely determine whether your organization can build an internal capability or needs to work with external vendors.

To determine your organization's readiness, you'll need to consider a number of variables involved in achieve this new operating capability: resources, capital expenditure, operating expenses, ramp-up time. Furthermore, operational readiness is largely strategic in nature. Your executive team may have the capability and the funding to deliver a process in-house, but may choose not to do so because management wishes to keep the organization strongly focused on its core competencies. This decision would ensure employees avoid distractions and focus on strengthening core functions.

4. WHAT IS YOUR BEST OPTION?

To answer this question, you'll need to undertake a traditional cost-benefit analysis of the various options available, and weigh each one to determine which is best suited for your organization. The cost-benefit analysis can be properly achieved only once you've identified your core competencies and evaluated both your operational readiness and the impact on your customers.

Choosing the Right Operating Model for Your Business

For customer-centric organizations considering how to perform certain business processes, there are multiple operating models available, each with various permutations. The main options, of course, are delivering the business process in-house or outsourcing it. A high-level understanding of each option will help you understand the key benefits and challenges it presents and help you select the particular option likely to suit your needs.

OUTSOURCING

Outsourcing requires an organization to have a defined business process and a set of business and technical requirements. The third-party vendor is typically a specialist in its field and has core competencies in the delivery of the business process to be outsourced. Pricing is typically based on time and material, transactions, or performance. Often these pricing components are used in combination and are not exclusive to one another. Service level agreements (SLAs) commit the third-party organization to deliver the goods or services according to agreed standards. Outsourcing tends to benefit CX-led organizations when it delivers a higher-quality, noncore business process and has low impact on customer experience.

INSOURCING

A business process is *insourced* or *captive* when the majority of costs (usually 70 percent or more) of delivering the business process are funded by the organization and directly delivered by its staff. Insourced business processes delivered by a customer-centric organization are typically core competencies and have a major impact on customer experience outcomes. The business process normally involves a customer touch point, and the organization has determined it has the operational readiness to deliver the function.

SHARED SERVICES

If your organization has identified a large amount of duplication in its various departments or divisions, it may decide to centralize some common functions and share some infrastructure (e.g., employees, facilities, and equipment) across departments. In this case, it would form a legal entity, called a *shared services operation*, with the primary focus of serving departments within the organization, or other legal entities owned by the organization, as a service provider. The idea behind shared services is to reduce costs by removing duplicate resources, and to make processes more efficient because the shared services team's employees develop greater expertise, specialization, and standardization that can be capitalized on using the shared services model.

Typically, shared services operations provide back-office functions such as accounting or recruitment, but they can also deliver customer-facing functions such as contact centers. These front-office customer functions are normally for multibrand entities wanting to achieve cost efficiencies from centralized operational delivery. Shared services are normally established by larger organizations operating across multiple locations and are designed to standardize and optimize business processes at the various locations.

The Different Forms of Shared Services

The different forms of the shared services model are as follows:

- **Joint venture.** Instead of remaining as the sole shareholder, the company may recruit external vendors as shareholders of the shared services. This may take the form of a joint venture between the two entities. The key reason for bringing in external parties would be to introduce new expertise to the shared services. Often organizations understand the benefits of a shared services operation, but lack the necessary expertise to operate it as though it were a service provider. Normally the partner selected would have outsourcing experience as a provider.
- **Outsourced labor.** The company may also seek a double benefit from the shared services by gaining some cost savings from the location from which the shared services will operate. So, in addition to creating a shared services model, the company may decide to relocate the services to a lower cost base so it can benefit from lower labor costs.

Alternative Operating Models

Beyond the typical operating models described above, there are a number of alternative operating models of various shapes and sizes that you can consider for your organization's needs. The options are limited only by your imagination. Some may be simple hybrid solutions of insourcing and outsourcing; others could be more inventive, even exotic. The danger of an alternative operating model is that it can become too complicated and ultimately may be unable to achieve the required business outcome. One of my golden rules in business is to always seek a solution with clear accountability and few moving parts. Complexity in an operating model can become a hindrance to a customer-centric organization, requiring high levels of collaboration and accountability to implement CX best practices.

Some of the alternative options, however, may offer certain organizations a better solution than the classic operational models of insourcing and outsourcing. An alternative option is usually selected by an organization that needs to overcome the challenges of each classic model. If executed properly, one of these options can help an organization create a branded experience in the marketplace and elevate its competitiveness.

There are four notable options available in this category—a commercial or business process outsourcing company (BPO), an equity carve-out (IPO or trade sale), and a strategic acquisition. Each is normally conceived as described in the following sections.

BUSINESS PROCESS OUTSOURCING COMPANY (BPO)

In this case, an organization has common business processes that it currently performs in-house and funds as a regular profit-and-loss cost department, but then realizes the in-house operation is inefficient and not operating using best practices. After reviewing the various options, the organization decides it would like to either outsource the function or invest further in the department to raise standards. The organization seeks control because it considers the processes as core functions, but it does not like the idea of increasing costs to improve standards. In the end, the organization decides to pursue an alternative: creating a new legal entity by partnering with an outsourcing specialist and jointly offering its services to the open marketplace.

This option enables the organization to fix its best-practices issues by utilizing the intellectual property of the partner organization. At the same time, it will be able to offset the costs of the former department by generating new revenue from clients and potentially making a profit with the new company.

This model has proven to be highly successful for organizations like GE, which originally formed Genpact to service its own lines of business but later—because it had become successful at delivering quality services efficiently—began offering BPO services to external business customers. Genpact was eventually listed on the NYSE in 2007, ten years after its founding. Its total revenue in 2016 was estimated to be in the vicinity of $2.62 billion.

However, not all ventures using this model have been as successful as Genpact. To make a BPO successful, careful evaluation of certain components is required:

- **Size.** The department that is being converted into an outsourcing entity needs to be sizeable enough to create the necessary revenues so the new entity can become commercially viable. For example, an organization with enough work for a 500-seat contact center will have a better chance of creating a business process outsourcing (BPO) company than will an organization with only enough work for fifty seats.

- **Expertise.** Attempting to establish an outsourcing company without prior experience or knowledge is likely to lead to failure. Do not assume new customers will come to your new entity simply because of your reputation elsewhere in the marketplace.

- **Flexibility.** The creation of this new outsourcing entity will require changes to the existing operations. The new equity partner is likely to make changes in areas such as people, processes, and technology. This is necessary if the new entity is going to make a profit without increasing costs for the delivery of services. By scaling outward, the parent organization is able to benefit from this new entity because the profits it generates from other customers will offset the cost of providing services to the parent company. The organization benefits from the efficiencies derived from serving multiple customers with similar requirements.

EQUITY CARVE-OUT—IPO

When a company decides to spin off or sell an existing department to a third party, it is called an *equity carve-out*. This third party can be a single company, or the department can be offered to the public via an initial public offering (IPO). The latter is usually only possible if the new subsidiary company to be carved out is worthy of public investment interest. Often a noncore part of the business is sold off to raise capital for core functions of the business or another venture. The classic 2001 carve-out case study was Philip Morris and the IPO of its partial holding in its subsidiary Kraft Foods. Philip Morris managed to retain control of Kraft Foods by selling only 15 percent of the company and using the proceeds to reduce debt incurred from acquiring Nabisco Holdings a year earlier.[23] Few companies take the IPO option, because few companies have sizable entities to warrant this type of sale.

EQUITY CARVE-OUT—TRADE SALE

The alternative option most companies adopt is a trade sale of an asset to a single organization. In the case of business services, the asset's value needs to be protected from erosion. To achieve this outcome, a separate agreement is made with the purchaser of the asset to guarantee services for a fixed, significant term (usually ten years minimum), ensuring revenues are realized by the purchaser at expected rates. The purchaser benefits because the equity increases in proportion to the revenues and profits it can generate. An example is the sale of the back-office functions of Goldman Sachs to State Street Corporation for $550 million in 2009. The proceeds from the sale helped Goldman Sachs repay part of the $782 billion it borrowed to bail out the company during the 2008 subprime mortgage crisis.

STRATEGIC ACQUISITION

Some organizations seek an alternative operational model when they are facing market pressure due to changes in their business model or technology that have resulted in dwindling revenues. An organization may have a significant number of employees and want to remain significant in size.

....

23   Espen Eckbo and Karin S. Thorburn, "Corporate Restructuring: Breakups and LBOs," Tuck School of Business at Dartmouth: European Corporate Governance Institute (ECGI), *Handbook of Corporate Finance: Empirical Corporate Finance*, vol. 2 (2008): 444–82.

It may consider outsourcing and downsizing, but an alternative approach could be a strategic acquisition that allows the organization to enter a new market or acquire a new competency. These acquisitions often require a strategic shift in order for the organization to maintain sustainability.

Strategic acquisitions are becoming more prevalent for organizations that feel the impact of digital disruption. Acquisitions are often a complicated and difficult option, but they can ultimately lead to survival by providing a new competitive dimension for the organization. One leading example is Xerox, which decided to enter the BPO industry by acquiring ACS for $6.4 billion in 2009. This strategic shift enabled the company to leverage some of its assets and avoid diminishing value from maintaining its existing business offering. More recently, Microsoft acquired LinkedIn for $26.2 billion in an attempt to capitalize on the business network's access to Microsoft product buyers.[24]

Performing a Cost-Benefit Analysis

As your organization develops a greater understanding of the characteristics that define excellent customer experience, your evaluation of the most suitable operating model will mature. Each of these options—from the traditional to the alternative—will have a significant impact on your ability to implement a sustainable branded CX program. And the innovation of operating models is not limited to the options outlined in this chapter.

The design of an operating model should be specifically customized to perfectly suit the needs of your organization. To achieve this outcome, the cost-benefit analysis should answer the following questions:

- How well do the various options fit into your overall customer experience strategy and business objectives?
- What are the primary drivers for your decision making? Are they strategic, tactical, or a combination of both? One driver must outweigh the other. Giving equal weighting to this question will likely lead to a flawed outcome.

....

24   "Microsoft to Acquire LinkedIn," Microsoft News Center, June 13, 2016, https://news.microsoft .com/2016/06/13/microsoft-to-acquire-linkedin/#sm.000014lkqw1b8bco2qdt4u0fxzfd2.

- What investment is required, and does this investment fit into the shareholder risk profile?
- What is the worst-case scenario? Don't base your decision making on the best-case scenario—it will only lead to embarrassment in the board room.
- What is the most likely payback for this investment?
- What are the key risks, and are they likely to be acceptable to the board?
- Does the operating model deliver the desired branded customer experiences?
- Do you have the resources and bandwidth to execute? If you intend to use mostly internal resources, this could lead to a major shift in focus from your core business. Working with a partner can ensure you are able to execute without loss of focus on your core business.
- What is your exit strategy? The lack of an exit strategy, or not knowing the triggers for exit, can lead to poor long-term outcomes.
- How will you enforce service levels, and what are the customer implications if they are not met?

Answering these questions will enable you to fine-tune your thinking and select the operating model for your organization that will deliver the most effective, efficient, and consistent branded customer experience.

KEY LESSONS

- Outsourcing can make an organization more agile in responding to customers' changing demands.
- Before you determine the best methodology to evaluate and manage outsourcing vendors, you need to ask, "Should my organization outsource at all?" and "If we don't outsource, what other options are available?"
- Executives who understand the relationship between outsourcing and effective customer experience implementation will consider a

multitude of variables as they evaluate potential outsourcing solutions.

- When making a decision about outsourcing for your organization, you need to consider the balance between immediate financial gain and long-term brand consequences.

- Customer-centric organizations able to clearly articulate their core business in terms of the value they deliver for customers have the foundation to determine properly whether a business process should be retained in-house, delivered by a third party, or performed using some other form of hybrid solution.

- Determining whether a business process is a core function and whether it impacts customers is critical when choosing an outsourcing solution.

- Operational readiness determines the organization's ability to deliver the business process according to your CX program's standards.

- There are multiple operating models for performing certain business processes, each with various forms; the main options are delivering a business process in-house or outsourcing it.

- If your organization has identified a large amount of duplication in its divisions, you may decide to centralize some functions and share some employees, facilities, and equipment that perform common tasks, such as recruitment and accounting.

- An organization that needs to overcome the challenges inherent in the classic operating models of insourcing or outsourcing may select an alternative operating model.

- The design of an operating model should be specifically customized to perfectly address the needs of an organization.

CHAPTER 17

Effective Governance of
Outsourcing Relationships

An organization that uses a structured framework based on best practices for effectively managing its outsourcing relationships has a higher probability of a satisfactory experience with its chosen providers. Gartner analysts' research has indicated that successful outsourcing is indeed built on a "network of relationships, not transactions" and that outsourcing governance is the most important factor in determining the success of an outsourcing engagement.[25] Yet when you look at the number of organizations that are unhappy with their outsource partner—42 percent of CIOs are dissatisfied due to poorly developed, under-budgeted, and under-resourced governance models, according to a survey by EquaTerra—it becomes clear that this is an area of concern.

A strained relationship between your organization and a provider detracts from the value generated by the provider and can compromise your customer experience objectives. Any expected benefits, such as reduced costs, greater innovation, or more agility, would be greatly endangered if the relationship degraded to mistrust, conflict, and disagreement. The demise of an outsourcing relationship incurs greater monitoring, auditing, and issue management by the organization, making it impossible to extract the expected value from the engagement. Given that poor management is one of the fundamental issues behind troublesome outsourcing engagements, I have devoted this chapter to a checklist that will help you identify any gaps in the best-practice management of your organization's outsourcing relationships.

....

25   Linda Cohen and Allie Young, *Multisourcing: Moving Beyond Outsourcing to Achieve Growth and Agility* (Cambridge, MA: Harvard Business School Press, 2005), 198–203.

Components of an Outsourcing Governance Model

An organization typically spends a significant amount of time and energy in selecting a provider, but very little in developing an outsourcing governance model or framework that will ensure you extract the expected value from an outsourcing relationship. This governance model assigns a team within the organization the responsibility of ensuring the expected value can be achieved. Members of the CX governance team should also be part of the outsourcing governance model, to ensure their interests are properly communicated to service providers that have an impact on the CX program.

To ensure your organization has the capacity to work effectively with an outsource partner and achieve the desired value from this collaboration, you need to develop a governance model before engaging the provider. Some organizations make the mistake of forgetting to perform an internal evaluation of how they will manage the relationship beyond procurement. Processes are not defined for managing the provider, and stakeholders are not trained to manage outsource partners. This leads to haphazard practices and poor management of the relationship. The application of best-practice governance models, on the other hand, provides clarity and structure to aid both parties.

A well-defined governance model will have seven components: a high-level mission statement, KPIs that are aligned with relationship goals, a fit-for-purpose governance model, engaged stakeholders, a separate governance team, defined team member roles and responsibilities, and standard reports and formats for managing information.

I. A HIGH-LEVEL MISSION STATEMENT FOR THE OUTSOURCING RELATIONSHIP

Many outsourcing engagements deteriorate because of a fundamental lack of understanding over long-term objectives. Develop a clear vision and mission statement about why you have entered into an outsourcing relationship and what business outcomes you expect from the engagement. This may change down the track, but only a solid starting point can give both parties shared goals to work toward.

2. ALIGNED KPIS

Misalignment of KPIs for the goals of the outsourcing relationship creates tension and undermines the ability of both parties to achieve those goals. This is particularly relevant for an organization seeking to differentiate itself in customer experience. If your organization is not yet fully customer centric, parts of the business may still utilize performance indicators based on operational efficiency, with minimal attention paid to customer outcome performance metrics. If these outdated KPIs form the basis for deliverables expected from the provider, then the provider may achieve the operational efficiency targets but still deliver a poor experience for customers.

Misaligned KPIs often stem from a lack of thought about the outsource provider's role within the larger strategic objectives of the organization. The provider will work toward achieving whatever KPIs are listed in the agreement, so be sure these metrics reflect your new customer-centric approach in order to achieve real value from the provider and deliver it to stakeholders.

3. A FIT-FOR-PURPOSE GOVERNANCE MODEL

The governance model for your outsourcing relationship needs to reflect the size and complexity of the outsourced function, and especially its impact on customers. Determine how strategically important the engagement is, and you will be able to identify the model that will capture the desired benefits over the term of the relationship. A temporary engagement with low customer impact will not need the same level of involvement from the same number of stakeholders as a strategic, long-term, high-impact outsourcing arrangement. Each governance model should be fit-for-purpose, meaning it extracts the expected value from the outsource partner for the function it has been engaged to perform.

4. ENGAGED STAKEHOLDERS

Just as you involved company stakeholders to develop your strategic CX program, you will need to involve people with vested interests in the outsourcing relationship. Identifying and engaging the right stakeholders, both from your organization and from the service provider, is critical for ensuring mutual involvement and desire to make the relationship work. Not all stakeholders need to be involved at the same level, but forgetting to involve even a minority stakeholder could lead to mistrust and conflict. When identifying stakeholders, you should select influential and senior employees who may not be directly involved but who can influence the outcome of the relationship should it face problems. Independent members without a direct vested interest can also act as arbitrators to resolve any issues with the provider.

5. A GOVERNANCE TEAM SEPARATE FROM OPERATIONS

When using an outsourcing governance model, you should always have two teams in place: operational and governance. Best-practice organizations use the governance team to oversee corporate structures and the operational team to report on operational issues of the business. The separation of the teams avoids potential conflicts of interest and ensures the necessary distance so decisions are made based on facts. There will be some crossover: The governance team may include some operational staff to assist nonoperational staff in better understanding the issues at hand, and operational staff can be included in governance meetings to explain issues without making important decisions regarding the relationship. Alternatively, some larger outsourcing engagements may require the appointment of a steering committee to make operational decisions, and may leave the governance team to make nonoperational, strategic decisions regarding the engagement.

6. WELL-DEFINED ROLES AND RESPONSIBILITIES

Although this may seem an obvious component, in some outsourcing engagements the roles and responsibilities are simply not defined. To avoid overlap, confusion among team members over their functions, and poor accountability, it is important to present clearly delineated roles and responsibilities for your teams. Effective governance of the engagement can be achieved only if team members know the who, what, and how of contributing to the engagement.

7. STANDARD INFORMATION MANAGEMENT

Good governance requires good record keeping and follow-up. It also requires stakeholders to base their decisions on empirical evidence and not on opinion. The governance team should outline the types of reports required in order to make fact-based decisions. These reports should also provide the governance team with the knowledge of how the organization plans to successfully extract the value from the relationship in line with the mission statement. The governance team should identify the frequency of meetings up front, send agendas and supporting reports prior to meetings, and share meeting minutes with specific action items and timelines for completion.

Applying these seven components of best practices to your governance model will help you better manage your outsourcing relationship. Good governance should proactively drive the relationship toward both parties achieving the desired value outcomes.

Taking an Active Role in Your Outsourcing Relationship

Value extraction will accelerate when the governance team plays an active role in developing the outsourcing relationship. A well-structured governance model will function better if the governance team takes a number of actions to support it.

FOSTER TRUST

The chief deciding factor for the effectiveness of an outsourcing relationship lies in the ability of the organization to trust the outsource partner. Building trust takes time and consistent behavior from both parties, but the governance team should proactively seek to grow trust with the provider rather than passively wait for trust to develop. Active development of the outsourcing relationship should involve developing a plan for building trust into the relationship through a partnership approach, under the guidance of the head of the governance team.

DEFINE TRANSPARENCY LEVELS

When an outsourcing relationship is in place, transparency usually becomes a topic of discussion. Often the service agreement will include a mandatory, reasonable level of transparency so the organization stays informed about the contracted services of the provider.

If there is any reason to question the trustworthiness of the provider, however, the level of transparency required may increase significantly. When an organization lacks trust in the relationship, or when a provider is not delivering components of the contract, it may be necessary to revert to full transparency. Certainly, if the provider is suspected of providing misleading information, then increased transparency is justified. But to avoid damage to the outsourcing relationship, the level of transparency should be defined from the outset and should be reserved for relevant, business-related reporting.

REDEFINE BUSINESS PROCESSES TO SUIT OUTSOURCING

A good governance structure will also define new business processes that appropriately incorporate the outsource provider into the organization's operations. If new procedures are not implemented, the various services may not be properly documented or signed off on. To ensure that services are uninterrupted when the engagement begins, individuals must be trained in the application of these new processes. Including sufficient flexibility in the agreement can accommodate variations to services as business needs change.

Having a governance structure in place without updating business processes to reflect the onboarding of the outsource provider is insufficient. These new processes should apply to the operations area, particularly when the organization's internal operations team is required to engage with the outsource provider to deliver part or all of a business process.

UTILIZE TECHNOLOGY

You can help effectively govern the outsourcing relationship with technology that properly captures critical operational documents, reporting, issues, and invoices. This software would be ideally integrated into internal enterprise report planning systems, but can easily provide both parties with visibility on performance, issues, and long-term objectives. Cloud-based software is now readily available, making it easier than ever to provide visibility of critical documents for parties in different locations.

CREATE A CLEAR PLAN FOR DEALING WITH ISSUES

Finally, any good governance structure needs a clearly documented action plan for addressing nonperformance and other legal issues. Develop a plan based on the governance model to resolve issues and ensure the provider achieves the desired outcomes. It is important not to alienate the provider with a rigid approach, as this could lead to a disengaged provider only willing to do the bare minimum as outlined in the agreement. If a misunderstanding or other barrier prevents the provider from going the extra mile, then your organization may not gain the desired value from the relationship.

Take a partnership approach to outsourcing so you can work cooperatively with the provider to achieve common goals and remedy any aspect of the service that does not meet expectations. Keeping the relationship on track and working cooperatively is a better outcome than taking a legal path and potentially creating irreparable damage.

The effective management of the relationship is the primary instrument determining success or failure in outsourcing arrangements. Given its importance, I have dedicated the next chapter exclusively to how to have a successful relationship with outsource providers.

KEY LESSONS

- The demise of an outsourcing relationship incurs greater monitoring, auditing, and issue management by the organization, making it impossible to extract the expected value from the engagement.
- You should develop a governance model before engaging an outsource provider.

- There are seven components to good governance:
  1. A high-level mission statement for the outsourcing relationship
  2. Aligned KPIs
  3. A fit-for-purpose governance model
  4. Engaged stakeholders
  5. A governance team separate from operations
  6. Well-defined roles and responsibilities
  7. Standard management information

- Active development of the outsourcing relationship should involve developing a plan for building trust into the relationship.
- A good governance structure is supported by appropriate and well-defined business processes.
- Effective governance over outsourcing relationships is best supported using technology that can effectively capture critical operational documents, reporting, issues, and invoices.
- Any good governance structure needs to include a clearly documented action plan for addressing nonperformance and other legal issues.

CHAPTER 18

Managing Outsourcing Relationships

Successful outsourcing is all about relationships and how they are managed. As in any relationship, both parties—the organization and the outsource provider—expect to gain benefits. Without a clear understanding from the outset of what these benefits are for each party, the outcome is likely to be disappointing. Unclear expectations will inevitably lead to disengagement with the vendor, and your organization will need to select an alternate provider or a different operating model. Either option is costly to the organization and can have a negative impact on your customers.

This chapter explores current and future trends in outsourcing, and discusses both the negative consequences associated with outsourcing and the opposite arguments for implementing such relationships. It also outlines ten principles, which I have formulated based on decades of experience providing and designing outsourcing services, to guide a successful relationship between organization and vendor.

Outsourcing in Modern-Day Organizations

Leading business strategist Peter Drucker famously wrote in the 1990s that organizations need to "do what [they] do best and outsource the rest"—a strategy that has been adopted by businesses all over the world. A recent survey identified that approximately 90 percent of companies outsource some component of their business.[26] This widespread practice has helped organizations accelerate their growth and reduce costs over the past thirty years.

....

26   Michael F. Corbett, *The Outsourcing Revolution: Why It Makes Sense and How to Do It Right* (Chicago: Dearborn, 2004).

Yet outsourcing has come under close scrutiny recently, with many economists and business strategists arguing against the value it can generate for an organization. According to a 2015 survey arranged by Sourcing Line Computer Economics from the Associated Press, 89 percent of economists believe job outsourcing hurts the economy.[27] Over the past decade, amid increasing analysis of the value generated from outsourcing, some organizations have returned components of their business—typically customer-facing ones—from outsource vendors back to in-house operations. As more organizations grapple with the changed competitive landscape, debate over the benefits of outsourcing will continue to occupy executive agendas.

Outsourcing will not disappear anytime soon. It plays an integral role in helping organizations compete effectively. The level of understanding about the role of outsourcing in modern-day organizations is in flux. This new thinking has brought new expectations of outsourcing vendors. Providers of outsourced services need to evolve their service offerings to adapt to these new organizational expectations. More organizations are moving away from traditional hands-off relationships and seeking greater participation with the outsourcing vendor. This is particularly relevant when the business process outsourced has a direct impact on customers. These changing expectations are largely driven by the acknowledgment of customer experience management as a competitive force.

I expect to see dimensions of outsourcing, on both the organizational and the vendor sides, return to increased relevance in business strategy. This trend will revolve around value. The trade-off between cost and benefit is ultimately what will determine the need for outsourcing. When the deliverables provided by a vendor are more valuable than the cost and effort combined, then outsourcing is preferred. The types of questions to determine the value of outsourcing were highlighted in the previous chapter, and these provide a guide as to whether you should even consider outsourcing for your organization. Assuming that some business process in your organization will be outsourced, whether you can extract the expected value from your

27   "Job Overseas Outsourcing Statistics," Sourcing Line Computer Economics, Associated Press, accessed November 16, 2016, http://www.statisticbrain.com/outsourcing-statistics-by-country/.

outsourcing relationship will depend on your ability to follow best practices. Not having a well-aligned relationship with your outsource provider can compromise your entire CX program and prevent you from achieving market-differentiated customer experiences over the long term.

Ten Principles for Successful Outsourcing

When selecting an outsource partner, your organization should look for significant characteristics that indicate the partnership will be successful. Compatibility with your organizational culture, for example, plays a major role in determining the longevity of the relationship and increases the probability of extracting value from it. The following ten principles are an overview of the previous two chapters, intended to provide both parties with a guide on how to make outsourcing work. Rather than go into how to select an outsource partner, the guiding principles focus on the foundation and management of the outsourcing relationship, as this tends to be the root cause of many problems.

I. ASSESS THE VALUE EXPECTED FROM OUTSOURCING

Too often organizations start outsourcing without properly evaluating the business process in question and determining whether outsourcing is even the correct path. They frequently engage with vendors based on organizational mandates driven out of short-term necessity rather than strategic positioning. As a result, the contract is normally awarded to the lowest bidder offering comparative services. Very little attention is given to the relationship or the strategic value the vendor can deliver in a long-term relationship. This short-term view of outsourcing relationships tends to hinder both parties from encouraging the relationship to mature and deliver new value.

A partnering organization must develop, before engaging with the provider, a thorough understanding of the potential value it expects from the outsourcing relationship. Without it, the services delivered by the vendor will be constantly questioned by stakeholders in the organization, creating tension and taking the relationship in opposing directions. This lack of strategic vision can mean the vendor's services are seen only in terms of lower costs rather than the value created for the organization's customers. The strategic basis for outsourcing forms the foundation for the relationship between both parties and clarifies the expectations from the relationship, beyond the rudimentary benefits associated with outsourcing.

2. TREAT OUTSOURCE PARTNERS AS PART OF YOUR TEAM

A successful outsourcing relationship involves a sense of ownership on behalf of the individuals or department managing the relationship with the outsource partner. It is not sufficient to consider an outsource partner as an entity that is providing services to your company. Instead, the outsource partner must be included as a team member and viewed as a colleague of equal standing.

A breakdown in the organization–vendor relationship often happens when the organization dominates the vendor and assumes a superior position because it writes the checks. This abuse of economic power undermines the true partnership, and the relationship evolves into one of master and slave, with clear dominance by the organization. In some cases this dominance leads to subversive acts by the vendor, such as falsifying operational reports and disguising problems. The root cause of this behavior is fear of the consequences imposed by the organization—namely, the fear of not getting paid for services rendered. The organizational representatives may feel they are tightly controlling the vendor through this dominance, but ultimately they are hindering the possibility of extracting value from the relationship.

3. SET REALISTIC GOALS

Another destructive act is when an organization sets unrealistic goals to test or show up an outsource partner. This type of action is unproductive and leads to tension and suspicion in the relationship between organization and provider. Remember, the outsource partner is an *extension* of your company; setting unrealistic goals negatively affects your company at the same time.

Outsourcing providers are a group of individuals who are committed to providing their best to service your organization, and it is quite rare that a partner does not have this work ethos. Outsource partners are normally specialists in a particular area of business, but this does not make them perfect. Expecting excellence is one thing; expecting perfection leads to frustration and disappointment. Providers are not immune from typical mishaps you may experience in your own organization. Expecting them to be infallible, and then punishing them for any problems, achieves nothing. A realistic level of failings should be expected and tolerated as a normal outcome from the vendor services.

4. FOCUS ON THE SOLUTION

When a problem arises, focus on how to solve it. Although this may sound like a simple and obvious principle, organizations tend to focus on the problem more when an outsource provider is responsible than if it had occurred internally. It's natural to expect a higher level of operational delivery from an outsource provider, but problems occur regardless of the provider's experience. Don't allow unrealistic expectations to blind you and create a barrier between you and a solution to the problem.

Moving toward solutions is critical in making an outsourcing relationship successful. Ideally, any problems are solved through cooperation. The accountability of the problem may rest with the outsource provider, but the organization's involvement in devising a solution will help build a stronger relationship between the two parties, shaping their relationship and the direction it takes. Building trust takes time and is achieved through the actions of both parties. Resolving problems by focusing on the solution enables trust to develop.

5. SIGN LONGER-TERM AGREEMENTS

One fundamental mistake when establishing a relationship with an outsource partner is the brevity of the contract. The short-term nature of outsourcing contracts is often an indicator that the organization has yet to define the value it expects from outsourcing. Service level agreements bind the provider to deliver services in accordance with set standards. Instead of using an SLA to define the limits of the relationship, however, the organization should view the agreement as only one component of the relationship.

The commercial agreement should provide enough time to enable both parties to deliver longer-term, sustainable value for the organization. When only a short term is agreed upon, it is difficult for each party to invest in the relationship. The relationship is fundamentally flawed, because neither party is willing to invest the energy and resources for long-term success. The term need not be ten years long, but a minimum of five years should provide both parties with good reason to invest in the relationship and should enable the organization to extract value from it. A long term will ensure a true sense of commitment by both the organization and the outsource partner and will enable a higher level of trust to develop between them.

The longer length of an agreement does not compromise the organization's ability to change strategy should market conditions or internal company thinking shift. Although the intention to work collaboratively with a strategic partner should be clearly communicated in the terms of the original agreement, flexibility to terminate the arrangement exists within all modern-day contracts. An agreement of greater duration gives both parties the necessary time to perfect the delivery of services with a solid understanding of what is expected from the provider to become a seamless extension of the brand.

6. ESTABLISH A SOLID GOVERNANCE MODEL

As discussed in chapter 17, good governance of the outsourcing relationship cannot be underestimated. It ensures clarity of communication and accountability from both sides. Outsourcing relationships have a tendency to deteriorate when there are too many different individuals managing the relationship. From the outset, there should be a well-defined framework that is understood by all and that outlines the involvement of all stakeholders, defining what they will do, how they will do it, and when they will report back. Poor governance of an outsourcing relationship leads to unclear communications and unmet expectations. Establishing good governance and maintaining discipline throughout the outsourcing engagement increases the probability the organization will successfully realize the value it expected.

7. LEVERAGE THE PROVIDER'S HIGH-PERFORMANCE CULTURE

Outsource providers that cannot demonstrate a high-performance culture are unlikely to deliver any meaningful value other than simple cost savings. A provider needs to demonstrate not only that it has a culture that matches the partner organization's, but also that it knows and can apply the principles of a high-performance culture. Of the several ways to identify a high-performance culture before you engage with a provider, one of the easiest is simply to ask employees working for the provider. Reliable knowledge of the vendor's culture ensures a decision can be made to engage the provider most likely to add value.

As outlined previously, highly engaged employees are willing to go the extra mile to deliver consistently branded experiences for customers. This requirement extends to the outsourcing provider. A provider that is able to demonstrate a high-performance culture will have highly engaged staff. Ideally, the provider also should have a customer-centric focus for conducting business and should provide examples of how this is practiced. Aligning the organization with a customer-centric provider means the organization can leverage this culture to help implement its own customer experience program.

8. LEVERAGE THE PROVIDER'S SPECIALTY AND EXPERIENCE

A business process is outsourced when it can't be delivered internally because of a lack of capability, a lack of resources, or both. Typically, as discussed in chapter 16, the outsourced process is not considered a core competency of the organization, but a function that the provider should have greater capability to perform. After all, it is a core of the provider's business. Once the organization selects a provider for its expertise, it's important to keep acknowledging that expertise. Some organizations, immediately after selecting the provider for its expertise, make the mistake of instructing the provider on how to operate its own business.

The ability to leverage the provider's area of expertise and experience adds to the value of the outsourcing relationship. If the organization does not trust the provider's track record in delivery of services, then there is a fundamental flaw in the selection criteria. If the organization does trust the process and the provider, it needs to give the provider some latitude in how it delivers services. Respectfully standing back and observing how the provider works is sometimes the best path to learning when outsourcing.

9. SEEK INNOVATIVE SOLUTIONS

Technology has played a major role in disruption of multiple industries. Outsource providers should be able to demonstrate how they use technology to innovatively deliver their services more effectively. Providers using innovative solutions are more likely to remain relevant for the organization for a longer period of time. The ability to innovate highlights the potential of the provider to contribute new value for the organization. A provider with a strong track record for innovation can compensate for the organization's deficiency in designing new operational solutions for customers.

10. BUILD TRUST AND FLEXIBILITY

It does not matter how many lawyers and advisors you speak to, or how ironclad your service level agreement is—there is no substitute for building a trusting relationship imbued with common goals. For a partnership to work, trust needs to exist on both sides. Although this principle is intangible, it remains one of the most essential ingredients to ensuring a successful outsource partnership.

The agreement formed with the vendor should reflect your desired relationship with that vendor. A clear understanding of the outsourcing relationship, its value, and what is expected from it enables the organization to form clear expectations for the provider from the outset. Clarity in expectations ensures no surprises for the provider and provides the foundation for trust to develop.

If the contract is established correctly from the outset, then you are likely to file it away once it is signed and rarely refer to it again. The legal agreement should not form the basis of determining the relationship or be pulled out to determine every bit of detail related to the delivery of services. The organization–provider relationships that generate the greatest value are based on mutual respect and trust. There is an expectation sometimes that requesting a deliverable not included in the agreement would be completed as a "value add" to the client, without referring to the agreement. On other occasions, the organization may give the provider new paying work because of the flexibility on other requests made outside of the agreement. This two-way level of trust and flexibility enhances the relationship and brings the provider closer to being considered part of the senior leadership team. Trust is earned, and as long as there is good footing, the long-term agreement should yield a positive and mutually beneficial understanding between the two parties.

Outsourcing has its place in any modern organization and will remain an important aspect of how organizations achieve competitive advantage. Sceptics of outsourcing may point the finger at the vendor and claim that no provider is capable of delivering the process as well as an organization can do it internally. This argument may be true for core functions of the organization, but as more organizations change their definition of *core business* in accordance with customer experience outcomes, the types of business processes considered suitable for outsourcing will change too.

In any case, effective outsourcing starts with the organization, not the vendor. The onus rests with the organization to evaluate vendors correctly and establish the governance model that will extract the expected values from the outsourcing relationship. A failure to predetermine the desired value from outsourcing often leads to poor vendor selection and poorly conceived, short-term agreements that conflict with the strategic value expected by some of the stakeholders in the organization.

In the majority of cases where outsourcing has not worked well, there has been a fundamental flaw in the relationship itself. Outsourcing is all about establishing a relationship and effectively managing that relationship on both sides. Unfortunately there has been minimal literature on this subject, as the focus for selecting an outsource partner has traditionally been on cost and service level agreements. Over time, a better appreciation of what elements compose a successful outsourcing engagement may reflect a balanced mix, by incorporating relationship management as part of the equation.

This chapter concludes our discussion of customer experience implementation. The next section of the book examines the future of customer experience management. A solid understanding of the forces shaping this future will allow you to modify aspects of your CX program to capitalize on emerging trends.

·· **KEY LESSONS** ··

- Successful outsourcing is about relationships and how they are managed.
- The level of understanding about the role of outsourcing in the modern-day organization has evolved as the competitive landscape has changed, as have new expectations from outsource vendors.
- The trade-off between cost and benefit is ultimately what will be debated in deciding whether to outsource.
- There are ten principles for successful outsourcing:
    1. Assess the value expected from outsourcing before engaging with a vendor.
    2. Treat outsource partners as part of your team.
    3. Set realistic goals, and do not be quick to chastise when a goal is not met.
    4. When a problem arises, focus on the solution.
    5. Sign longer-term agreements with your outsource partners.
    6. Establish a solid governance model for managing the out-sourcing relationship.
    7. Leverage the provider's high-performance culture.
    8. Leverage the specialty and experience of the provider.
    9. Seek innovative solutions.
    10. Build trust and flexibility.

- The onus rests with the organization to evaluate vendors correctly and establish the governance model that will extract the expected values from the outsourcing relationship.

Part 3

THE FUTURE OF CUSTOMER EXPERIENCE MANAGEMENT (CEM)

CHAPTER 19

How Data Will Define
the Future of CEM

The final part of this book is dedicated to the future of customer experience and the directions it will most likely take. Nobody can precisely predict the future, but a careful evaluation of the forces shaping customer experience can produce a reliable forecast. Understanding the likely impact of these forces on branded customer experience should provide you with the necessary insights to position your organization so it can capitalize on future trends.

To better understand the future of customer experience management (CEM), we first need to acknowledge its history and why it has become a popular business practice.

Understanding the History of CEM

The past twenty years have seen an evolution in how businesses view, analyze, and manage our customers. Customer experience management began with the adoption and practice of customer relationship management (CRM): the discipline of building loyalty by focusing on improving the *relationship* between a company and its customers, through personalized marketing. Although the concepts of CRM emerged in the 1960s, they really started acquiring stature in the 1980s and 1990s when authors like Don Peppers published books on the subject of one-to-one marketing. The mid-'90s saw the movement gain momentum largely because technology had caught up with personalized mass marketing. Previously, companies had not adopted the ideas due to technological limitations.

The evolution from CRM to CEM was driven by advancements in

technology and changes in consumer behavior, similar to how the Internet has changed how consumers behave before and after a purchase. Large numbers of consumers now research products and services prior to making a purchasing decision, and some make online purchases, bypassing traditional brick-and-mortar channels. Later, these consumers use review sites to post opinions about items they purchased. Social media also has created a means for customers to publicly voice their views about products and services and to reach large groups of consumers with common interests.

All these Internet-related changes have led to a shift in what is considered important in the management of customer relationships. The proliferation of information and applications on the Internet has also changed consumer expectations. Now consumers demand increased channels to conduct business, and they expect organizations to take their reviews of products and services seriously. For companies, this has meant dealing with the challenge of serving customers across multiple channels and delivering consistent quality of service.

In addition, organizations have become painfully aware that review websites provide a large audience for any disgruntled customer. Power has shifted from the masters of marketing and brand management within an organization to a lone customer with a large following on social media and review websites. This paradigm shift has formed the basis for a lot of the ideas behind customer experience management. In a growing conversationalist culture, customer word of mouth now defines a lot of what is known about a brand.

Simultaneous with this shifting control over brands, globalization has started to impact companies. Countries have formed free trade agreements to take advantage of emerging markets and capabilities. Advanced technology and lower cost bases have driven many organizations to transfer manufacturing to new countries.

By the time these new countries developed their manufacturing capabilities, in about 2008, it had become apparent that organizations could no longer rely on product differentiation. The ease of manufacturing increased the level of competition in most industries. Meanwhile, e-commerce was gaining momentum, and with globalization in full force, organizations could now compete without ever manufacturing anything or selling goods through a physical store. The combination of technological evolution, globalization, and shifting consumer behavior changed the competitive landscape.

Defining how best to compete in an age characterized by point-click-buy behavior led thought leaders to isolate the emotional relationship with customers as a unique differentiator. Business publications started highlighting customer experience as the final battleground for differentiation. This concept is based on the notion that customer *experiences,* if properly managed, are unique and define the *emotional* relationship with a brand. Imitating this emotional relationship through experiences is difficult for a competitor.

CRM evolved into CEM to address the total sum of customer interactions throughout a customer's life cycle and how important it is to shape a customer's emotions and attitudes toward an organization. The ethos behind customer experience management required organizations to broaden their view of customer service to include experiences at every touch point of the customer's life cycle. Correlations were made between positive emotional experiences and corporate growth. If the organization had a positive emotional experience with its customers, then there was a higher probability customers would continue using its products or services and bring in more business via word-of-mouth recommendations. If a company had consistently negative emotional experiences, then the converse would occur.

CEM evolved into the discipline we know today with the following business goals:

- To determine how competitive an organization is in the marketplace compared with its peers
- To influence the rate at which an organization can acquire new customers and keep existing ones
- To help determine how profitable an organization will be in the future

The possibility that CEM could provide an organization with these insights elevated its importance until it became a leading business practice. These objectives are of equal importance to both business leaders and shareholders. The rise of CEM shifted the focus of customer management away from centralized departments, such as customer care, so that it became the concern of the entire corporation. To achieve this outcome, organizations needed to seek technology solutions that enabled the entire company to deliver experiences to customers that would produce the greatest economic value.

Changed consumer behavior, brought on by the Internet and smartphones, now requires organizations to adopt new technology solutions that monitor and effectively manage customer interactions. This requirement has led to the evolution of data-centric solutions that enable organizations to potentially deliver consistently great branded customer experiences. These solutions highlight the importance of data in the CEM equation.

Intelligent use of customer data enables organizations to take action according to customer expectations and needs. Not knowing what customers value is like a business organization shooting at an invisible target. Data gives an organization the telescopic sight required to aim its efforts at a clearly defined target.

Raw data, and the analytics required to convert it into meaningful information, has become a major force in effective CEM. The maturity of larger data sets accumulated over years of digital usage by consumers has led to new data sets known as *big data*. The manipulation of these large amounts of data from disparate sources has become economically possible only because of the exponential growth in the digitization of information during the past ten years. Organizations now have access to internal customer data and these new big data sets to create and manage customer relationships.

The Rise of Big Data

To truly appreciate the future of customer experience management requires a more in-depth understanding of big data and its likely role in the evolution of CEM. Big data has become prominent as emerging technology has made huge amounts of data not only digital, but available for analysis. This has led to researchers uncovering new insights.

For example, just a few years ago it would have been difficult to know confidently the best time to purchase cheap airfare. Then in 2004 an Internet company called Farecast developed an algorithm to predict the best time to purchase airfare based on destination and time of travel. The company used 12,000 price observations from travel websites to create its predictive model. The Farecast site was making the right fare predictions 75 percent of the time when Microsoft snapped up the company for $115 million and integrated it into its Bing search engine in 2008.[28] The service offering was later ditched by Microsoft in 2014 and replaced by a new, more advanced offering using a sophisticated machine-learning algorithm.

The Farecast example is one of many that depict how big data can be used to influence consumer behavior. Big data could have one of the most significant impacts the business world has ever seen on businesses and how we manage our customers. More and more companies are beginning to understand the economic value of the huge amounts of data they currently possess or can access using the Internet.

What does big data mean for businesses that manage their customers? I believe the answer provides a clue to the next evolutionary step in customer experience management: Just as the evolution from CRM to CEM was driven by the shift in power from organization to consumers, the effective use of data empowers the organization and helps it reclaim some of the lost control over brand definition. The potential for organizations to regain control of consumer behavior using big data is likely to push the boundaries of customer experience management toward customer *prediction* management. The ability to predict customer behavior will become the next logical differentiator for companies.

What Is Customer Prediction Management?

Organizations can now tap in to mass amounts of data stored in silos and identify patterns that reveal correlations between variables. Like Farecast, they are able to develop algorithms that will isolate new value for their consumers and will influence purchasing decisions. Having the tools

....

28   Viktor Mayer-Schonberger and Kenneth Cukier, *Big Data: Revolution That Will Transform How We Live, Work, and Think* (Eamon Dolan/Houghton Mifflin Harcourt, 2013), 5.

to predict, with a high level of confidence, future consumption of goods or services by consumers will shape every aspect of customer experience management. Prediction will become the driving force in generating economic value and giving organizations a competitive edge—particularly when companies learn to use this data with artificial intelligence (which I will explore further in chapter 21), opening up tremendous opportunities to predict consumer behavior and create unique customer experiences.

Steve Jobs's approach to product design at Apple is a great example of the power of customer prediction management. Jobs believed customers didn't really know what they wanted and asking them was a waste of time—by the time a product was developed to accommodate their requests, it would no longer be relevant. So the design and launch of the iPhone and iPad were based purely on predictions about what customers wanted. These predictions, made without the use of big data, led to phenomenal economic success for Apple. Remarkable entrepreneurs like Jobs are rare, and his ability to predict consumer response to new products and services is not something that can be easily taught; however, the intelligent manipulation of data sets creates a discipline that *can* be taught to organizations so they can practice prediction management.

There are also tactical examples of how data is being used to predict consumer behavior. The Australian supermarket chain Coles has begun to use data in an intelligent, tactical way in its campaigns to provide contextual offers to customers, tapping in to its customer data to generate personalized marketing campaigns. The company achieves this by accessing customers' loyalty card database to identify what they buy frequently and from which store. Coles then sends emails with special discounts for only the member's most purchased products and directs the member to his or her most visited store.

This clever use of smaller customer data sets highlights how organizations are starting to use their data to secure greater loyalty among their customers. By personalizing promotions down to the level of product and store location, Coles is contextualizing its marketing to customers, thereby elevating its relevance for them. The impact of these campaigns is largely tactical, because it helps drive new sales into the stores but does not uniquely differentiate the brand of Coles in the marketplace. Still, these contextual offers make the shopper feel special and help create a loyalty barrier around the customer, making it more difficult for a competitor to poach the customer.

Big data has the potential to go one step further. We can hypothesize that if the same small data sets were used with big data, such as purchasing and cellular network data, then Coles could determine the next most common place the same shopper went to after completing his or her purchases at Coles. An analysis of such data would give Coles a greater understanding of what types of products the store should be stocking or, alternatively, which other stores it should partner with to gain greater loyalty and "fence in" its customers. The ability to predict what products or commercial arrangements are likely to appeal to customers beyond its supermarkets would help Coles gain a unique market advantage over competitors. This strategy would enable Coles to move from tactical uses of data to strategic applications, by creating a branded experience for their customers to differentiate Coles from competitors.

The Emergence of Customer Prediction Management

Customer prediction management is no longer an enigma based on hypothetical best guesses. We are now on the verge of making it a formal craft that uses scientific methods to increase the accuracy of predictions. By tapping in to various sources of data, organizations can better understand customers and their behaviors.

Google is one company that understands the value of big data and its potential to influence markets. Every search term used on the Google search engine site is collected and used to predict areas of interest, and this information is used in turn by marketers to determine future demand. Similarly, movie distributors are able to determine the likelihood of box office success using big data analytics to isolate the movie formulas most likely to attract consumers. The economic value of such insights is undeniable.

Big data is about understanding the correlation of two or more variables.

It is not about understanding *why* something happens, but about simply recognizing *that* it happens. Once you confidently understand that an event occurs every time X happens, you have the ability to determine how this affects customers' behavior in the future.

For example, take easily available data about the topics customers access most commonly in a support knowledgebase. If the topic most requested of a car manufacturer is how to convert gasoline engines so they can use cheaper fuel such as liquefied petroleum gas (LPG, or autogas), then there is a high probability that fuel efficiency is a major consideration for customers. Using this insight, manufacturers and marketers can deduce that fuel-efficient vehicles are more likely to appeal to customers than excessive fuel–consuming vehicles. This is a simple example of the data that exists in organizational databases and can be used to predict future customer behavior and shape product design.

The increasing adoption of digital channels by consumers benefits CEM professionals because of the footprint left behind every time a customer uses the channel. These digital imprints give clues about consumer behavior, offering organizations a multitude of information about what customers want and don't want. These clues are embedded in the hordes of data contained in data warehouses and are available from organizational databases or websites that sell big data. The clues come in many forms, ranging from the type and tone of conversations used by customers when making calls into the contact center, to topics of interest based on a number of "likes" on Facebook.

Customer experience management going forward will likely be about the ability to harness these digital clues and then apply scientific methods to make educated predictions about what customers are likely to want in the future. The effective analysis of multiple data sets to predict and manage future customer behavior will ultimately determine the future competitiveness and sustainability of organizations in most industry sectors. Predicting future customer behavior and creating products and services to *elevate* customer experience is the logical evolutionary step for organizations that wish to achieve competitive advantage.

Customer Prediction Management as a Future Competitive Advantage

CEM is about how well organizations interact with their customers and the ability to create positive experiences throughout the customer life cycle. The customer journey narrative is typically written in the present tense to capture what is *currently* occurring. If the next evolutionary stage is to *predict and manage* how customers will feel about products and services in the *future*, defining the customer journey in terms of future customer aspirations and desires will enable the organization to better plan and release value propositions to achieve first-mover advantage.

The supply of big data has increased the capability to tap in to multiple disparate sources of data to devise new insights on consumer behavior. Telefonica, one of the largest telecom operators in the world, is now monetizing the massive amounts of data captured from its network of customer locations by selling anonymous data to retailers through a subsidiary company called Telefonica Digital Insights. Predicting the future using scientific means will soon become a common practice for retailers and other organizations. It's not yet an exact science, but it will be refined over time using modified algorithms, artificial intelligence, and innovative use of technology.

Customer prediction management is not only going to be a reality, but is fast becoming an important competitive advantage for organizations. The ability to accurately predict future customer behavior, and to release products and services to capitalize on this knowledge before competitors do, will position organizations as market leaders. Disciplines such as behavioral analytics and speech analytics are likely to be combined into a single category known as *prediction management.* The practice and importance of this discipline will be elevated in the typical business organization when it becomes identified as a key enabler for the innovation engine.

Predictive management and innovation go hand in hand. An organization will not be able to innovate if it does not have the facts to support why an organization should make investments in any particular innovation idea. Predictive analytics fuel innovation and help focus the efforts of organizations, giving products and services a higher probability of success in the marketplace.

Historically, organizations have relied on a high degree of experience, instinct, and anecdotal facts to determine what products and services to release and which channels to use. The risk of making an ill-conceived investment was high. Predictive analytics can dramatically reduce the commercial risks associated with launching new value offerings. The ability to accurately match products and services with future customer needs and desires will become a key competitive advantage for organizations.

The Ethics of Customer Prediction Management

The use of data to gain a competitive advantage is a reality, and it will continue to shape how organizations design and manage their customer experiences. With organizations gaining access to highly private and sensitive data about customers, people have begun to question whether it's ethical to use such information for commercial purposes. More consumers are now aware of the digital breadcrumbs they leave behind when using digital channels, and there is growing concern about who is using the data and what for.

Data protection became front-page news in early 2016, for example, when Apple refused to grant the FBI access to data from a suspected killer's iPhone. Apple argued that protection of customer data was its highest priority, not to be breached even by a legal order. The data was eventually retrieved by the FBI, but the case made by Apple was supported by a number of digital giants, such as Facebook and Google.

The use of customer data for commercial reasons will continue to be hotly debated and can be best summed up using a line from Marvel's *Spider-Man:* "With great power comes great responsibility." Having access to rich data sets and the tools to analyze them to gain insights about consumer behavior is an amazing power. This power does not come without its own inherent risks. Business leaders need to understand both the risks and the potential benefits in order to determine how best to use customers' data for the good of their organization.

Technology is advancing at a faster pace than the legal system can provide laws or guidance for business leaders. This has led consumer groups to debate whether there are basic principles for data ownership and whether organizations should have access to such data without consumers' explicit permission. A number of issues around privacy and ownership need to be carefully considered before an organization decides to use sensitive data sets.

Specifically, business leaders need to understand four key areas when a data-centric project is presented for consideration:

1. Is the organization considering monetizing internally sourced data by selling it to a third party? If so, is this data properly sanitized, and does it protect confidential and private customer information? Does the organization have a legal right to sell sanitized data?
2. Is the project likely to breach any privacy laws?
3. If no laws are broken by this project, does it meet the ethical standards of the organization?
4. Does the potential payback outweigh the risks?

These questions and answers are likely to create a level of debate among leadership teams. Although big data and its analytics are certainly open for misuse, there are some real business benefits that simply cannot be ignored. The potential to gain sustainable competitive advantage over the competition should be a focus for any organization aiming to lead its sector.

KEY LESSONS

- The evolution from CRM to CEM was driven by advancements in technology and changes in consumer behavior.
- The combination of technological evolution, globalization, and shifting consumer behavior has changed the competitive landscape.
- The rise of CEM has shifted the focus of customer management away from centralized departments, such as customer care, so that it is now a concern for the entire company.
- To achieve a branded customer experience, organizations needed to seek technology solutions that enabled the entire organization to deliver experiences to customers that would extract the greatest economic value.

- The management of interactions across multiple channels has led to the evolution of data-centric solutions.
- Raw data, and the analytics required to convert it into meaningful information, has become a major force in effective customer experience management.
- The potential for organizations to regain control of consumer behavior using big data is likely to push the boundaries of customer experience management toward customer prediction management.
- Big data is about understanding the correlation of two or more variables. It is not about understanding *why* something happens, but about recognizing *that* it happens.
- The future direction of customer experience management lies in the ability to harness digital clues left behind by consumers and then apply scientific methods to make educated predictions about what customers are likely to want.
- The ability to accurately predict future customer behavior, and to release products and services before competitors do, will position organizations as market leaders.
- A number of issues around privacy and ownership need to be carefully considered before an organization decides to use sensitive data sets.

CHAPTER 20

How Technology Will
Define the Future of CEM

Although data may give us the power now to make educated predictions about future customer behavior, the analysis on its own is insufficient to support investment in a new innovation, product, or business model. Customer experience management is only beginning to evolve into the predictive management of customers' behavior, as I proposed in the previous chapter. Data analytics forms only part of the equation. The other part is knowing how to incorporate emerging technology-based megatrends into your analysis.

Once you have incorporated both data analytics and technological megatrends, you will have a better basis for your plan about what to offer your customers. The value proposition is likely to resonate more powerfully with customers if it's closely aligned with customer expectations that have been shaped by popular technology solutions offered in the marketplace.

This chapter takes a closer look at what popular technologies are emerging as megatrends—and at the likely impact on customers and their expectations.

Understanding the Trajectory of Technology

As I mentioned in the introduction to this book, World Economic Forum economists have labeled this period of history the Fourth Industrial Revolution. The label signifies two major ideas: The first idea is that current and emerging technologies will have a significant impact on industry, and the second idea is that this technology will revolutionize many traditional ways of conducting business. The basis for this argument is simple: There has never been a period in our history when so many emerging technologies are becoming commercial realities. The convergence of multiple new technologies creates significant commercial opportunities and threats for organizations. A technological tsunami is coming in the next ten years, and those businesses that are unprepared could feel the impact severely and negatively. But those that are prepared and are able to capitalize on changing customer expectations will have the opportunity to dominate markets and new industries.

According to a 2015 survey by the Global Center for Digital Business Transformation, business leaders from twelve industries in thirteen of the world's largest economies predicted four out of ten highly ranked global companies would fold sometime in the next five years—victims of rapid technological change, shifting business models, and compelled mergers. "Not just lone companies, but entire industries are being side-swiped by these effects," said James Macaulay, co-author of the study. "Digital disruption now has the potential to overturn incumbents and reshape markets faster than perhaps any force in history."[29]

The fear expressed by business leaders is largely based on a fundamental concern about their ability to adapt quickly enough to the disruptive forces of these technologies. In fact, many of these leaders are betting on the fact that a large number of incumbent organizations won't be able to adapt in time.

What makes our current industrial revolution different from the previous revolution, during which technology liberated people from physical labor, drudgery, and constraints of mass production, is that this latest revolution has technology displacing people and industry. Past industrial revolutions tended to create new economic growth by enabling new industries to produce more and better-quality goods and services. Job growth was a normal by-product. However, unlike previous revolutions, this one has the potential to disrupt our lives, industries, and governments, and to detract jobs from the world's economies.

It's not difficult to see the disruption in the lives of taxi drivers all

....

29   Global Center for Digital Business Transformation, *Digital Vortex: How Digital Disruption Is Redefining Industries*, June 2015, 1.

over the world because of the success of Uber. The demonstrations of taxi drivers against Uber services have escalated, drawing attention to how this technological revolution is already affecting both their industry and their lives. The influence of this revolution is a work in progress, and our attention is focused on customer experience. Understanding the key drivers behind these technological developments and the likely effect on customer experience will help you formulate a strategy for your organization to achieve future competitive advantages.

A Shift Toward Life-Enhancing Technologies

A number of new technologies are about to become commercially available in the near future. Most of the technologies referenced in this chapter are either in early production or waiting on final approval before widespread distribution. I've narrowed down a list of those I believe will have the greatest impact on customer experience and the competitive landscape of an industry sector. The assumption here is that the technologies with the greatest financial investment are the ones most likely to achieve the necessary momentum in the marketplace and to have the greatest impact on consumers' lives.

There are few organizations with the necessary financial muscle and execution capability to influence markets using technology innovations:

- Google
- Apple
- Microsoft
- Facebook
- Amazon
- Samsung
- SoftBank

At the same time, I can't ignore some of the emerging companies producing the technologies that larger organizations and the investment community are funding:

- Huis Ten Bosch
- Tesla
- Magic Leap
- SmartThings
- iRobot
- Riken-SRK Collaboration Center for Human-Interactive Robot Research
- AeroMobil
- MemoMi

Some of these companies, such as Google, are investing in a large and diverse range of technology. The following technology categories are where the largest investments are being made and where the greatest potential lies for changing customer behavior and experience:

- Robots
- Process automation
- Artificial intelligence (AI) used for predictive solutions
- Internet of Things (IoT), which makes devices such as fridges and mirrors "smart" through software applications and connections to data networks
- 3-D printing
- Self-driving vehicles
- Contextual applications using technology such as facial recognition
- Flying cars (yes, you read that correctly!)
- Augmented/virtual reality applications

Many of these technologies are being turned into effective disruptive tools through innovative applications of multiple independent technologies. For example, self-driving cars by companies such as Google only recently entered the testing phase because of the advancement of multiple complementary technologies such as advanced driver assistance systems (ADAS), sensors, cameras, GPS tracking, and robotics. These minor technologies have matured to the point companies can assemble new innovative solutions capable of changing the way we live and interact. This is disruption, and in many cases it's closer to becoming a commercial reality than most people realize. These technologies are at different stages of commercialization, and some are already appearing in certain marketplaces today.

What value propositions do these emerging technologies offer consumers? My research has identified future trends in customer experience management and has indicated that attitudes are beginning to change toward CEM concepts. Traditionally, CEM is defined in terms of customer expectations and values: how a company can provide a branded experience throughout the entire customer journey and generate loyalty and advocacy at every touch point. According to my research, the more impressive technology companies have a slightly different view of how to create long-term loyalty with their customers. They are pushing the traditional boundaries of CX beyond customer–organization interaction and into new areas where experiences can generate longer-lasting loyalty to the brand. These tech companies are less focused on the transactional aspects of customer experience management and more interested in delivering innovative technology solutions to elevate their customer's life experience.

The primary difference in these companies' thinking is the shift from consumerism toward life-enhancing products and services. It can be argued that their goal is to help people define their very *raison d'être* and to deliver greater life satisfaction and a sense of accomplishment. Some of these companies focus on higher humanitarian objectives, such as improved learning, development, and health care, or bringing electricity to regional locations and providing better support for those who are physically challenged. These pioneering organizations are driven by the fact that the next technological wave will influence almost every aspect of our lives. It will no longer be sufficient to manage the customer–organization relationship through interactions—this approach will be too limiting because it largely examines the customer's relationship with the organization in isolation from the outside world.

The proliferation of technology in almost every aspect of our lives will require organizations of the future to define their offering to people relative to a larger ecosystem of life-enhancing technologies. Their view of the customer must incorporate how their customer functions on a daily basis and interacts with different technologies to ultimately improve their life.

The shift toward life experience management will be the main focus for organizations delivering the technological solutions that change our future lives. Car manufacturers such as Toyota, Mercedes, and Jaguar, for example, are already designing vehicles that will incorporate their customers' digital lives. Most new car models already integrate seamlessly with smartphones, access the Internet, and remotely locate themselves using mobile applications. When lifestyle behaviors are properly considered and integrated into the overall value solution, the experience provided—in this case, by the car manufacturer—extends beyond the product in question.

Beyond Traditional Disruption

Technological disruption is not new. People have been innovating and creating since the dawn of time. Just think of how the discovery of electricity changed the way we live and opened the doorway for life-changing technologies such as the light bulb, the elevator, the movie camera, and ultimately computers. Traditional disruption from technology can be grouped into four key categories—not based on historical evolution of disruption, but rather on the impact on people's lives.

UPLIFTING HUMAN ASPIRATIONS

The categories are:

1. **Productivity technology** helps us by reducing inefficiencies and the number of daily tasks we have to do.
2. **Health enhancement technology** reduces risks to our health and well-being.
3. **Control technology** facilitates the manipulation of our surroundings with minimal effort and greater capability.
4. **Human aspirations technology** enhances our existence as human beings by addressing a fundamental human drive through technology.

Many of the disruptive technologies we have seen in the past fifty years can be grouped into the first three categories. Their disruption is largely utilitarian in nature, changing a particular aspect of our lives in a specific manner. Years ago, the development of large cranes led us to build tall buildings. More recently, eBay empowered consumers to easily buy and sell goods from each other without the need for a corporate retailer.

The fourth category presents the most interesting concept related to future technological disruption, and it requires some illustration. Electricity, for example, led to the invention of the motion camera. The motion camera led to the evolution of cinema. A movie in a dark theater taps in to the human psyche in a way that is similar to dreaming. While we don't yet fully understand the impact of why humans dream, we do know that every human does it, and therefore it plays an important part in who we are as humans. The technological invention of moving pictures enabled us to "share a dream" with others and thus to explore human emotions such as love and fear. Therefore this technological invention can be grouped in the fourth category, as it enhances our existence as human beings.

The next technological wave will bring an unprecedented number of technologies focused on this fourth category of innovation. These technologies aim to go beyond the traditional objectives of utilitarian disruption, to enhance our lives by appealing to and potentially satisfying deep psychological and emotional needs.

Companies like Magic Leap are working on bringing back magic into the world with the commercial release of supposedly groundbreaking technology. Although details are scarce, we do know that Google is investing heavily in the start-up by leading capital-raising efforts to the tune of $542 million. According to *The Wall Street Journal*, Magic Leap's technology currently operates like a pair of augmented reality glasses; however, instead of displaying images on the inside the glasses or projecting the images outward, Magic Leap's glasses reportedly project the image right onto the wearer's eyes—creating stunning effects. Digital objects in your vision appear to exist in the world around you. Thomas Tull, CEO of Legendary Pictures, reported his experience with the glasses as "incredibly natural and almost jarring." As he described it, "You're in the room, and there's a dragon flying around; it's jaw-dropping and I couldn't get the smile off of my face."[30]

....

30   Jacob Kastrenakes and Ben Popper, "Google Leads $542 Million Funding of Mysterious Augmented Reality Firm Magic Leap," The Verge, October 21, 2014, http://www.theverge.com/2014/10/21/7026889/magic-leap-google-leads-542-million-investment-in-augmented-reality-startup.

The human fascination for magic and wondrous experiences enables Magic Leap to tap in to all sorts of possibilities, beyond pure entertainment, that are related to a user's higher and deeper engagement, and potentially "positively transform the process of education" by providing students with an immersive experience to elevate learning.

Another recent invention, released by SoftBank Robotics Corp. in Japan, is a robot called Pepper, claimed to be the world's first robot able to intuit human emotions by sensing changes in voice and facial expressions. Pepper was specifically created to be a robot buddy. A lot of robots are being developed as emotional companions, especially for children, the elderly, and hospital patients. This is particularly important in Japan, which has the fastest-aging population in the world. Technological inventions such as Pepper are being released to enhance the lives of many, by providing a synthetic companion that helps people overcome loneliness. SoftBank says the robot has one overriding aim: "He tries to make you happy."

Furthermore, with its own emotions—a feature that's been added since the robot was initially announced—Pepper also addresses the parental urge of being needed through its ability to express its own "emotional" need for companionship. Pepper had a limited release in Japan in June 2015. The initial one thousand units had an up-front retail price of $1,610 plus maintenance contracts for three years, taking the total cost to $9,380. The robots sold out in one minute.[31]

Are these robots attractive in the marketplace simply because they are cool? The cool factor of owning a robot will no doubt drive demand for robots such as Pepper. However, we cannot ignore the large appetite for technologies that have the potential to improve our lives overall rather than simply enhancing a single aspect of life.

The underlying urge for a better life is different for all individuals. Some may experience a strong urge to better their living conditions, while others may have more altruistic urges. Technology companies are starting to capitalize on various desired life experiences by creating life-changing technology solutions. This will see the evolution of traditional CX thinking

....

31   Angad Singh, "'Emotional' Robot Sells Out in a Minute," CNN, June 23, 2015, http://www.cnn .com/2015/06/22/tech/pepper-robot-sold-out/.

shift toward "whole of life" experience management as opposed to simple interaction management.

EVOLVING CONSUMER EXPECTATIONS

Environment, upbringing, and major life-changing events largely drive the evolution of people's expectations and values. The on-demand generation is living a digital life with new, different expectations. Shorter attention spans and digital access to information have redefined their expectations around, for example, accessing product and service information, and purchasing options. Current technologies such as smartphones and e-commerce sites that shape consumer behavior have focused on increasing our productivity, making us more efficient, and giving us more control over our world. Consequently, these technologies have created a world where time is effectively shrinking.

Everything in our world is now taking less time to perform. It takes us less time to shop, find a tradesperson, book a flight overseas, measure our fitness, and pay our bills. The reduced effort of performing many everyday tasks means that we now have a generation of people with different expectations of time. Many of the mundane everyday activities we perform already take less effort thanks to technological solutions. There is always going to be potential for newer and more efficient solutions, but many of these will provide minor improvements to existing solutions. Once access to a product or service has been reduced to the single push of a button, the only evolutionary step then becomes the eradication of the need for the product or service altogether.

It can be argued that the primary objectives of many current disruptive innovations have been the reduction of effort and time and the elevation of consumer control. The primary aim of the coming wave of technology will be to improve the lives of people by eradicating negative emotions associated with deep-seated human aspirations. The by-product of these technologies will help people focus on a higher quality of life, and there will be a stronger focus on the emotional payback offered by these technologies. The emotions generated from these technologies can lead to an enriched life.

The complicated relationship between technology and people was well depicted in the 2013 movie *Her*, released by Warner Bros. Pictures. In the movie, a loner's life is enriched though an odd relationship with a "female" artificial intelligence program. This storyline highlights the artificial relationships we humans are beginning to form with technologies, and illustrates what the desired emotional paybacks of the future might be.

Value Creation around Pleasure and Time

Technologies of the fourth category, human aspirations, are intended to create value for consumers by providing the user with a valuable life event through a more pleasurable experience. Pleasure can be defined in multiple ways. Some people can derive pleasure by knowing that their favorite climate settings and lighting are set the minute they walk into their house. Others can derive pleasure from knowing they have been able to help someone less fortunate than themselves. The use of technology to provide appropriate and sustainable pleasure will partially determine the value of a product for its user and ultimately decide its usefulness in the user's digital world. The ability to deliver more free time for the user will also contribute to its value.

Future technological solutions need to be effective in eradicating negative emotions if they are going to enhance customers' lives. The focal point for mass consumer products and services will be to eradicate negative emotions in order to create more pleasure and free time. A number of organizations have already designed products and services with this aim, targeting the negative emotions that have the highest impact on us. The higher the impact, the better potential for the organization to gain long-term customer loyalty. Following is a list of the main negative emotions that emerging technologies are trying to eradicate:

- Anger
- Frustration
- Loneliness
- Despair
- Fear
- Insecurity
- Instability
- Boredom

Having reviewed the products and solutions offered by the select group of companies, and how these technologies were likely to impact people's live, I performed an evaluation aimed at determining the products that are likely to create new value by attempting to replace negative emotions with positive ones. The summary is provided in table 20.1:

TABLE 20.I: TECHNOLOGY INNOVATORS AND FUTURE SOLUTIONS SUMMARY

COMPANIES FOCUSED ON DIVERSE TECHNOLOGY SOLUTIONS

Company	Technology Solution	Negative Emotions Targeted for Eradication	Positive Emotions Targeted for Creation
Google	Google is the most diversified. They have a large range of patents from emotional expressive toys to downloadable personalities for robots. Their current investments are focused around three main areas: • Google self-driving car • Augmented reality for future computing and gaming • Artificial Intelligence and Robotics for a range of applications	Frustration Boredom Fear Instability Anxiety Laziness Procrastination	Joy Serenity Interest Amusement Safety
Apple	Apple is investing in: • The Internet of Things (IoT). Their recent move into tech wearables such as the Apple Watch will lead them down the path of providing consumers with more smart devices that will seamlessly connect to the Apple ecosystem. iBeacon is an example of an IoT business application able to provide hyper-contextual content to customers. • iCar–self-driving car code-named "Titan" • Advanced forms of Siri to perform robotic automation of household processes such as climate control	Boredom Disconnection Isolation Repression Rejection	Desire Pride Confidence Connection
Microsoft	• Microsoft is betting on the next computing evolution with what they term as "holographic computing" via their user interface called HoloLens. • Microsoft's recent US$1 billion investment in Uber indicates its survival strategy is hedged on the success of other tech companies. Uber could also be an indirect investment into self-driving vehicles and also to utilize Microsoft's Azure cloud computing platform.	Chaotic Confusion Hopelessness Uninformed Loss Boredom	Confidence Inspiration Satisfaction

Company	Technology Solution	Negative Emotions Targeted for Eradication	Positive Emotions Targeted for Creation
Amazon	Amazon is continuing to invest in technologies of the future in the way customers shop online. Recent technology releases include: • **Echo** (Amazon's voice-activated, cloud-connected wireless speaker, who talks back to you and acts as kind of a personal assistant.) • **Fire Phone** • **Dash Replenishment Service** (one button push to buy products) It is also investing in becoming the infrastructure powerhouse for the IT industry by expanding and providing new solutions around data centers and cloud offerings.	Manipulation Uninformed Frustration Controlling Disadvantaged	Serenity Relief Satisfaction Confidence Pride

COMPANIES FOCUSED ON ROBOTICS AND ARTIFICIAL INTELLIGENCE

Company	Technology Solution	Negative Emotions Targeted for Eradication	Positive Emotions Targeted for Creation
SoftBank	SoftBank released Pepper the robot on the 20th of June, 2015. This is the emotion-sensing robot that is designed to "make you happy."	Loneliness Depression	Kindness Sympathy Love
Riken-SRK Collaboration Center for Human-Interactive Robot Research	Produced Robear: a high-tech "Robot teddy with a mission" helps take care of the elderly in the future. Robear is designed to perform tasks such as helping elderly patients stand up, or lifting them from a bed into a wheelchair.	Lonely Dependence Victimization	Kindness Respect Independence
Huis Ten Bosch	In Japan in July 2015, this company launched the first hotel to be fully operated by robots. Humanoid robots greet Japanese-speaking guests at reception, while English-speaking guests are met by a robotic dinosaur! The robots are able to engage in intelligent conversations. More functional droids are on hand to cart luggage to the hotel's 72 rooms, staff luggage lockers, and clean.	Complaining Neglected Dominated	Relief Relaxation Surprise
iRobot	iRobot offers robots for business and the defense and security industries. Its home robots are revolutionizing the way individuals clean their living and working spaces. Its RP-VITA, a roving communications protocol, allows a doctor to visit a patient without leaving his or her office, thus facilitating more doctor-patient face-time.	Dependence Desperation Annoyance Frustration	Independence Relaxation Joy

COMPANIES FOCUSED ON VIRTUAL AND AUGMENTED REALITY

Company	Technology Solution	Negative Emotions Targeted for Eradication	Positive Emotions Targeted for Creation
Magic Leap	Magic Leap's technology currently uses an apparatus like a pair of glasses. Rather than displaying images on the glasses or projecting them out into the world, Magic Leap's glasses reportedly project the image right onto the wearer's eyes—creating stunning augmented reality.	Unhappiness Boredom Controlled Reclusive	Enchantment Fascination Awe Amusement
Oculus	Oculus produces a range of virtual reality wearables able to provide a much-improved, high-presence experience to engage the user more completely than previous devices. The equipment utilizes a gaming platform (DK2), wearable glasses (Rift), and a device to turn Samsung phones into a mobile VR system (Gear VR).	Boredom Bullied Lost Timid	Energized Inspiration Fascination Confidence

COMPANIES FOCUSED ON THE INTERNET OF THINGS

Company	Technology Solution	Negative Emotions Targeted for Eradication	Positive Emotions Targeted for Creation
SmartThings	SmartThings produces software that helps control everything from door locks to light switches in homes. Samsung acquired the company for $200 million.	Impatience Disorganization Disconnection	Connection Relaxation Confidence
MemoMi	MemoMi, in collaboration with Neiman Marcus, has built the Memory Mirror, a new technology that has transformed the customer experience. This giant video screen and camera allows shoppers to view outfits from 360 degrees, and also to compare clothing options side by side. It also remembers what customers have already tried on. The mirror records an eight-second video, which is password protected and can be emailed so shoppers can instantly see and share the results from their own personal devices.	Impulsiveness Confusion Conflict Manipulation	Empowerment Pride Desire Relief

COMPANIES FOCUSED ON ENERGY AND TRANSPORTATION

Company	Technology Solution	Negative Emotions Targeted for Eradication	Positive Emotions Targeted for Creation
Tesla	This electric motor vehicle company is also becoming an energy company able to provide new and improved ways of battery storage of electricity.	Egocentricity Arrogance Self-obsession	Confidence Courage Satisfaction
AeroMobil	The AeroMobil 3.0 prototype is a flying car. The company has been flight-testing its hybrid transportation option in real conditions since 2015 and anticipates a commercial launch in 2017. The new model is reportedly capable of taking flight from a grass strip.	Anger Frustration Confinement Rage	Joy Freedom Confidence Relief

The Whole Is Greater Than the Sum of Its Parts

As outlined at the beginning of this chapter, one key characteristic of the upcoming technology wave is the convergence of a number of technologies that will create disruptive solutions. A better understanding of which major technologies are being used in the next wave will help you identify areas for further investigation and investment.

ARTIFICIAL INTELLIGENCE (AI)

AI technology has taken major leaps in recent years. A number of new start-up companies are developing AI solutions, and most notable are the investments made by Google, including the acquisition of British start-up DeepMind in 2014 and the recruitment of two big hitters in the field: Ray Kurzweil and Professor Geoffrey Hinton. Professor Hinton is working on a concept called "thought vectors" whereby every word is given a specific set of numbers (or vector) and a computer can be trained to understand the actual meaning of these words using number codes. The result is that a computer could decipher the meaning for words used in a sentence in a way more closely resembling how we process language instead of simply matching words to their equivalent references. DeepMind made headlines in 2016 after its AlphaGo program beat a human professional Go player for the first time.[32] This was identified as a milestone for the science behind AI, because the program displayed reinforced learning, making AlphaGo a lot more humanlike in its use of information. The evolution in AI is the basis for many of the technology solutions we are seeing, such as conversational robots and complex problem-solving machines.

BIG DATA

Big data is not a technology in its own right, but the diversity and richness of data sets is the basis driving predictive technologies and contextual solutions.

SMART TEXTILES AND MATERIALS

Smart materials are opening up new possibilities for wearables, automobiles, and the future of our everyday clothing.

CLOUD COMPUTING

Cloud computing has removed the tendency of hardware to become a barrier for technology solutions. The maturity of cloud computing is enabling companies to control the "smarts" in their devices and create new disruptive solutions. For example, Pepper the robot and Amazon's Echo both have their intelligence based in the cloud.

SENSORS, FACIAL RECOGNITION, AND SPEECH ANALYTICS

All these technologies are driving the Internet of Things and the commercialization of smart home devices. Facial recognition and speech analytics technologies enable devices to recognize facial expressions and speech in order to process the correct action or response.

BROADBAND SPEED, RELIABILITY, AND COVERAGE

These broadband characteristics are the fundamental connectivity requirements for all these technologies to reach commercial viability. Companies

....

32   BBC News, "Artificial Intelligence: Google's AlphaGo Beats Go Master Lee Se-dol," Technology section, March 12, 2016, http://www.bbc.com/news/technology-35785875.

like Google know this and have invested significant funds in preparing for the upcoming technological wave. Google has invested an estimated $1 billion in a company called SpaceX, which launches low-orbit satellites to enable low-cost broadband access around the world.[33]

Be Cautious of Future Technologies

The unique combination of these individual technologies forms the basis of many of the world's cutting-edge technologies. Some of the companies behind these technologies have the opportunity to increase their market size, revenues, and customer base substantially and become megacorporations. Hopefully we won't see the type of megacorporation portrayed in the 2008 Pixar movie *Wall-E*—it dominated Earth's economy and governments, leading to our planet's (fictional) demise. However, the movie does serve as a warning to all of us.

With the fusion of life-enhancing technology with our everyday lives comes the danger of achieving the opposite effect: Instead of our lives becoming better, we could end up disrupting our own lives for the worse. The negative consequences of disruption are obvious, and without progressive thinking about how to address the social and economic implications, we could end up living a reality that is very different from what was intended. People can end up losing jobs or being displaced, and the divide of wealth could accelerate to unacceptable levels. Governments are not acting quickly or sufficiently to address the conflicting forces of disruption and its impact on employment and human lives. Not all innovation is ultimately good for society, and unless governments can direct efforts of business toward desired areas of innovation, the consequences could be dire.

The impact of technological advancement on individuals doesn't come without its dangers, particularly with the evolution of AI. Renowned thought leaders in the technology industry, such as Stephen

....

33   Alan Boyle, "Liftoff! SpaceX Gets $1 Billion from Google and Fidelity," NBC News, Science, January 20, 2015, http://www.nbcnews.com/science/space/liftoff-spacex-gets-1-billion-google-fidelity-n289866.

Hawking, Bill Gates, and Elon Musk, warn of the dangers of a *techno-logical singularity*: the point at which artificial intelligence exceeds man's intellectual capacity and produces a runaway effect.[34] While it may be some time before an apocalyptic army of robots overcomes the human race, as depicted in movies like *I, Robot* or *The Terminator*, there is still real concern about the moral, legal, and ethical limits and boundaries for potentially powerful technologies like AI. Governments need to introduce legislation to control the release of AI technologies and any technology that may be used to harm humanity. Recently, the US Congress effectively shut down a research laboratory that had discovered how the Ebola virus could be spread without being airborne. It was said that the research, if it got into the wrong hands, could lead to weaponization of the virus for warfare.

The evolution of technology and its application in our daily lives is a reflection of the evolution of mankind. Our sense of wonder and excitement about the possibility of living in a futuristic, automated utopia like many of us grew up watching on *The Jetsons* drives us to invent new solutions to make our lives easier. The rise of robots shouldn't be seen as the beginning of the end. Instead, we should view the possibilities these robots can offer to change our lives for the better. As our companions in business and pleasure, they can diminish the cognitive heavy lifting required in problem solving, reduce menial tasks, and increase the amount of time we have for creative pursuits and personal aspirations.

The future wave of technology will bring an exciting array of possibilities and risks. Our ability to adapt as businesses, as communities, and as humans will determine whether there is a consequential long-term enhancement or detriment to our lives.

....

.... **KEY LESSONS** ....

- The convergence of many new technologies creates significant commercial opportunities and threats for organizations.
- Those prepared and able to capitalize on changed customer expectations derived from the next technological wave will have the opportunity to dominate markets and new industries.
- There are a few organizations with the necessary financial muscle and execution capability to influence markets using technological innovations.
- It can be argued that the goal of leading organizations is to help people define their very *raison d'être*, and to deliver greater life satisfaction and a sense of accomplishment.
- Innovations in human aspirations technology aim to enhance our lives by appealing to and potentially satisfying deep psychological and emotional needs.
- The primary aim of the coming wave of technology will be to improve the lives of people by eradicating negative emotions associated with deep-seated human aspirations.
- Future technological solutions need to be effective in eradicating negative emotions if they are going to fulfill their promise of enhancing consumers' lives.
- Not all innovation is ultimately good for society, and unless governments can direct efforts of business toward desired areas of innovation, the consequences could be dire.
- Governments will need to introduce legislation to control the release of AI technologies and any technology that may be used to harm humanity.

CHAPTER 21

The Impact of the
Digital Workforce on CEM

With emerging technologies poised to revolutionize traditional business and industry, the future of customer experience management will be influenced by the adoption of a nonhuman workforce. This adoption has recently accelerated in many blue chip organizations because of sophisticated software being designed that automates business processes and provides cognitive support. The augmentation or replacement of a human workforce with a digital one will impact customers and create new opportunities for value creation. However, the inclusion of a digital workforce also has the potential to negatively disrupt the human workforce and affect the high-performance culture required to achieve the true customer centricity that delivers a branded customer experience.

This chapter provides some insight on what this new digital workforce could look like and suggests a number of considerations to help you make the necessary adjustments to your customer experience program so you can better adapt to this emerging trend.

Understanding the Digital Workforce

Different varieties of digital workers are appearing in the marketplace, and it's important to be able to distinguish them so you can determine how they may impact your CX initiatives.

Digital workers exist in the world of bits and bytes. They are not physical robots, but software applications in an IT network. Unlike normal software programs, however, digital workers are defined by their ability to perform multiple tasks in a business process normally performed by a human. They cannot exist as stand-alone programs; they must interface with other data and applications in order to achieve their objectives. Their interdependence on other IT systems is a key characteristic of these programs.

This highlights the importance of having good data and applications to execute business processes in the first instance. Without these IT components, the organization will be at a disadvantage when it comes to capitalizing on the business benefits of a digital workforce.

The different technologies can be classified into four different categories, each of which measures the software on a certain functional dimension:

1. **Data:** The level of sophistication in dealing with business data (structured or unstructured)
2. **Task:** The type of task predominately performed (rule-based or requiring knowledge from multiple sources to complete the process)
3. **Interoperability:** The level of collaboration (whether work is performed in a single application or across multiple applications and platforms)
4. **AI:** The level of artificial intelligence (none, machine learning based on pattern recognition and statistics, or emerging true AI)

These four dimensions enable us to identify the types of tasks performed by the digital workers (DW), the applications they can access, and the level of cognitive computing they offer. The DW capability model (see figure 21.1) was designed to provide categories for the key characteristics of each offering based on these dimensions:

DIGITAL WORKERS CAPABILITY MODEL

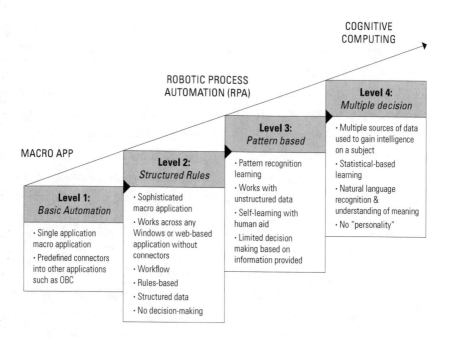

The solutions currently available in the marketplace broadly fit into the categories of this capability model. At the lower end of the spectrum, the digital workers simply follow defined business rules and behave like a macro within a defined workflow. On the higher end of the spectrum, the programs display humanlike intelligence by learning and applying knowledge from unstructured data sources. No software company has currently been able to demonstrate true artificial intelligence (a program that has intelligence capable of reasoning, knowledge, planning, learning, natural language processing, perception, and the ability to move and manipulate objects).[35] A number of key organizations such as Google, IBM, and IPsoft are making major inroads into creating true AI, but at this stage there are minimal commercial applications in the marketplace. Google's DeepMind is the company closest to achieving true AI, but even they

35   This list of intelligent traits is based on the topics covered by the major AI textbooks, including Russell & Norvig (2003), Luger & Stubblefield (2004), Poole, Mackworth, & Goebel (1998), and Nilsson (1998).

acknowledge the challenges in achieving an independent program that is self-aware and capable of manipulating its own environment.

Ultimately, true AI will become a reality, and a fifth category will join the capability model. The definition of AI used to categorize digital workers today is mostly based on machines using fuzzy logic algorithms and statistical probability as the basis for making "intelligent," humanlike decisions when completing a business process. The closest commercially available application of AI that is able to augment and potentially replace front-office workers is IPsoft's Amelia. The latest release of Amelia uses sophisticated algorithms to process unstructured data, respond to natural language, and display appropriate emotive responses in conversation with customers. Meanwhile, a number of companies have used IBM's AI, known as Watson, to improve cognitive-based, back-office business processes such as creating new marketing campaigns.

Robotic Process Automation

The most widely adopted variety of digital workers is currently the automation of repetitive, rules-based, back-office business processes using structured data. The automation provided by these programs takes place when software "robots" carry out processes or tasks normally completed by humans. Several names are used to define these programs and the function they perform, the most widely of which is robotic process automation (RPA). RPA is positioned in the marketplace as an offering that belongs to the next wave of digital disruption. Because the software has the ability to replace or augment human workers and change business models, these technologies have the disruptive capabilities outlined in Klaus Schwab's book *The Fourth Industrial Revolution*.

RPA's adoption rate has been gaining momentum over the past two to three years largely due to the increasing attention these technologies have received from tier-one consulting firms and to the increase in IT vendors providing RPA solutions and releasing more sophisticated versions of the software. This momentum has increased in countries such as the US, the

UK, and Australia largely because of the high cost of labor and the maturity of IT systems in the execution of business processes. The adoption of RPA is expected to increase in many organizations as its value is better understood.

It's inevitable that category four and five (AI-focused) implementations of digital workers will eventually be introduced into business, thereby making the evolutionary step from a "dumb" software robot to cognitive-based computing. Their introduction into commercial organizations will add value to business processes by increasing the level of analytics and predicting customer and business outcomes in a more insightful, commercially useful manner.

Currently, organizations appear to be comfortable with the introduction of software to automate repetitive business processes, as opposed to the introduction of knowledge-based digital workers. The main reason rests with the low-value aspect of these processes and the minimal impact on internal organizational resources. Typically, the business processes better suited to RPA have some common characteristics:

- Repetitive and rule-based
- Accesses structured data sets
- Utilizes applications on a Windows or web-based platform
- Well documented and standardized in practice
- Three or more staff are hired to complete the process
- Data input is prone to human error

The popularity of RPA in automating back-office processes is growing because previously the only option to cost-effectively deliver these processes was to outsource them. Despite being of low strategic value, these processes are necessary in the daily operations of most businesses. RPA solutions are helping companies reduce errors and deliver more efficient interactions with their customers, while at the same time freeing up the humans performing those tasks to work on higher-value work.

For example, in the finance and banking sector, the customer experience is enhanced by automating new account verification, form filling, and financial claim processing. Other industry sectors—insurance, telecommunications, health care, retail—are benefiting as well. Common transactions, such as retrieving customer data to handle a support or sales inquiry, normally take several applications to process. The delays and errors experienced by customers can be eliminated when an organization implements an RPA program to assist the human employee by performing all the mundane functions of opening applications, retrieving data, and filling in customer information multiple times.

Internal departments of organizations are also able to benefit from this type of assistance, particularly with some of the key processes well suited for RPA:

Finance/Accounting
- Invoice processing
- Accounts payable and accounts receivable
- Reporting
- Bank reconciliation
- Fixed assets analysis
- Master data management
- Vendor and customer account creation
- ERP logging from another system

HR
- Employee onboarding
- Leave of absence management
- Populating employee data into multiple systems
- Performance appraisal management

IT
- Creating new accounts
- Software installations and updates
- Batch processing
- Printer setups

Processes that can be automated do not always require a high volume of work as justification for RPA. Digital workers can be multiskilled and shared within a department to undertake multiple low-value, but essential, processes. A shared digital resource can help a department or shared services center focus time on higher-value tasks that are more strategic and able to commercially benefit the organization overall. For example, a finance department could have a large team of accountants spending a significant proportion of their time on manual data entry. The introduction of RPA for data entry would free up this staff to perform more knowledge-based functions such as analyzing important financial records.

Organizations are constantly looking for ways to improve all aspects of their operations. Business processes over the past decades have undergone multiple revisions ranging from mapping, standardizing, and reengineering to outsourcing and transformation. The most recent big transformation related to extracting value from business processes has focused on cost reduction and improving outcomes by outsourcing, centralizing, and creating global shared services centers. The results from these initiatives have been mixed. Some organizations have been successful in extracting the value from such projects, while others have not.

Offshoring back-office processes to low-cost labor forces in countries such as India and the Philippines has been an option in recent years for any company seeking to optimize its operations and yield a greater result for its shareholders. Over time, however, this strategy has uncovered risks that have organizations reconsidering their offshoring model:

- Higher likelihood of errors
- Risk of data theft
- Loss of control over the process, thus limiting improvements
- Higher costs for supervision
- Rising labor costs that erode the cost benefits
- Business disruption due to climatic and political issues
- Fluctuating currencies that impact financial gain

COST COMPARISON OF BACK-OFFICE WORKER TO RPA

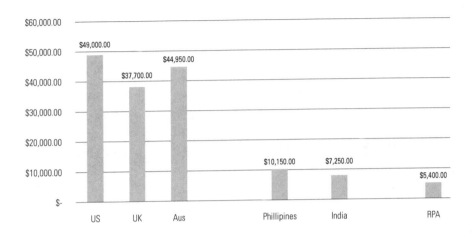

RPA offers organizations the opportunity to take these processes back in-house at a lower cost than is currently offered by their outsource vendors. Consider a cost comparison[36] of RPA versus a full-time equivalent staff member: The cost of a back-office worker in three similar markets (US, UK, Australia) reveals that an onshore staff member would cost approximately 85 percent more than an RPA software license. At the same time, the RPA solution is approximately 50 percent cheaper than a Philippines-based worker and 34 percent cheaper than an offshore worker in India.

These cost comparisons are based on a captive operation in both the onshore and offshore locations. The costs would be approximately 35 percent higher if a vendor were providing the services to an end client. The cost comparison includes labor on-costs of 35 percent and software on-costs of 20 percent.

This high-level cost comparison is more attractive when a more detailed analysis compares the costs benefits of RPA with hiring a human equivalent. Additional components to consider include

....

36   Cost comparison based on PayScale (www.payscale.com) salary comparisons across companies in the BPO sector.

- support staff,
- attrition,
- hiring,
- training,
- vacant real estate and utilities, and
- agent errors.

These components need to be considered when you present the case for RPA because, unlike a human worker, the digital equivalent does not

- make the same amount of errors,
- call in sick,
- work only one shift,
- need to take rest breaks,
- resign from work to seek career advancement,
- have holidays,
- need refresher training,
- cause HR issues,
- need physical working space, or
- need severance payment if no longer viable.

All these components should be considered when you present the commercial business case for RPA. The case for RPA in general is compelling enough to predict it will become a growing consideration for many organizations.

How Digital Workers Can Elevate the Customer Experience

If implemented correctly, digital workers can offer far-reaching benefits to companies beyond the obvious cost savings of reducing human worker counts. On the surface, it may appear that digital workers provide only cost optimization for the operations of an organization. However, this is a narrow view of the benefits associated with digital workers. In fact they can generate new value, because they can potentially enhance customer experience and help an organization accelerate market differentiation though the delivery of a branded customer experience.

Many of the back-office functions described as suitable for digital automation have an indirect and a direct impact on customers' experiences. For example, when highly repetitive tasks are required, humans are prone to errors. These errors could lead to a delay in a medical claim or an incorrect account name; collectively, they could urge your customers to fast-track their search for an alternative offered by your competitor. Similarly, customers calling a contact center to inquire about their account are often subjected to the same security questions several times, as the agent is required to open multiple applications to process an inquiry. This highly repetitive task creates frustration for both the customer and the human worker processing the inquiry. Human workers performing such repetitive tasks are less focused on delivering a superior customer interaction.

A digital workforce can elevate customer experience by making business processes

- more efficient,
- largely error free,
- faster, and
- more effortless.

Automation of these processes releases frontline, customer-facing human employees to focus their efforts on emotional aspects of customer interactions. With RPA performing the more clear-cut functions, human employees can ensure the customer

- receives proper attention,
- is treated courteously,
- receives personalized responses,
- has his or her needs more fully identified and matched to products and services, and
- is able to resolve more complaints on the first interaction.

The reason for most substandard customer experiences is the poor execution of business processes. A digital workforce is capable of remedying this by faultlessly executing the essential processes that impact customers' experiences.

Assessing the Impact on the Human Workforce

There are clear opportunities to enhance the customer experience using a digital workforce. Before deciding on your strategy for digital workers, however, you will need to carefully consider the impact on human workers, company culture, and overall business objectives.

A number of strategic considerations need to be carefully evaluated before your organization incorporates digital workers. The following questions should help you answer *how* and *if* you should implement digital workers in your organization:

- Will digital workers augment human efforts during some processes or replace them entirely?
- How will digital workers elevate your current customer experiences?
- What is the likely impact on company culture?
- Should the stakeholder for digital workers be the IT department or a business-focused department?
- Which areas of the business could benefit from a digital workforce?
- Which processes are currently standardized and ready for automation?
- Which processes need reengineering prior to implementing a digital workforce?
- Is there a road map for a phased approach for the introduction of different varieties of digital workers?
- How will communication about the digital workforce be managed internally?
- Will you utilize a change management process to implement the digital workforce?

- What is the governance model for managing the digital workforce vendor?
- If existing processes are outsourced, will a digital workforce enable these processes to be brought back in-house?
- How (and by whom) will the digital workforce be supervised?
- What role will humans play in helping execute a process largely managed by digital workers?
- Will you retrain humans being replaced or fire them?
- Are there any union considerations if you intend to make people redundant?
- Will you reduce headcount though natural attrition instead of redundancy?
- How will you communicate your initiative to the public and shareholders?

These questions should be answered, or at least considered carefully, before your organization introduces digital workers. This change has the potential to disrupt employees, making them feel threatened, and could undermine all previous CX enhancements you have implemented.

It's important to distinguish between what digital workers offer in the CEM equation and the role played by humans. With proper implementation to achieve strategic customer experience, digital workers elevate the services delivered to customers by human employees. Human-to-human interaction will remain, in my opinion, the preferred form of interaction when customers need to manage more complex issues. By perfecting repetitive processes or accessing knowledge-based information faster and better, digital workers can complement human employees and help them achieve better outcomes for customers.

Realizing New Value from Digital Workers

Already, a number of organizations are at varying stages of incorporating digital workers, ranging from proof of concept (PoC) to outsourcing multiple business processes, and headcount reductions are happening.

ANZ, one of the top four banks in Australia, announced its use of RPA in 2015, which helped validate RPA use in blue-chip organizations. The case study[37] for the ANZ implementation summarized the benefits as follow:

- 235 processes automated using RPA
- Cost savings of greater than 40 percent
- 20 percent fewer full-time employees used

By automating processes—such as transaction investigations, funds tracing, audit certificates, funds disbursements, and address changes—ANZ has been able to elevate its customer experience by reducing the delays and errors that occur when humans perform these tasks. Having reduced the cost of processing these low-value functions using RPA, the bank now has the flexibility to pass these savings to customers and become more competitive.

Other companies such as GM, Dell, and Uber have also automated some of their business processes to achieve similar cost savings. How these organizations use these cost savings will determine the value they deliver for customers. For example, will they choose to retain the cost savings for their own commercial gain? Or will they use part of the cost savings to retrain staff on performing more strategic functions for their customers, or to invest in other, similar CX initiatives. If they select the latter, then they have the potential to use this investment to further differentiate themselves through their branded customer experience.

On the AI end of the digital workforce spectrum, companies will be able to elevate the customer experience by reducing the cognitive heavy lifting and effort required at various stages of the customer life cycle. Pattern-matching AI programs can be used to create an effortless, highly customized customer experience, for the simple reason that customer behavior is largely pattern based. People tend to follow repetitive behavior when shopping based on visual cues, and organizations of the future will be able to capitalize on this.

....

37   ANZ RPA case study compiled and published under permission by the ANZ by Midfields Consulting, 2015.

Take, for example, the online shopping experience. Consumers tend to follow a pattern in how they search and purchase goods. An AI program can recognize this pattern of behavior and then manipulate the user's experience, providing a highly contextualized and personal experience by presenting pages and images most likely to appeal to the user. The AI programs can achieve this contextualization only if there is preexisting data on user behavior. Programs like Mixpanel capture the raw user behavior from websites that is required for AI programs to provide a personalized experience for online shoppers.

Other pattern-matching AI solutions capable of elevating the user's experience include image recognition and natural language processing. Programs such as CloudSight or IBM's Visual Recognition enable companies to build applications that allow a user to take a picture of anything with a smartphone and have an immediate response about what the item is or how it fits with other items. In a shopping context, this reduces the customer's effort in searching for the item, and it can provide the user with similar products at the lowest price point and in close proximity, all in a matter of seconds.

Digitized support functions can often frustrate customers, because a self-service knowledgebase tends to be cumbersome and costly when trying to retrieve information and live support from a human. But with natural language processing (NLP) using AI, a company can provide an interactive experience for customers without a human employee. AI programs are being used to leverage existing corporate information (such as user manuals) and to manage support calls in order to provide a faster, more accurate response to customers seeking support.

Digital workers will play an important role in how organizations deliver new value for customers and, consequently, will shape future CX strategies. Organizations that are able to capitalize on the digital workforce's abilities can elevate their customers' experiences and strategically improve competitive positioning. The risks to human workers should not be underestimated, but careful evaluation and planning will help mitigate these risks and secure the full benefits of using digital workers.

KEY LESSONS

- The future of customer experience management will be influenced by the adoption of a nonhuman workforce.
- Different varieties of digital workers are appearing on the marketplace.
- The most widely adopted variety of digital workers is the automation of repetitive, rules-based business processes using structured data for back-office processes: robotic process automation, or RPA.
- The adoption of RPA is expected to increase in many organizations as its value is better understood.
- Currently, organizations appear to be comfortable with the introduction of software to automate repetitive business processes, as opposed to the introduction of knowledge-based digital workers.
- RPA offers organizations the opportunity to return back-office processes in-house at a lower cost.
- The commercial business case for RPA is compelling enough to predict it will become a growing consideration for many organizations.
- There are clear opportunities to enhance the customer experience using a digital workforce.
- A number of strategic considerations need to be carefully evaluated before an organization incorporates digital workers.
- With proper implementation to achieve strategic customer experience, digital workers elevate the services delivered to customers by human employees.
- The risks to the human workforce should not be underestimated, but careful evaluation and planning will help mitigate these risks and secure the full benefits of using digital workers.

CHAPTER 22

Final Thoughts on Strategic CEM

Strategic customer experience management is like a good Swiss watch: A craftsman pieces together many intricate and precise components to make what is arguably the world's highest-quality timepiece. When the purchaser of the watch looks inside, however, it's difficult to truly understand the level of detail and engineering that defines it. Nor do we really care about the details of the machinery. All that we value in our Swiss watch is that it looks good and tells time with great precision and reliability. Our relationship with the Swiss watch is with the *face* of the watch, not the inside of the machine. When we raise our wrist to view the time, we might feel happy and proud of owning a beautiful, high-quality timepiece. We are less concerned about how it is able to tell the time. We are more concerned with what the Swiss watch stands for: reliability, beauty, and quality.

As customers, our relationship with a company is at the same level. We don't care too much for what is inside the organizational machine and how it functions. All we care about is that the product looks and feels good, and that the company can deliver on its promises consistently and reliably. Our emotional relationship with the watch or other product, and with how it makes us feel, is simply the total sum of our experiences with the *brand*.

Customers experience only the final output of many internal processes, technologies, and efforts from a large number of people. Delivering on the simple promise of providing customers with the most reliable timekeeping piece has taken Swiss watchmakers years of development, refinement, and engineering. Out of the great complexity of creating a branded customer experience comes a very simple concept: that the key to achieving success is your organization's ability to *consistently deliver a highly valued customer promise.*

The journey toward achieving a branded customer experience is not an easy one. It requires careful thought, deep domain knowledge, good planning, and the capability to execute properly. Not many organizations have all the components required to achieve success. As difficult as the journey may be, however, the rewards are worth it.

This journey has no end point—only lookout points where you can admire the view of momentary success. The rewards come along the way as you progressively achieve each initiative in your customer experience program. Once you step back to view what you have achieved, you will realize that collectively the sum of your program's parts yields a great reward for your organization and its customers.

As with the Swiss watch, each component has a purpose and a place in your overall machine. Neglecting the importance of even a single component of your CX program will not deliver the precision you are after. The key is to focus on each component and allocate the necessary effort to shape it according to your plans.

This process takes time. I don't make apologies for this.

Avoid taking the easy road, or applying a quick fix, as this will simply take your organization back to tactical outcomes and short-term results. Sustainable market differentiation that achieves long-term rewards is for a handful of elite organizations, the best of the best—the ones that dare to leap ahead of their competitors and lead from the front.

I leave you with this final quote from author Joseph Bruchac to sum up the journey ahead:

The best teachers have showed me that things have to be done bit by bit. Nothing that means anything happens quickly—we only think it does. The motion of drawing back a bow and sending an arrow straight into a target takes only a split second, but it is a skill many years in the making.

Appendix

THIRTY STAGES TO CREATE YOUR BRANDED CUSTOMER EXPERIENCE

Stage	Desired Output
1. Identify whether your organization can benefit from improving its customer experience, and set your vision and mission for your program.	A comparative financial analysis of your nearest competitor, and a clear vision and mission for your program
2. Identify the financial areas you would like to generate a commercial benefit.	A financial analysis of customer metrics and the profit and loss statement
3. Identify by how much you would like to change the metrics.	Objectives and targets for each area selected for change
4. Provide a clear ROI for the investment in your customer experience initiative.	A summary of the net commercial benefits, required investments, and expected time frame for achieving the financial targets
5. Evaluate the organization to determine how customer centric the employees are.	An empirically based analysis identifying problem areas in the organization
6. Identify the impact of the lowest-scored components on customers and the company.	An analysis outlining the impacts and their underlying causes
7. Identify the areas within the organization that will have the greatest impact on your financial goals.	A list of organizational areas targeted for change as part of your customer experience program
8. Identify what actions you will take to achieve the changes in the organization you desire.	A list of actions you will take to remedy specific areas in the organization that affect customer experiences
9. Map your customer journey.	A comprehensive customer journey map that incorporates all customer touch points
10. Evaluate your customers to determine what they value most and what they like least.	An empirical analysis based on customer research that identifies customer values and problem areas
11. Evaluate what your competitor's customers like least about their products or services.	Identification of marketplace gaps that are opportunities to win new customers

Stage	Desired Output
12. Summarize your customer research, and identify the areas you wish to improve with a weighted system.	A weighted list of customer issues that form part of the case for your CX initiative
13. Use the customer research to allocate a ratings score to each touch point in your journey map, identifying which have the most negative impact.	Identification of the organizational pain points that should be remedied to elevate customers' experiences
14. Use the competitor research to identify opportunities to win new customers.	A list of new initiatives that are likely to lead to new customers
15. Use the breakdown of the reasons customers left in the previous year to identify the top 2–5 reasons.	A list of the top pain paints to rectify in order to improve retention
16. Use a breakdown of the top customer values and initiatives to win new customers, and identify the 2–5 points that are most likely to generate new customer wins to include in the business case for your CX program.	A list of the top new customer value initiatives that will lead to achieving your customer acquisition figures
17. Review your top customer acquisition and retention initiatives, and identify how you can achieve any defined cost or improved margin targets.	A list of initiatives to achieve your cost reduction and/or improved financial targets
18. Summarize all initiatives to achieve your financial targets, and allocate time frames and resources to complete them.	High-level time frames and a list of how resources for each initiative's completion are allocated
19. Using the organizational evaluation for customer centricity, identify the top 2–5 areas you need to change to achieve sustainability for your CX initiative.	A list of the key organizational changes needed to achieve sustainability for your CX program
20. Design a customer-centricity program specifically addressing the areas in the organization most likely to impact the sustainability of any financial benefits generated from your CX initiative.	A program designed to permanently change the key areas identified in the organization as impacting improved CX sustainability
21. Allocate time frames and resources for your sustainability initiatives.	Detailed time frames and resources for each initiative
22. Identify stakeholders for initiatives, and note the ones that may pose risks in completing your tasks.	A list of stakeholders for each initiative and possible risks in completing your tasks
23. Select a change methodology best suited to transform the organization.	A suitable method for managing changes that result from the CX program
24. Position customer experience management as a strategic imperative in the organization.	Direct accountability of customer experience management to C-level (reports directly to the CEO)
25. Plan customer implementations using appropriate methods.	An implementation plan with tasks following practices of a suitable methodology
26. C-level sponsored communication to all staff prior to the launch of the program.	CEO-sponsored communication that clearly explains the journey of change and rationale

Stage	Desired Output
27. Implement the plans for the organization and customer initiatives.	Progressively implemented organizational and customer initiatives, and engaged employees
28. Mentor and train staff in new work behaviors.	Staff's consistent demonstration of new behaviors
29. Establish a CX governance unit and the organizational structure to maintain and elevate the CX program after its implementation.	A CX business unit that maintains, fixes, and elevates the customer experience on an ongoing basis; customer-centricity behaviors that are embedded in the organizational culture
30. Implement a continual cycle of improvement by measuring, monitoring, and innovating customers' experiences to maintain differentiation in the marketplace.	Identification and prioritization of CX innovations to ensure ongoing market differentiation; operational delivery adapted to changing customer expectations

Index

A

accountability, employee, 202–3
accounting departments, RPA in, 333
adaptation, happiness and, 237
ADKAR® model, Prosci, 160
Adrià, Ferran, 226
advocacy, customer, 40–41
AeroMobil, 323
Agile methodology, 164
airline customer journey mapping, 106
aligning CX program to objectives
  cost of proposed initiatives, 135–38
  executive summary, 141–45
  gap and opportunity analysis, 125–35
  overview, 124–25, 145
  reviewing financials, 139–41
AlphaGo program, DeepMind, 323–24
alternative operating models, 271–75
Amazon, 33, 223, 258–59, 321
Amelia, IPsoft, 331
analysis phase, 46–47, 146–53. *See also*
  aligning CX program to objectives;
  customer journey maps; financial
  aspects of CX
ANZ bank, 340
Apple, 22, 232–33, 242, 267, 303, 307,
  320
artificial intelligence (AI), 321, 323–26,
  329, 330–31, 340–41
augmented reality, 322
authenticity, 188–89, 257
autonomous governance units, 217–18

B

baby boomers, 199–200
back-office processes, 332–35, 337–38
banking, online, 114
behavior
  culture-building strategies, 200–206
  customer, capturing, 89
  and mobile devices, 252–55
  recognizing and rewarding new, 193–94
beliefs, 77–79, 177, 191–92, 199–200
benchmarking, 149–50
BI Intelligence, 250
big data, 301–2, 304–5, 324
bill shock, eliminating, 102
boxes, thinking in new, 227–30
Brabandere, Luc De, 227–30
brainstorming, 110–13, 140
brand promise, 97, 267–68
branded experience, 1–5. *See also* customer experience; customer experience management
broadband, 324–25
Bruchac, Joseph, 344
budget, 46–47, 139–41, 213–14
business analyst, 219
business case for CX programs, 47–48,
  57–59, 141–45. *See also* aligning CX
  program to objectives; customer
  journey maps
business model, changing, 226–27
business process outsourcing company
  (BPO), 272–73

business processes
    automation of, 332–35
    and CX, 23–24, 337–38
    operating models and, 269–71
    outsourcing, evaluation of, 265–69
    redefining to suit outsourcing, 283

C

call centers, KPIs at, 121
capability model, digital workforce,
    329–31
captive business processes, 270
cause and effect, in customer journey
    mapping, 95
CCScore (customer centricity score),
    14–15, 59–61, 64–68, 80–83
CEO. *See also* leadership
    change management sponsorship, 161
    in employee engagement, 189–90
    importance of CX support by, 17
    outsourcing decisions by, 264–69
    role in CX, 174, 175, 182
change
    and employee engagement, 183–86
    employee resistance to, 196–99
    governance model and, 20
change agents, 162–63, 201–2
change management, 160–63, 169–71,
    174–75. *See also* implementation;
    leadership; scaling CX excellence
change manager, 163
channel strategy, 259–60
chief of customer/chief of customer
    experience, 219
churn rate, 34–35
cloud computing, 324
CloudSight, 341
coaching, 21. *See also* training
cognitive computing, 330, 332
Coles supermarket chain, 303–4
collaboration, 60, 66, 81–82, 119–20, 127
collaborative software, 167
Collins Dictionary, 209–10
commitment, 15–16, 176
communication, 161–62, 175–76, 188–90

company environment, 11–12
company processes, 11–12. *See also*
    business processes
comparative analysis, 13–14, 28–34,
    48–49
competitor variance analysis, 28–34,
    48–49
competitors, benchmarking against,
    149–50
consistency, 150–51, 264
consumers. *See* customers
contextualization capabilities of mobile,
    251, 252
contextualized marketing, 303–4
contracts, outsourcing, 290–91, 293–94
control, 191, 210–12, 254, 256–57
control technology, 315–16
convergence phase, innovative thinking,
    229–30
cool, in digital age, 238–39, 259
core business, 265–67
core services, 231–32
cost of customer acquisition (CAC), 34
cost-benefit analysis, 135–38, 269,
    275–76, 335–36
Costco, 244–45
courage, in leaders, 178–79
creative thinking, 227
culture, 22–23, 152–53, 199–206, 232–34
current experience map, 100–109
customer acquisition cost (CAC), 34
customer centricity. *See also* strategic CX
    programs
    allocating actions for change, 80–84
    business case, adding substance to,
        57–59
    commercial benefits related to, 18
    core business and, 266
    customer journey maps, 19
    customer research, 20–21
    embedding in corporate DNA, 152–53
    employee empowerment and, 23
    employee engagement and, 22–23,
        70–73
    employee engagement program, 77–80

employee evaluation, 59–61
evaluating, 14–15, 17–18
executive appreciation of, 15–17
governance model for, 19–20
leaders as fostering, 177
overview, 57, 69, 70, 84–85
root cause analysis, 62–68
work environment supporting, 151
customer experience (CX). *See also*
    specific CX phases and aspects;
    strategic CX programs
aligning with value to customer, 149
business processes and, 267–68
digital workforce and, 336–38
employee engagement and, 184
evaluating current strategy, 12–26
general discussion, 2–5
importance of, 1–2
innovation, importance to, 223–24
leadership, role in, 174–75
measuring effectiveness, 18
positioning within organization, 161
rules of excellence, 146–53
tactical, 9–10
thirty stages to create, 346–48
training in, 21
customer experience management
    (CEM). *See also* future of CEM;
    specific CX phases and aspects;
    strategic CX programs
emerging technologies and, 314
final thoughts on, 343–44
general discussion, 2–5
history of, 298–301
overview, 308–9
rise of big data, 301–2
customer experience manager, 219
customer initiatives
cost of, 138
in executive summary, 144
gap and opportunity analysis, 130–34
implementation planning, 158, 164
customer innovation manager, 219
customer journey maps
by airline, 106

bill shock and, 102
brainstorming process, 110–13
characteristics to consider, 88–89
creating new customer journey, 110–18
customer segments, 92
defined, 87–88
digitizing, 119–20
dimensions of, 95–96
evaluating current customer journey,
    102–7
future, designing, 107–10
goals of, defining, 90–91
key performance indicators, 120–22
logical flow of components, 100
measuring effectiveness of, 120–22
overview, 19, 86, 122–23
phases of customer journey, 93–95
researching customers, 91–92
rolling out new experience, 118–19
selecting customer segments to map, 93
structure of, 100–101
style and design elements, 99–100
telling customer's story, 89–90
testing new customer journey, 113–18
time frame, 101
workshop methodology, 96–101
customer life cycle, 88
customer lifetime (CL), 34–35
customer lifetime value (CLV), 35–37
customer prediction management, 302–8
customer relations manager, 219
customer relationship management
    (CRM), 298–300
customer research, 20–21, 86–87, 91–92,
    146–47. *See also* customer
    journey maps
customer retention cost (CRC), 38
customer segments, 88, 92, 93, 252–53
customer service, 2
customers. *See also* emotions, customer;
    on-demand generation
aligning KPIs to emotions of, 204
of competitors, analyzing, 30
contribution to ROI, 37–38
deep understanding of, 146–47

in evaluation of CX strategy, 13
evolution of expectations, 318–19
expectations for digital solutions,
 255–58
happiness of, focusing on, 203–4
mobile domination, 250–55
new, 13, 30, 32, 34, 93
pain points, fixing first, 147
reducing effort for, 148
shift of control to, 210–12
strategic CX programs and, 12
touch points, 19

D

data analytics, 215, 301–2. *See also*
 customer prediction management
data protection, 307
deductive thinking, 229–30
DeepMind, 323–24, 330–31
delighting customers, 106–7
design phase, 46–47, 146–53, 157. *See also*
 aligning CX program to objectives;
 customer journey maps; financial
 aspects of CX
digital customer dashboard, 172
digital solutions
 customer expectations for, 255–58
 customer prediction management, 305
 designing successful, 258–61
 emotional sculpting in, 244
 mobile domination, 250–55
 overview, 249, 261–62
 in retail settings, 247
 tracking digital revolution, 249–50
digital workforce
 and customer experience, 336–38
 impact on human workforce, 338–39
 overview, 328, 342
 realizing new value from, 339–41
 robotic process automation, 331–36
 understanding, 328–31
digitizing customer journey maps, 119–20
disruptive technology, 230, 311, 315–16.
 See also specific technologies;
 technology

disruptive thinking, 148
divergence phase, innovative thinking,
 229
divisional organizational structures, 212
doubt, and innovative thinking, 228
Drucker, Peter, 286

E

earnings before interest tax depreciation and amortization (EBITDA),
 43–44, 53–54
eBay, 316
effort, reducing for customers, 148,
 255–56
emotions, customer. *See also* customer
 experience
 capturing, 89
 in CX innovation engine, 224–25
 evaluating, 103, 106–7
 mood, understanding, 242–44
 technology targeting, 319–23
employee engagement
 best practices for increasing, 188–94
 causes of problems with, 72
 evaluating, 22–23
 during implementation, overview, 183,
 194–95
 importance to CX programs, 184
 improving, 73
 knowing what determines, 186–87
 program for, 77–80
 surveys of, 185, 188
 transformative programs, impact on,
 183–86
 value of, 70–71
employees. *See also* teams
 accountability, 202–3
 customer centricity of, 59–61
 empowerment, 23, 178, 202–3
 governance unit, 219–20
 impact of digital workforce, 338–39
 ownership, 179–82, 205–6
 recruiting right people, 206–7
 resistance to change, 196–99
 root cause analysis, 62–68

strengthening organizational culture,
200–206
work environment, 151
empowerment
employee, 23, 178, 202–3
of teams, 191
energy
face-to-face interactions, 242–44
organizational, 75–77
positive, 76–77
technology solutions in, 323
engagement. *See also* employee
engagement
change management stakeholder,
161–62
customer, 243–44
individual, 74–75
organizational, 73–77
outsourcing stakeholder, 280–81
EquaTerra, 278
equity carve-out, 274
established companies, CX value for,
43–44
ethics, customer prediction management,
307–8
evangelists, 201–2
execution, in executive CX maturity,
15–16
executive summary, 141–45
executives. *See also* CEO; leadership
appreciation for customer centricity,
15–17
outsourcing decisions by, 264–69
expectations, customer, 255–58, 318–19
experience, customer. *See* customer
experience; customer experience
management
experience maps, 89–90. *See also* customer
journey maps
external parties, getting input from,
147–48

F

Facebook, 236
face-to-face interactions, 240–47

facial recognition, 324
facilitator, workshop, 97
Farecast, 302
finance departments, RPA in, 333, 334
financial aspects of CX
amount of change needed, 41–42,
51–53
areas needing change, 40–41, 49–51
budgeting process, 46–47
comparative analysis, 28–34
example case, 48–54
metrics for identifying issues, 34–38
need for strategic CX, overview, 27,
48–49
overview, 27, 55–56
presenting case for, 47–48
reviewing, 139–41
ROI for investment, providing, 42–47,
53–54
targets, revising, 141
tracking overall financial targets,
171–72
vision and mission for CX program,
39–40
when testing new customer journey,
115–17
fit-for-purpose outsourcing governance
model, 280
Five Whys technique, 63–64
Forrester, 211
Fourth Industrial Revolution, 1–2,
310–12
functional organizational structures, 212
future of CEM. *See also* technology
customer prediction management,
302–8
in CX innovation engine, 225
overview, 298, 308–9, 310
relation to history of CEM, 298–301
rise of big data, 301–2

G

Gallup organization, 71, 72, 185
gamification, 257–58
gap and opportunity analysis, 125–35

Gartner analysts, 278
GE, 273
Generation X, 253
Genpact, 273
Gilovich, Thomas, Dr., 237
Global Center for Digital Business
    Transformation, 311
globalization, 299–300
goals. *See also* aligning CX program to
    objectives
  customer journey map, 90–91
  outsourcing relationship, 289–90
Goldman Sachs, 274
Google, 223, 225–26, 242, 304, 320,
    323–24, 325, 330–31
governance model, CX
  adopting, 216–17
  implementation planning, 165–67
  need for, 19–20
  overview, 158–59, 209, 221
  positioning governance unit, 217–19
  staffing governance unit, 219–20
governance model, outsourcing
  components of, 279–82
  issues, dealing with, 284
  and outsourcing relationship,
    282–84, 291
  overview, 278, 284–85
gross margin, 13, 31, 32
growth imperative, 180–81

H

happiness, adaptation and, 237
Harvard Business School, 71
health enhancement technology, 315–16
Her (film), 318–19
hierarchical organizational structures,
    212–14
high-performance culture, 291–92
Hinton, Geoffrey, 323
Hollister, 244–45
honest communication, 188–89
Huis Ten Bosch, 321
human aspirations technology, 315,
    316–23

human resources (HR), 163–64, 333
human workforce, 338–39
hyperconnectivity, 209–10, 213. *See
    also* digital solutions; on-demand
    generation

I

IBM, 223, 331, 341
image recognition, AI, 341
implementation. *See also* leadership;
    outsourcing; planning for CX imple-
    mentation; scaling CX excellence
  allocating actions for change, 82
  budgeting for, 47
  as CCScore area, 61
  customizing for different teams, 190–91
  employee engagement during, overview,
    183, 194–95
  gap and opportunity analysis, 128
  in root cause analysis, 67
  team, structuring, 157
independent governance units, 217–18
individual changes, KPIs for, 169–70
individual engagement, 74–75
information management, 282
initial public offering (IPO), 274
innovation
  impediments to, 233
  importance to CX, 223–24
  organizational culture and, 232–34
  by outsource provider, 293
  overview, 222, 234
  prediction management and, 306
  promoting, 215
  to reduce effort for customers, 148
  in traditional organizational
    structures, 214
innovation engine, CX
  customer emotional states, 224–25
  future, considering, 225
  impediments to, 233
  overview, 224
  selecting CX to innovate, 231–32
  team thinking processes, 226–30
  testing, 225–26

insourcing, 270
Internet, 209–10, 299. *See also* digital
  solutions; technology
Internet of Things (IoT), 313, 320, 322
investment, in executive CX maturity,
  15–16
Iny, Alan, 227–30
IPsoft, 331
iRobot, 321
IT, RPA in, 333

J

Jobs, Steve, 22, 232–33, 267, 303
joint ventures, 271

K

Kalanick, Travis, 230
key performance indicators (KPIs),
  120–22, 169–71, 204, 280
Kraft Foods, 274

L

labor, outsourced, 271
leadership
  allocating actions for change, 81
  appreciation for customer centricity,
    15–17
  as CCScore area, 60
  commitment to realizing vision, 176
  communication of vision, 175–76
  convincing others to commit to vision,
    176–77
  courage, 178–79
  in customer centricity, 15–17, 22
  in customer experience, 174–75
  data-centric projects, factors to
    consider, 308
  defining, 175
  and employee empowerment, 178
  by example, 163
  fostering customer-centric belief sys-
    tem, 177
  gap and opportunity analysis, 126
  overview, 182
  ownership, championing, 179–82

in root cause analysis, 65–66
in traditional organizational
  structures, 214
vision, role in, 175
Lean Six Sigma, 165
life-enhancing technology, 312–23,
  325–26
LinkedIn, 275
Loehr, James E., 74–75
logical thinking, 227
Lowen, Alexander, 247

M

Macaulay, James, 311
Magic Leap, 316–17, 322
management. *See* CEO; executives;
  leadership
margin, 13, 31, 32
market maturity, 29–30
market share, 33
marketing, personalized, 298, 303–4
Maslow's hierarchy of needs, 236–37
matrix structure, 215
McDonald's, 229–30, 266
meaning, organizational culture providing, 205
MemoMi, 322
memorable customer interactions, 246–47
mentoring, 192–93, 200–206
metrics, CX, 34–38, 40–42, 49–53. *See
  also* specific metrics
Microsoft, 180, 242, 275, 302, 320
millennials, 199–200, 253
mission, 39–40, 77–79, 279
Mixpanel, 341
mobile carrier bill shock, 102
mobile domination, 250–55
mobile revolution, 250
mood, understanding, 242–44
Moore's law, 249

N

narrative, customer, 89–90. *See also*
  customer journey maps
NASA, 78

National Center for Biotechnology
    Information, 254
natural language processing (NLP), 341
negative customer moments, 103, 106–7,
    109–10, 319–23
net present value, 37
net promoter score (NPS), 18, 120
network organizational structure, 215–16
new customer journey, 110–19
new customers, 13, 30, 32, 34, 93
new experience map, 100–101, 107–10
Nielsen Consumer Research, 211

O

objectives. *See also* aligning CX program
    to objectives
  customer journey map, 90–91
  importance to governance unit, 217
Oculus, 322
offshoring back-office processes, 334–35
omnichannel access, 256
on-demand generation
  cool, redefining, 238–39
  expectations of, 318
  face-to-face interactions, 240–47
  overview, 235, 248
  understanding, 235–38
online banking, 114
online shopping, AI use for, 341
operating margin, 31, 32
operating models, 269–76
operational capability, 268–69
operational team, in outsourcing, 281
opportunities. *See* gap and
    opportunity analysis
organization. *See also* customer centricity
  deep understanding of, 146–47
  defined, 74
  internal input, 147–48
organizational culture, 199–206, 232–34,
    291–92
organizational energy, 75–77
organizational engagement, 73–77
organizational initiatives
  change management, 160–63

cost of, 136–37
in executive summary, 143–44
gap and opportunity analysis, 125–30
implementation planning, 158, 159–64
organizational structure, 209–16, 220–21
outsourcing
  cost-benefit analysis, 269, 275–76
  debate over benefits of, 287
  evaluating potential solutions, 265–69
  labor, 271
  in modern-day organizations, 286–88
  operating models, 269–76
  overview, 263, 276–77, 295
  principles for successful, 288–94
  reasons to choose, 263–65
  relationships, importance to, 286
  solutions, focusing on, 290
  value of, 287–89
outsourcing governance model
  active role in relationship, 282–84
  components of, 279–82
  effect on outsourcing relationship, 291
  issues, dealing with, 284
  overview, 278, 284–85
ownership, 179–82, 205–6, 289, 307–8

P

pain points, fixing first, 147
Pepper robot, 317
Peppers, Don, 298
personal space, digital, 254
personalization, of digital solutions, 256
personalized marketing, 298, 303–4
Philip Morris, 274
physical customer experiences, 240–47
planning for CX implementation
  collaborative software, 167
  customer implementation, 164
  governance model, 165–67
  KPIs, setting, 169–71
  mitigating risk, 167–68
  organizational implementation, 159–64
  overview, 156, 172–73
  primary implementations, 157–59
  structuring implementation team, 157

tracking overall financial targets, 171–72
pleasure, technology producing, 319–23
positive customer interactions, 246–47
positive emotions, technology targeting, 320–23
positive energy, 76–77, 243–44
positive reinforcement, 193–94
Power of Full Engagement, The (Loehr and Schwartz), 74–75
predictive CLV, 36–37
privacy, data, 307–8
probe the possible phase, innovative thinking, 228
Process Excellence, 165
process excellence manager, 219
processes. *See* business processes
productivity technology, 315–16
products, benchmarking, 149–50
profit and loss statement (P&L), 30–31
project performance, KPIs for, 169
Prosci ADKAR® model, 160
purpose, organizational culture providing, 205

Q

quality, in CX strategy, 150–51
quality assurance manager, 219
quality management system (QMS), 203–4

R

recruiting employees, 206–7
reevaluation phase, innovative thinking, 230
relationships, in CRM, 298–300. *See also* customer experience
relationships, outsourcing
issues, dealing with, 284
in modern-day organizations, 286–88
overview, 286, 295
principles for successful, 288–94
taking active role in, 282–84
research
customer, 20–21, 86–87, 91–92, 146–47

before purchases, 254
resistance to change, 196–99
retail interactions, 240–47
retention, customer, 38, 93
return policies, 257
returns on investment (ROI), 37–38, 42–47, 53–54
revenue, 30–31, 32, 37
review websites, 254, 299
Riegel, Klaus, 180
Riken-SRK Collaboration Center for Human-Interactive Robot Research, 321
risk, 118–19, 167–68
robotic process automation (RPA), 331–36, 337, 340
robots, 317, 321
rollout, customer experience, 118–19
root cause analysis, 62–68, 80–83, 188
root causes, fixing, 152

S

sales, focus on, 213, 215
scaling CX excellence
employee resistance to change, 196–99
organizational culture, 199–200
overview, 196, 207–8
recruiting right people, 206–7
strengthening culture, 200–206
Scherer, Klaus R., 243
Schwartz, Tony, 74–75
scribe, workshop, 97
self-service movement, 255, 257
senior managers. *See* CEO; executives; leadership
senses, shaping CX with, 244–45
sensors, 324
service level agreements (SLAs), 290
shared services operations, 270–71
silos, 213, 214
simple organizational structures, 212
Sleeping Duck, 257
smart textiles and materials, 324
SmartThings, 322
Smith, Adam, 212

social media, 299
SoftBank, 317, 321
software, 119, 167, 283–84. *See also* digital
 solutions; digital workforce
Sourcing Line Computer Economics, 287
SpaceX, 325
speech analytics, 324
stakeholders, 160, 161–62, 280–81
standard happiness procedure (SHP), 204
standard operating procedures (SOPs), 203
start-up companies, CX value for, 45–46
State Street Corporation, 274
Statista, 250
story, telling customer, 89–90. *See also*
 customer journey maps
strategic acquisitions, 274–75
strategic CX programs. *See also* customer
 centricity; specific CX phases and
 aspects
 allocating actions for change, 80–84
 amount of change needed, 41–42,
  51–53
 budgeting process, 46–47
 comparative analysis, 28–34
 evaluating current strategy, 12–26
 final thoughts on, 343–44
 financial areas needing change, 40–41,
  49–51
 general discussion, 10–12
 metrics for identifying issues, 34–38
 need for, overview, 27, 48–49
 overview, 9
 presenting case for, 47–48
 ROI for, 42–47, 53–54
 vision and mission for, 39–40
surprise, customer, 107

T

tactical CX programs, 9–10
Taj Hotel, India, 206–7
team organizational structure, 215
teams
 customizing implementation for,
  190–91

empowering to control changes, 191
 innovation, 226–30, 232
 outsourcing, 281
 treating outsourcing partners as part
  of, 289
technological singularity, 326
technology. *See also* digital solutions; digital workforce; specific technologies
 big data, 301–2
 consumer expectations for, 318–19
 in customer experience, 23–24
 disruptive, 315–16
 future wave of, 323–26
 governing outsourcing relationship,
  283–84
 historical evolution of CEM, 298–300
 human aspirations, 315, 316–18
 life-enhancing, shift toward, 312–15
 outsource provider use of, 293
 overview, 310, 327
 trajectory of, 310–12
 value creation, 319–23
Telefonica, 306
Tesla, 233, 323
testing, 113–18, 225–26
Thinking in New Boxes (Brabandere and
 Iny), 227–30
thought vectors, 323
touch points, 19
trade sale, 274
training, 21, 192–93, 200–206
transformative programs, 183–86. *See
 also* change management; implementation; leadership; scaling CX
 excellence
transparency, 257, 283
transportation, technology in, 315, 323
trust, 185–86, 282, 283, 293–94
Tull, Thomas, 316

U

Uber, 20, 230, 312, 320
understanding, in executive CX maturity,
 15–16

V

value
  from digital workforce, 339–41
  importance to CX strategy, 150–51
  of new customers, 13
  of outsourcing, 287–89
  technology creating, 319–23
values, 191–92, 199–200
Virgin Australia, 239
virtual reality, 322
vision, 39–40, 77–79, 175–76, 279
Visual Recognition, IBM, 341
Vodafone, 231–32

W

Wall Street Journal, The, 316
Wall-E (movie), 325
Wal-Mart, 24, 180
winning, training for, 192–93
word of mouth, 41, 299
work environment, 151
workforce. *See* digital workforce
workshops, customer journey mapping,
    96–101, 110–13

X

Xerox, 275

Z

Zappos, 266, 267, 268

Consulting and Resources

JOE TAWFIK invites you to visit www.experience mybrand.com, a website dedicated to providing additional resources to help you achieve your branded customer experience. The website contains toolkits and valuable information to further enhance your journey.

The author and his team also offer consulting on a worldwide basis. If you would like to discuss your consulting needs, you can reach him by email at joe.tawfik@experiencemybrand.com. Feel free to also connect on LinkedIn!